HEALING : MIND, BODY AND SOUL

Are we merely complex biological organisms, or spiritual beings, residing for a time in a physical body? Believe it or not, how you answer this question may well affect your health.

In 1999, researchers from the University of Texas, Austin, published a study in the journal *Demography*, which documented the dramatic effects of religious belief on longevity. In a study of 21,000 adults in the USA, researchers found that on an average, deeply religious people lived seven years longer than those who never attended worship services, even after taking into consideration such obvious healthy habits as not smoking, avoiding alcohol and having a network of friends. Overall, non-religious people, according to research findings, had four times the rate of diabetes, lung and infectious diseases, in comparison to religious people.

Healing: Mind, Body and Soul explores the fascinating connection between health and spirituality, reviewing exciting research findings and examining their implications for our health. Moreover, the book thoroughly analyses the role of food in health and reviews breakthrough findings in the field of nutrition. Writing from the perspective of a Baha'i, Alan Bryson gives the reader his personal insights on such important health issues as diet, spirituality, attitudes, emotions, faith, virtues, prayer, stress management, vegetarianism, complementary medicine, finding the right physician, and discovering our own inherent healing potential.

Healing: Mind, Body and Soul is an ideal book for anyone interested in venturing forth on the road to health, loaded with useful information, practical tips, and exciting ideas for achieving and maintaining optimal physical and spiritual well-being.

HEALING
MIND, BODY & SOUL

ALAN BRYSON

New Dawn

NEW DAWN
a division of Sterling Publishers (P) Ltd.
L-10, Green Park Extension, New Delhi-110016.
Ph.: 6191784/5, 6191023 Fax: 91-11-6190028
E-mail: sterlin.gpvb@axcess.net.in
ghai@nde.vsnl.net.in

Healing: Mind, Body & Soul
©1999, Alan Bryson
ISBN 81 207 2205 1

Important Notice

This is a book about health and not about illness. Always discuss any ideas or suggestions contained in this book with your physician prior to adopting them into your lifestyle, and never substitute them for proper medical attention.

The ideas in this book represent my own personal opinions. They do not characterise an official Bahá'í view, nor are they necessarily shared by other Bahá'ís.

Published by Sterling Publishers Pvt. Ltd., New Delhi-110016.
Lasertypeset by Vikas Compographics, New Delhi.
Printed at Prolific Incorporated, New Delhi.

To my wife Angela for her invaluable advice and assistance.
She and nurses like her are the compassionate face and hands of medicine.
And to Dr. G. for providing my parents with such wonderful primary care.

CONTENTS

CONTENTS

INTRODUCTION

Know thou that the soul of man is exalted above and
is independent of all infirmities of body or mind.
...The soul of man is the sun by which his body is
illumined, and from which it draweth its sustenance,
and should be so regarded.

Bahá'u'lláh

Diet, physical activity, lifestyle, hygiene, attitudes,
emotions, community, relationships, spirituality, faith,
virtues, prayer, stress management, breathing,
imagination, awareness and choosing a physician are the main
components of what we term proactive health. We will explore
these various topics, review exciting and important research
findings, and discuss their implications for the maintenance of
health. An ancient Chinese proverb makes clear the inadequacy
of taking health for granted:

Treating someone who is already ill
is like beginning to dig a well after you have become thirsty.

Classical Chinese physicians were emulated and consulted, not
only in matters of health, but also in questions of wisdom and
morality. According to modern Western medicine a man can be
pronounced in perfect health, even though he has a ruthless and
abject nature. The classical Chinese physician would require that

one's body, movement, thoughts, morality, emotions and actions be in harmony with the forces of the universe before he could be deemed healthy. In these areas, through counsel and example, the classical Chinese physician educated his patient, who in the final analysis played the primary role in sustaining his own health. In contrast to modern medicine, the classical Chinese physician received his fee only as long as his patient remained healthy, at the onset of illness payment stopped. The goal was to attain balance within one's own self and with the universe at large.

There was a time when Western medicine had much in common with both classical Chinese and Indian medicine, for example, all three shared a belief in the concepts of harmony and life force. Hippocrates (ca. 460-377 B.C.), the acknowledged father of Western medicine, maintained:

> *Health depends on a state of equilibrium among the various factors that govern the operation of the body and the mind; the equilibrium in turn is reached only when man lives in harmony with his external environment.*

Confucius (ca. 500 B.C.) taught:

> *This Equilibrium is the great root from which grow all the human actings in the world, and this Harmony is the universal path which they all should pursue. Let the states of equilibrium and harmony exist in perfection, and a happy order will prevail throughout heaven and earth, and all things will be nourished and flourish.*

With respect to the body, the Chinese identified the life force as *chi*, which they believed had to flow properly throughout the body to maintain health. The Indians used the term *prana* and Hippocrates designated *pneuma* as the life force. What led to a rejection of the concepts of harmony and life force in Western medicine? How has the reductionist scientific model influenced the role of the physician? What caused the shift of emphasis from maintaining health and treating patients, to abating symptoms and fighting diseases? While exploring these questions we will also examine how the dissociation of faith, attitude, emotions, spirituality and God from the *science of medicine* has undermined the *art of healing*. In this context we will examine the ramifications of treating a human being solely as a biological machine. By denying the spiritual dimension of a human being, modern Western medicine has come to view death as the ultimate enemy, to be fought at all costs. This completely materialistic interpretation of existence has had a tremendous impact upon the practice of medicine, often stripping patients of dignity and control. By failing to see death as a transition and a natural aspect of existence, we've created an environment of fear, denial, guilt, isolation and sometimes protracted and needless suffering.

Medicine has become ever more specialised, focusing primarily on systems which are viewed as more or less autonomous. History does indeed repeat itself as Herodotus's (ca. 440 B.C.) description of ancient Egyptian health care reveals:

> *Medicine is practised among them on a plan of separation;*
> *each physician treats a single disorder, and no more: thus the*
> *country swarms with medical practitioners, some*
> *undertaking to cure diseases of the eye, others of the head,*
> *others again of the teeth, others of the intestines, and some*
> *those which are not local.*

Fortunately, things are changing and a growing number of medical practitioners are beginning to see the individual as a whole and not merely as an assemblage of independent parts and systems. For example, two decades ago a textbook dealing with the immune system would scantly mention the nervous or the endocrine systems; now, however, scientific research is forcing the medical community to recognise that these systems are interconnected to a degree which challenges many aspects of conventional medical thinking. The development of psychoneuroimmunology (PNI) has spawned a wave of scientific research which is beginning to prove that the mind and emotions are demonstrably conjoined with the body. Sheepishly some researchers, while stressing that their personal feelings are neither quantifiable nor scientifically admissible, are even beginning to conjecture the existence of a human spirit. One very positive aspect of this development is the recognition that the *art of healing* is vitally important to the practice of medicine. Just as we've come to understand that not everyone in charge is a natural leader, it is becoming evident that not everyone who practices medicine is a natural healer. Healers have always understood the significance of the mind and spirit in the healing process, even before their effects were confirmed by scientific research. We will delve deeply into this matter and also discuss the importance of seeking and finding a physician who practises the *art of healing*.

I would be remiss not to acknowledge that my faith and personal experiences have influenced my orientation to health and healing. As Bahá'ís we are taught the importance of medical science:

> *This knowledge (of the healing art) is the most important of all the sciences, for it is the greatest means from God, the Life-giver to the dust, for preserving the bodies of all people, and He has put it in the forefront of all sciences and wisdoms.*

Bahá'ís are also enjoined:

> *Resort ye, in times of sickness, to competent physicians; We have not set aside the use of material means, rather have We confirmed it through this Pen, which God hath made to be the Dawning-place of His shining and glorious Cause.*

There are numerous references to health and healing in the Bahá'í teachings, however, it would be inaccurate to give the impression that a Bahá'í system of medicine exists. Indeed, Bahá'ís are cautioned against selecting specific references from the *Holy Writings* in order to advance a particular theory or school of medicine. The Bahá'í teaching offer broad guidelines which will no doubt come to influence the practice and development of medical science in the future. Any passages from the Bahá'í teachings included in this book should be seen in that light.

As we have seen, the knowledge of the art of healing and medical science are the most important branches of science according to the Bahá'í teachings. Moreover, ministering to the sick and practising medicine are considered praiseworthy acts, equivalent to worship:

> *In the Bahá'í Cause arts, sciences and all crafts are worship....*
> *Briefly, all effort and exertion put forth by man from the*
> *fullness of his heart is worship, if it is prompted by the highest*
> *motives and the will to do service to humanity. This is*
> *worship: to serve mankind and to minister to the needs of the*
> *people. Service is prayer. A physician ministering to the sick,*
> *gently, tenderly, free from prejudice and believing in the*
> *solidarity of the human race, he is giving praise.*

Unquestionably, conventional Western medicine has made tremendous strides during the 19th and 20th centuries, and the future appears full of promise, yet with each new high-tech and mechanistic solution, one senses that the practice of medicine is growing progressively colder and increasingly depersonalised. Compounding this problem are the constraints put upon physicians and care givers by insurance companies and governments seeking to control costs. The greatest potential for cost saving lies in encouraging a proactive approach to health, yet paradoxically, budget cutters, who deem such programmes "non-essential", frequently target these areas for cuts. Fortunately, some insurers and government planners are beginning to rethink this strategy.

At the individual level there are a number of factors which undermine the maintenance of health. First and foremost in the developed nations are diet, stress and an unhealthy self-indulgent lifestyle. Ironically, many otherwise virtuous people are reticent about actively pursuing personal health, associating it with a selfishness and egotism. This is unfortunate, for in reality it is a virtue and an obligation to care for the temple of the soul. For example, Buddha, an absolute paragon of selflessness, taught:

> *...the self-indulgent man is a slave to his passions, and*
> *pleasure-seeking is degrading and vulgar. But to satisfy the*

*necessities of life is not evil. To keep the body in good health is
a duty, for otherwise we shall not be able to trim the lamp of
wisdom, and keep our minds strong and clear. Water
surrounds the lotus flower, but does not wet its petals. This is
the middle path, O bhikkhus, that keeps aloof from both
extremes.*

Mahatma Gandhi left us this advice:

*The body is the home of the soul. Can its mysterious tenant
find rest and unmixed joy within its chambers if daily exposed
to sharp and shivering shocks through its aching joints or
quivering nerves?...If God has bestowed upon you the
inestimable gift of good health and a good constitution, it is
your duty, as a rational creature, to preserve it.*

Beyond our own physical well-being the Bahá'í Writings
encourage mankind to:

*Let your vision be world-embracing, rather than confined to
your own self.*

Indeed, we should all be aware that a proactive orientation to
personal health has far-reaching implications, not just for the
individual, but for mankind as a whole. We should recognise that
by maintaining our health tremendous financial and professional
resources will be set free. We then need to allow our vision to be
world-embracing with respect to how we allocate these resources.
In the coming decades a responsible proactive approach to
personal health will gain in significance as our collective resources
are strained and our social conscience tested.

Think Globally, Act Locally

The chaos theory postulates that the seemingly insignificant
flapping of a butterfly's wings in the rain forest could conceivably
have an impact upon the global climate, correspondingly your
decisions regarding lifestyle, nutrition, fitness and spirituality will
have far reaching consequences, not only for you, but also for your
world. Although this book will deal with issues which affect the
individual, it's certainly worthwhile to briefly consider how your

health and lifestyle can impact upon the exigencies of global health.

According to the World Health Organisation, WHO, the number of people in developing countries over 65 years of age will increase by between 200 and 400 per cent over the next thirty years. As we increase the human lifespan we will be confronted with dramatically increasing health care challenges. Currently, at least 22 million people globally, one in every five persons over 80 years of age, are affected by dementia, in particular Alzheimer's disease. Numerous studies in a variety of countries have demonstrated that elderly people are particularly susceptible to chronic diseases such as stroke, heart disease, dementia and cancer. Globally at least 165 million people, mostly elderly, suffer from rheumatoid arthritis and one in three women over 50 years of age have osteoporosis. Conventional Western medicine, while efficacious in treating many bacterial, fungal and parasitic infections, and managing trauma and surgical emergencies, has not been nearly as effective in dealing with chronic degenerative diseases, autoimmune diseases, psychosomatic illnesses and many forms of cancer. The good news is that proactive health can diminish, albeit not eliminate, the statistical probability of you suffering from many forms of cancer and chronic diseases. For instance, lack of exercise, smoking and diet are all factors under the control of the individual, and these factors are linked to half of all fatal cancers.

Through proactive health and stress reduction Herbert Benson, MD, Associate Professor of Medicine at Harvard Medical School, estimated that in the United States nearly forty per cent of all visits to the doctor could be eliminated. This represents huge sums of money and resources at a time in which half of the world's population, according to the WHO, lacks access to medical treatment and essential medications. Every eight seconds a child under the age of five dies of an acute respiratory infection, or more than 4 million children annually. Three million children die of diarrhoeal diseases, while malaria and measles kill over a million children per year respectively.

In the developed countries we tend to forget the impact of communicable diseases. Forty per cent of the over 50 million deaths last year resulted from communicable diseases, however, ninety-nine per cent of deaths from communicable diseases and from maternal, perinatal and neonatal factors were registered in the developing nations. In developed nations seventy-five per cent of deaths resulted from noncommunicable diseases, many of which are lifestyle-related, such as cancer and heart disease. In addition, 500 million people suffer neurotic, stress-related and somatoform illnesses, and an additional 200 million are afflicted with mood disorders such as chronic and manic depression. By the year 2000 it is estimated that nearly 100 million people will suffer from a form of diabetes which is strongly linked to lifestyle, unsound diet and lack of exercise. Simultaneously, a million people are killed annually by hepatitis B, which is preventable by vaccine, and schistosomiasis, known as snail fever, affects 200 million people in seventy-four countries, although the cost of treatment is only 30 cents per patient. Viewed in this context, proactive health isn't just about individuals living longer and healthier lives, it's also about freeing up medical and financial resources to help alleviate the world's health problems.

Shamefully, 1.1 thousand million people are addicted to tobacco in a world in which nearly a third of the world's children are undernourished and more than twenty per cent of the world's population live in extreme poverty. The WHO has identified smoking as the world's largest single preventable cause of illness and death. Based on current trends it is expected to kill 10 million people annually by the year 2020. The amount of resources devoted to growing, processing and distributing tobacco stagger the imagination, as do the costs of treating the various cancers, respiratory and heart diseases linked to tobacco use. The WHO has determined that between seventy-five and eighty-five per cent of smokers would like to stop, yet fewer than half of all smokers manage to quit before reaching the age of sixty. Despite these facts some governments continue to subsidise tobacco cultivation.

Although this is only a cursory review of global health problems, we haven't, for example, even mentioned HIV or tuberculosis, it should be clear that humanity faces a problem of immense proportions. Imagine if just 1,000 readers of this book practised proactive health and were thus able to avoid heart bypass surgery, which they otherwise would have required. This could represent savings of $50,000,000 or more. In the United States alone upwards of 12,000 million dollars are spent annually on bypass surgery, and 4,000 million dollars on angioplasties. As mentioned previously, Herbert Benson has estimated that visits to the doctor could be reduced by nearly forty per cent, which in the United States means an additional savings of over 50,000 million dollars annually. The list goes on, but the point is clear, if the peoples of the developed nations begin practising responsible proactive health, they will be in a much better position to assist the developing nations in providing their populations with adequate health care.

Finally, I would like to emphasise that the suggestions and information in this book are intended as an aid to maintaining health and are not meant to supersede medical treatment. You should discuss these topics with your personal physician before dramatically altering your diet, lifestyle and physical exercise regime. An even better approach before making any major changes would be to undergo a thorough physical examination, taking advantage of the considerable diagnostic capabilities available. By documenting your weight, blood-pressure and blood-chemistry, etc., you will be in a much better position to evaluate the advantages of a proactive approach to health.

2

LETTING NATURE
TAKE CARE OF IT

Happy are those who spend their days in gaining
knowledge, in discovering the secrets of nature, and
in penetrating the subtleties of pure truth!

'Abdu'l-Bahá

God heals and the doctor takes the fee.

Benjamin Franklin

With respect to health, strangely the terms *nature* and *natural* are often considered simple and mildly effective when compared to medical technology. In reality, the self-healing potential of living organisms is so incredibly complex that after two centuries of scientific investigation we have only scratched the surface. In fact, scientists have described the human brain as the most complex structure in the known universe. The ingeniously complex chemistry, mechanics, structures, and functions of microscopic parts of the human body continue to defy the comprehension of even the greatest minds. This inability to understand one's own self must lead to a sense of wonder for the Creator of such magnificence.

Having recognized thy powerlessness to attain to an adequate understanding of that Reality which abideth within thee, thou wilt readily admit the futility of such efforts as may be attempted by thee, or by any of the created things, to fathom the mystery of the Living God, the Day Star of unfading glory, the Ancient of everlasting days. This confession of helplessness which mature contemplation must eventually impel every mind to make in itself the acme of human understanding, and marketh the culmination of man's development.

BAHÁ'U'LLÁH

We need to think of nature as a manifestation of God's will and the most powerful ally we have in maintaining health. In this chapter we will briefly review but a fraction of the mind-boggling healing mechanisms in the human body, with the aim of awaken a sense of confidence in the power of the divine will expressed in our own bodies. The greatest healers have always recognised this power.

Nature is God's Will and is its expression in and through the contingent world. It is a dispensation of Providence ordained by the Ordainer, the All-Wise.... It is endowed with a power whose reality men of learning fail to grasp. Indeed a man of insight can perceive naught therein save the effulgent splendor of Our Name, the Creator.

Bahá'u'lláh

One of the most remarkable physicians in the history of Western medicine was unquestionably Galen (ca. 130-200). Thanks to the foresight of Muslim scholars who translated Galen's works in the ninth century, many of his medical writings not only survived, but continued to exert a profound influence on medical humanists of Renaissance Europe 1,400 years after his death. Galen, of Greek heritage, was born in Pergamun, in Asia Minor, and began his medical training in Smyrna. He travelled extensively and eventually settled in Rome where he became physician to the Emperor.

Galen greatly advanced the science of anatomy by dissecting animals, both living and dead. In addition, by treating the wounds of gladiators he gained valuable insights into human anatomy. His medical and philosophical thinking was influenced by Aristotle's belief that nothing in nature is superfluous. Galen taught that by examining nature we can derive God's purpose. Galen believed in therapies such as diet, rest and exercise to encourage the natural healing process, declaring:

The physician is nature's assistant.

In his work, *On The Natural Faculties*, Galen credits Hippocrates for first recognising the power of nature:

Now Hippocrates, who was the first known to us of all those who have been both physicians and philosophers inasmuch as he was the first to recognize what Nature effects, expresses his admiration of her, and is constantly singing her praises and calling her "just". Alone, he says, she suffices for the animal in every respect, performing of her own accord and without any teaching all that is required. Being such, she has, as he supposes, certain faculties, one attractive of what is appropriate, and another eliminative of what is foreign, and she nourishes the animal, makes it grow, and expels its diseases by crisis. Therefore, he says that there is in our bodies a concordance in the movements of air and fluid, and that everything is in sympathy.

Hippocrates himself wrote:

Wherefore it appears to me necessary to every physician to be skilled in nature, and strive to know, if he would wish to perform his duties, what man is in relation to the articles of food and drink, and to his other occupations, and what are the effects of each of them to every one.

As if nature's healing mechanisms were somehow inherently inferior to modern medicine, some people resent being told, "Let nature take care of it." Indeed, many people feel cheated if they leave a physician's office without a prescription or some tangible medical treatment. No serious healer has ever underestimated the effectiveness of our natural healing mechanisms. Dr. Albert Schweizer put it quite well:

> *It's supposed to be a professional secret, but I'll tell you anyway. We doctors do nothing. We only help and encourage the doctor within.*

Some experts have estimated that science has explained about ten per cent of the precise functioning of the immune system. That is by no means a trivial accomplishment, indeed, one can only imagine how thrilled Galen or Hippocrates would have been to have had access to such a wealth of knowledge. Unfortunately, the medical and biological sciences have developed such extensive technical vocabularies that it's difficult for an ordinary person to grasp what is going on.

If we can overcome this difficulty and gain a more thorough understanding of our own healing mechanism, we will be in a better position to assist our own "doctor within". Therefore, using broad strokes and avoiding phrases like, "the reticuloendothelial system mediates the phagocytic response", we will highlight some of the body's healing mechanisms.

Your Inner World

Surely anyone who has studied human anatomy is humbled by the intricacy, precision, ingenuity and capacity which resides in his or her own frame. Imagine if you will that your body is a universe or a world in and of itself. Be aware that perhaps 300 trillion (300,000,000,000,000) separate living entities (cells) reside in your world. Every minute some 600 million of these citizens of your world are created and perish. Astoundingly, each cell carries around a complete blueprint and owner's manual of the entire universe. Each one of our 100,000 genes is determined by an exact sequence of four chemical letter, which, if represented as a string of letters, would take up 750 megabytes of computer storage. Just think, all that in the pocket of a cell not even visible to the naked eye!

Headquarters

About a trillion cells, of which 100 billion are nerve cells, reside, quite fittingly, in headquarters. Each second countless messages are received and processed. Light rays are gathered on a two-dimensional surface and transmitted to headquarters to be converted into three-dimensional visual images, which in turn are analysed and stored for later use. Sound waves are also registered, analysed and stored, as are tastes, smells and various sensations. The citizens of headquarters have an amazing communications network which operates using organic chemistry. Each of the 100 billion nerve cells can have between 1,000 and 6,000 friends and acquaintances with whom it communicates (some estimates go as high as 25,000). Thus headquarters has a capacity for around 100 trillion interfaces. When your doorbell rings, it simply rings, but the doorbells of the citizens of headquarters have various intensities, which in turn have different meanings. Thus, the capacity for communication is even further enhanced, perhaps 10 to the trillionth power, according to Professor Paul Churchland of the University of California. Little wonder that Professor Gerald Fischbach of Harvard University considers the brain the, "most complex structure in the known universe."

When the nerve cells of headquarters are at rest their membranes, or filter coverings, allow more atoms of potassium to enter their space. But if they are put on alert, their filter coverings are changed to allow more sodium atoms to enter. These sodium atoms, which quickly rush in, have a positive electrical charge which results in an impulse. An impulse then gives rise to the release of a "neurotransmitter", or chemical messenger, which can then travel to another nerve cell. To receive a message, a cell needs a receptor for the neurotransmitter, or chemical messenger. Although they aren't as effective as copper wires in carrying a message, they are ten times faster than an Olympic sprinter, reaching speeds of about 100 metres per second. Since the first one was identified in 1921, scientist have been able to identify sixty different neurotransmitters.

It would be incorrect to imply that the brain is simply a mass of more or less identical nerve cells. In reality, there is a tremendous diversity among the nerve cells of the brain with respect to structure, molecular distinction, function, size and wiring. Cells group together in divisions to perform specific functions. Some cells communicate with their neighbours, some communicate with other operating units outside their group.

As is widely known, the brain is divided into two hemispheres, which are connected and constantly exchange information. For example, generally we hear music with the left side of our brain, but we feel or experience it with the right side. The neocortex and cortex (from the Latin word for bark of a tree, or the outer layer) are the portions of the brain which have developed faster in man than any other animal. Although the neocortex, according to evolutionary theory, is the youngest portion of the brain, it accounts for nearly 75 per cent of all brain cells. Among many other things it is responsible for the correlation of data, associations, intellectual activity and the higher levels of personality.

The brain's base is known by its Latin equivalent, the medulla (literally marrow), which regulates functions such as respiration, circulation and digestion. These functions are considered autonomic, i.e., occurring involuntarily. Its neighbour is the cerebellum which coordinates muscular movement. In the middle of the of the brain is the thalamus (Latin for inner chamber), which is a sort of central switching station, or executive secretary. With the exception of smell, all sensory information is filtered by the executive secretary (thalamus) before being passed on to the higher regions of the brain.

Smells, or olfactory sensations, go directly to the limbic system, which from an evolutionary perspective is held to be the oldest part of the brain. Among other things the limbic system is responsible for emotions and long-term memory. Specifically, smells are registered in the hypothalamus, which simply means, beneath the inner chamber (later we will see why proponents of aroma-therapy deem this significant). The hypothalamus carries out a number of vital functions, but for the sake of example we might think of the hypothalamus as a maintenance department, which, among other things, regulates temperature, water metabolism, appetite, sleep and pleasure. We shouldn't, however, underestimate the importance of the hypothalamus, which if damaged, can result in immediate death. But how does the hypothalamus affect healing ?

Nature's Thermostat

The most obvious example would be a fever produced by regulating the body's internal thermostat. Certain cells in the hypothalamus continuously register the temperature of blood flowing by and initiate various responses to produce the proper body temperature. Muscular activity produces heat as we all know. What you might not know is that your muscles are constantly, albeit almost imperceptibly, vibrating several times every second. In extreme cold this activity becomes noticeable as we begin to shiver. Conversely, when it's too hot the hypothalamus turns on the body's air-conditioner, i.e., perspiration occurs and heated water evaporates, releasing heat from the body into the atmosphere. Thus to produce a fever, the body will reduce perspiration and increase the intensity of muscular vibrations, even to the point of shivering.

A fever is sometimes wrongly considered a disease or symptom to be promptly overcome by medication or cold compresses. Toxins (a Greek word for poison into which arrows are dipped) are proteins produced by invading organisms and their presence in the body can bring about a fever. This elevation in temperature accelerates the destruction of protein molecules in the invading organism. This of course is the desired outcome, however, life-essential proteins are also placed in jeopardy at high temperatures. Thus the body seeks to sustain a temperature high enough to kill invading bacteria, without endangering its own survival. Therefore, it is advisable to seek the advice of a physician before routinely intervening to reduce a fever.

Over the years physicians have noticed that high fevers sometimes result in improvement of various conditions including arthritis and even the remission of cancer. Of particular interest was the discovery in 1891 by a New York surgeon, William B.

Coley, that sarcoma, a soft-tissue cancer, often went into remission after patients had recovered from erysipelas, a severe streptococcal infection. Dr. Coley ultimately devised a treatment for cancer which involved injecting patients with a mixture of heat-killed bacteria. Shortly thereafter the patient would be overcome by a raging fever which usually persisted for about a day. Then the procedure would be repeated. Those with the highest fevers (102°F - 105°F / 38.9°C - 40.5°C) achieved the best results. The treatment was most effective against soft-tissue cancer — 50 per cent survived five years or more. For cancer of the lymph nodes a 38 per cent survival rate was reached.

After the rise of chemotherapy and radiation the "Coley Toxins" fell by the wayside. Forty years after Dr. Coley's death, researchers in 1976 began experiments on mice to identify what was going on. They were able to identify a chemical, tumour necrosis factor (TNF), which appears to be produced by the immune system in reaction to tumours and fever. In addition to serving as a chemical messenger between certain cells in the immune system, it appears that some tumour cells have receptors for TNF. In a cancer cell the presence of TNF can cause the cell to self-destruct. TNF has now been genetically cloned and used on patients in clinical trials.

The Master Gland

The hypothalamus, our indispensable maintenance department, is also in very close "chemical" communication with the pituitary gland, which is sometimes referred to as the master gland. When they were passing out names the pituitary gland was appallingly short-changed. Pituitary (Latin for phlegm) came about because it is located above the nasal passages and was therefore believed by the ancients to supply the nose with mucus. This master gland, about the size of a kidney bean, is extremely important despite what its size might imply. About a dozen bodily functions and almost all the glands of the endocrine system (adrenal, thyroid, parathyroids, male and female gonads and pancreas) are regulated by hormones secreted by the diminutive pituitary gland.

Among these vital functions is a response to distress which was (and is) critical to our survival. Primitive man was regularly in life-threatening situations which required him to fight or flee. For such occasions a response developed which enabled the body to react ideally. A noted authority on stress, Hans Selve, M.D., broke the "stress response" down into three distinct stages. During the first stage the body is alarmed by a distressful situation and prepares to fight for survival or escape danger. In this state we are highly alert: our pupils dilate, our breathing intensifies, our blood sugar increases, we slow our digestion to make more blood available and our heart pounds in order to better supply our muscles with sugar-and oxygen-enriched blood. During the second stage, called resistance, the body takes care of any damage brought about by the alarm stage. So far so good, however, chronic stress, the third stage, severely compromises the body's ability to maintain health. The immune response is weakened and physical maladies called "Stress-Related Disorders" may develop. This has proved to be a major affliction for civilised man, because something as insignificant as an insulting remark or gesture, a traffic jam or a deadline can elicit a major physical response designed to ensure our survival. As we will learn later, managing stress is vitally important to maintaining health.

Members Only

Think of your skin as an extensive physical barrier to countless invaders which seek entry into your world. Your skin does a fantastic job of preventing these invaders (bacteria, viruses, fungi and parasites) from gaining entry. Stomach acids kill their share of invaders as do enzymes in tears and saliva. But in spite of these precautions, some invaders do manage to gain entry. Those which do, have to contend with our immune system, which we can think of as a tremendous internal security agency. The cells in our bodies not only carry a detailed blueprint of themselves and their world, but all cells also carry an identity card.

In our societies we photograph, fingerprint and catalogue criminals. The immune system operates much more effectively against much more dangerous antagonists. Instead of fingerprinting and photographing intruders, the immune system uses an ingenious chemical identification process. When cells called "lymphocytes" encounter intruders without proper identification, they manufacture (or synthesise) a protein molecule called an "antibody". An antibody is manufactured to perfectly fit on to the surface of an intruder (called an antigen), like a key in a lock. There are millions of different types of antibodies circulating in our bodies which we've either inherited or produced ourselves. Imagine, in a single drop of blood there can be as many as a quadrillion antibodies (1,000,000,000,000,000)!

If an antibody happens upon its natural enemy several possible outcomes can occur. Some antibodies can inactivate their foes themselves and render them harmless. Others attach themselves to the intruders and aid special cells which engulf the intruder and annihilate it. Some antibodies damage the surface of the intruders so that other molecules (called complements) can destroy them. This, by the way, is the basis of a vaccination in which organisms are killed by heat or chemicals and then introduced into the body so that antibodies can be produced. (Sometimes live organisms are also used, however, they are first altered, "attenuated", so that they can no longer produce disease.) Once antibodies are present the immune system is one step ahead of the intruders and can mount a swifter and more effective response.

As ingenious as this defence is, our bodies also have to deal with exceedingly cunning enemies. A virus, for example, is a very clever infiltrator. Imagine walking around streets (your blood vessels) with security agents constantly checking your fingerprints and picture. If you are caught, punishment is swift and deadly. Viruses seek to survive and avoid detection in a very clever manner. A virus is so small, between 20 and 100 nanometres in width (one nanometre = one millionth of a millimetre), that it can't be seen with a conventional microscope. It actually has no real life of its own, rather it is a tiny bundle of DNA or RNA encased in a protein envelope. A virus is constantly on the lookout for a host cell. Once inside the host, the cell's enzymes remove the protective envelope and in an ingenious fashion the virus uses the cell to replicate itself. Since this goes on inside the cell the virus is safe from most of the body's defences and in some cases can live on for years in a cell. But, as you can imagine, our bodies have developed special defences against viruses.

Once a cell has been infiltrated by a virus it transports the virus' discarded protein envelope to the outside of the cell membrane to alert the body that it has been taken over by a virus. Special white blood cells (see below) recognise the infected cell and take steps to destroy it and along with the virus. The presence of viruses also stimulates cells to produce a protective chemical. In 1957 a British/Swiss team discovered a protein which they called interferon which is produced by our cells. Interferon causes cells to produce other proteins which inhibit the spread of a virus, in a process which isn't yet completely understood. In addition to fighting viruses, interferon has also shown promise as a treatment for cancer. In clinical trials interferon seems to retard the growth of malignant meningioma, a type of brain tumour which so far has been especially difficult to treat.

Pharmaceuticals, which have been so effective against bacteria, have as yet shown very meagre results against viruses. Currently our bodies themselves offer the best defence against viral infection, but the collective intelligence of medical researchers may well devise an effective treatment for viruses in the future. For example, by targeting an enzyme which the flu virus needs to replicate, researchers hope to develop a therapy for influenza. As our understanding of the body's own defences grows, treatments designed to emulate and enhance our natural resistance appear particularly promising.

There is no doubt that our bodies have tremendous defences. For instance, the body has an internal security force of about a 1,000,000,000,000 white blood cells. Like any good security force, the white cells have to be adept at *recognising* invaders (antigens) or terrorists (cancerous cells), *recalling* how they were handled before, and *reacting* effectively to a menace or a threat. The white cells have developed specialised functions in order to better recognise, remember and react. White cells are produced in various locations: bone marrow, tonsils, spleen, lymph nodes and lymphoid patches in the small intestine.

T-Cells are white blood cells which are trained in the thymus gland (thus the T), a walnut-sized gland behind the breastbone. The T-lymphocytes are the most numerous form of lymphocytes, accounting for up to 70 per cent of the total number. They directly engage and destroy antigens (invaders). T-cells secrete numerous chemicals called "cytokines" which help to regulate the immune response. For example, they can increase or suppress a response and instruct certain cells to multiply and mature more rapidly. Among other things it appears that white blood cells learn to differentiate between "self" and "foreign" in the thymus gland. When things are functioning properly the thymus gland won't allow cells into the blood stream which can't make this distinction.

Helper T-cells — these cells recognise antigens which are presented by special cells (APC). They also activate plasma cells and killer cells.

Killer T-cells — these cells recognise and destroy cells which have been invaded by viruses. It's possible that they also destroy tumour-cells.

Memory T-cells — these are a special type of long-term helper cells against a specific antigen. Memory cells are able to "chemically" remember the response (like a detective taking notes) so that the same intruder can be better dealt with in the future.

Natural killer-cells — especially active against tumour cells, but also against cells infected by a virus.

B-Cells are named after the "b" in bone marrow, which is a bit misleading, since T-cells also originate in bone marrow. B-cells cluster in the lymph nodes (lymph comes from Latin *lympha* meaning spring water) where they busily manufacture antibodies. When B-cells encounter an antigen (invader) they can transform themselves into two different cell types: memory cells which recall how to attack the invader, or plasma cells which manufacture antibodies against the invader. These cells are truly fantastic security guards. Just imagine, on the exterior of these cells there are *millions* of different receptors which are highly efficient at recognising the antigens produced by invaders. It would be like having security guards who naturally recognise millions of different invaders and immediately initiate an attack specifically designed for a particular invader. After a battle is over the memory cells go into a kind of suspended state and should the invader appear again, they can then transform themselves even faster into plasma cells to manufacture antibodies to fight the "remembered" enemy.

There is also a group of polymorphs called **granulocytes** (because of granular cellular fluid) which are the most numerous cells in the blood with a nucleus. They have a lifespan of about one or two weeks. If they encounter an invader (antigen) which has been tagged by an antibody or complement protein, they engulf the invader and destroy them with powerful enzymes which are contained in their cytoplasm (cellular fluid). There are also special cells in this group (**eosinophiles** and **basophiles**) which attack parasites. The **neutrophiles** (which make up over half of all white blood cells) aren't as particular, if they are called into action they will devour anything in their path — fungi, bacteria or viruses.

The largest white cells, **monocytes**, are also the rarest. They only live for a day or two in this state, but gradually they make their way to the tissue and develop into **macrophages**, which behave somewhat like neutrophiles.

P53

P53 is neither a fighter plane, nor a public school in New York City. The "p" stands for protein and "53" is the molecular weight of a substance, first discovered in 1979, which was named "molecule of the year" by the journal *Science* in 1994. In 1982 a scientist discovered the gene responsible for p53 on the short arm of chromosome 17. Initially it was believed to be a cause of cancer, a fact which didn't generate a great deal of enthusiasm. However, in 1989 researchers discovered that p53 was actually a first-line defender against cancer. In the meantime, over 5,000 studies have been published about p53 and it is certain to gain tremendously in importance as thousands of researchers turn their attention to it.

P53 is involved in several metabolic processes, in cell proliferation and growth, and in the reading (transcription) of DNA. As mentioned before, every minute up to 600 million new cells are created, each with a genetic code equivalent to 750 megabytes. If an error occurs during the copying of this enormous account of genetic data, steps have to be taken either to correct the mistake, or to destroy the copy. When we are exposed to radiation, toxic chemicals, chemotherapy or UV rays there is considerable potential for mistakes to occur and cells have devised strategies to cope with mistakes. Now p53 has been added to the list of known safeguards. Cells maintain a small and steady supply of p53 which is routinely replenished, however, in the event that a copying mistake occurs, somehow the cell steps up the production of p53. P53 then initiates steps to shut off the copying process until the mistake can be corrected.

The gene responsible for p53 is made up of over 2,500 "chemical" letters and it too is susceptible to mutation. When this occurs the cell loses a powerful anti-cancer agent. A damaged p53 gene has been linked to a great number of cancers. Aflatoxins produced by mould which can contaminate crops such as peanuts and corn have been shown to alter one amino acid in p53. Cigarette smoke has also been demonstrated to alter p53 and thus promote lung cancer. Also it is known that the (HPV) human papilloma virus, highly linked to cervical cancer, produces a protein which assists in the destruction of p53.

Once again it's clear that understanding our body's own defences is of the utmost importance. Not only is it useful for the average person to better understand the effects of such things as smoking and over- exposure to the sun, but physicians, armed with the knowledge of new developments such as p53, can better deal with diseases. For example, cancer therapies such as radiation and chemotherapy can be effective if the p53 gene is intact, however, if that isn't the case other measures may be indicated.

Again it appears that when researchers are able to emulate or stimulate the body's natural defences there is cause for hope. Recently, researchers at the University of Texas manipulated

viruses to carry a normal p53 gene. They then injected the virus
into nine patients with lung cancer. In three of the patients the
tumour stopped growing and in three others the tumours even
shrank. Surprisingly, it doesn't appear necessary to infect every
tumour cell with the jury-rigged "p53" virus. Tumour cells which
weren't infected by the "p53" virus, were somehow influenced by
neighbouring cells which were infected.

Paradoxically researchers at Onyx Pharmaceuticals employed
a defective p53 gene to attack tumour cells. In an experiment
researchers infected a mouse tumour with a manipulated virus
with a faulty p53 gene. Under normal circumstances the p53 gene
would suppress the virus in the cell, however, due to the defective
p53 gene the virus replicates unchecked until the tumour cell
ruptures. The spreading virus eventually destroyed the remaining
tumour cells. The next stage in the research will be to determine if
the virus can elude the immune system.

Such possibilities offer a ray of hope for those instances in
which the defective p53 defence is compromised, but we should be
aware that an intact p53 gene defence is ceaselessly thwarting
outbreaks of cancer. Indeed, nature is taking care of things in a
staggeringly effective manner.

It Doesn't Stop Here

Unfortunately, this could only be a cursory description of a small
aspect of the healing and health maintenance functions performed
by the human body. It should, however, be clear how
magnificently nature has provided for our protection. It's
important that we understand and never underestimate our own
healing potential. Throughout the remainder of this book we will
explore practical ways to aid *the physician within* to act as *nature's
assistant*. We also need to learn how to consciously fortify our
healing potential by striving towards wholeness or oneness. Until
recently the immune system described above was held to be nearly
autonomous, impervious to our thoughts, attitudes and emotions.
In the next chapter we will review recent findings which
demonstrate that our healing mechanisms and our mental state
are linked to a remarkable extent.

Perhaps as we reflect upon this extraordinary achievement of creation, the human body, we can develop an attitude of humility and stewardship towards this precious temple which has been placed at our disposal.

> *It is neither seemly nor befitting that such a noble creature, endowed with intellect and lofty thoughts, capable of wonderful achievement and discoveries in sciences and arts, with potential for even higher perceptions and the accomplishment of divine purposes in life, should seek the blood of his fellowmen upon the field of battle. Man is the temple of God. He is not a human temple. If you destroy a house, the owner of that house will be grieved and wrathful. How much greater is the wrong when man destroys a building planned and erected by God!*

'ABDÚ'L-BAHÁ

3

THE FORMATIVE STAGES
OF MIND AND BODY
MEDICINE

I n the preceding chapter we examined how brain cells
communicate by secreting and receiving various biochemical
messengers. Recently, the medical establishment was stunned
by the discovery that not only brain cells, but all of the primary
cells of the immune system are equipped with receptors for
neurotransmitters and neuropeptides. In fact, at first this idea
seemed so preposterous that it was denied by the medical
community for several years. Then came an even more startling
discovery: not only do the cells of the immune system receive
messages from the brain, but they also produce the same
biochemical messengers with which they can transmit messages to
the brain. Two medical researchers, Eric Smith and Edwin
Blalock, discovered in 1981 that white blood cells produce the
hormone ACTH, yet they were hardly able to get their results
published. At the time it was universally accepted that ACTH
could only be produced by the pituitary gland, so the editors of
various medical journals deemed Smith and Blalock's results
erroneous, the product of sloppy experimentation. A prominent
British scientific journal even went so far as to label them radical

psychoneuroimmunologists and it took four years before their results were confirmed by other scientists! Fortunately things are changing and the idea of an autonomous immune system is heading toward the scrap heap of history.

Still, well-entrenched ideas die slowly. In the 17th century Galileo wrote to Kepler to express his frustration at the refusal of his peers to gaze through a telescope and view the planets and moons for themselves. His disappointment is obvious, "Verily, just as serpents close their ears, so do men close their eyes to the light of truth." Although the "mind/body" connection has now engaged the public's attention, it still isn't as well received by the medical establishment as one might expect. In 1995 the noted physician and author, Andrew Weil, wrote that few in the medical establishment take the field of mind/body medicine seriously, indeed, he maintains that those who establish priorities and determine funding are contemptuous of colleagues who are involved in mind/body research. We, however, needn't involve ourselves in this dispute. After all, time is truth's champion and history has amply demonstrated that closed-minds cannot contain the truth.

Nature's Morphine

For quite some time medical researchers had supposed that there must be some sort of receptor process at work in the body to regulate biochemical reactions. In 1973 Dr. Candace Pert, then a graduate student, was able to devise a means of establishing the existence of receptors by radioactively tagging a drug and measuring its absorption in animal brain tissue. Shortly thereafter "opiate" receptors in the brain were identified. Naturally this begged the question, if the cells have opiate receptors, does the body produce its own opiate? The answer was, yes, it does. Actually a number of **endo**genous **morphines** have been identified and they are referred to by the contraction **endorphins**. Mothers in labour and long distance runners experience the analgesic and euphoric properties of endorphins.

Endorphins are actually chains of amino acids, which in turn are the building blocks of proteins. These chains of amino acids are called peptides, and endorphins are part of a group known as neuropeptides. Once endorphins were identified researchers began a search to determine if a system of neuropeptides is at work. Then in 1976 Nicholas Plotnikoff of the University of Illinois in Chicago discovered receptors for opiates on immune cells.

P-Mail

Our cells communicate by a system we'll call P-Mail, not in honour of Dr. Pert, but to represent the countless peptides involved in cell communication. Dr. Pert gives a good graphic representation of cell communication. Imagine a cell as having millions of different satellite dishes all over its surface, each individual dish is designed to receive a specific biochemical message. Molecules, especially peptides, instruct cells when to divide, which protein to produce and which genes to activate. There are twenty-three different amino acids, which are the building blocks of proteins and peptides. Think of the endless possibilities we have, to produce words with the twenty-six different letters of our alphabet. Similarly, the body has an almost infinite number of possibilities to produce "chemical" words using the twenty-three amino acids. There are some short words like enkephalin (the brain's own morphine) which has only five letters, and extremely long words like insulin, which is a chain of a few hundred amino acids.

Lysergic Acid Diethylamide (LSD) is a bit like a postal worker who sorts the P-Mail with a sense of reckless abandon. LSD, heroin, ecstasy, angel dust, caffeine and many psychoactive drugs work by altering neurotransmitters or their receptors. In the case of LSD, the brain stem, which regulates the alertness of the brain, is stimulated and the limbic system is subdued. This highly exaggerated state of alertness is probably responsible for the feeling of expanded consciousness associated with LSD. There is, however, also a diminishing perception of personal identity (or a dissociation of self), sometimes accompanied by terror and a sense of losing self-control. The processing of sensory information is also distorted, colours might be tasted, smells felt, and the perception of time and space is also altered. Sometimes the effects of hallucinations, a false sense of omnipotence, or paranoia, can result in potentially dangerous behaviour. Using the P-Mail analogy we can see that even a minuscule amount of LSD can send millions of confusing P-Mail messages to the cells responsible for the delicate balancing act of controlling consciousness.

Illnesses such as Parkinson's disease and schizophrenia appear to be a breakdown in the P-Mail system. In the case of Parkinson's disease the body loses the ability to produce sufficient amounts of the chemical messenger "dopamine". In the case of schizophrenia, emerging brain research seems to point to an impairment of the brain's ability to utilise dopamine to properly regulate the stimulation of nerve cells. Dopamine is sometimes found in abnormally high levels in people suffering from schizophrenia. There isn't, however, complete agreement among medical authorities as to the cause of schizophrenia.

Biochemical Aspects of Emotions

René Descartes, the 17th, century French philosopher and mathematician played a predominant role in the separation of the mind and body. In order to placate the Roman Catholic Church, which felt threatened by the study of anatomy, Descartes argued that since the body didn't need the mind to function, it could be thought of as independent. The mind, soul and emotions would, in his argument, rightly remain the domain of the church. Before we judge Descartes too harshly, we need to consider the power and the prevailing attitude of the Roman Catholic Church during his lifetime. For example, even in 1829 Pope Leo XII decreed that smallpox was a judgment of God and that anyone who received a vaccination was challenging Divine Will and could no longer be considered a child of God.

In any case, Candace Pert and many of her fellow researchers see current attitudes towards mind/body research as a legacy of this reductionist argument. They sometimes refer to the neuropeptides and their receptors as the biochemical correlates of emotion. That kind of talk is not only controversial in medical circles, but it can easily upset some religious people who have come to view the mind and the brain as being independent of the body. Dr. Pert, however, sees emotions as the bridge between the physical and the mental. In her view, various biochemical substances are responsible for specific "feelings" or emotions. A complex biochemical blend of neurotransmitters and neuropeptides is responsible for our "feelings", not only in the brain, but in cells throughout our bodies.

As we saw in the review of the immune system, it could conceivably be argued that the cells of the immune system demonstrate an intelligence of sorts, i.e., the ability to learn from experience and react according to what they have learned. Nature has endowed the brain and the cells of the body with the ability to communicate with each other and that needn't threaten one's beliefs. On the contrary, it's actually an ingenious design and the blending of the physical and mental unquestionably enhances the experience of being alive. Indeed, it's surely no accident that the terms *feelings* and *emotions* are often used interchangeably. It's interesting that Dr. Pert even found receptors for neuropeptides in the lining of the intestinal tract, perhaps adding a bit of credibility to the term "gut feeling". In any case she makes the point that in reality your mind is in every cell of your body, not just in your brain.

She gives an example of how the biochemical equivalent of *thirst* is understood by various parts of the body. Thirst is associated with a peptide called angiotensin. Angiotensin causes your mind to register thirst, but that very same peptide present in your lungs and kidneys causes them to conserve water.

The Nerve Connection
In 1963 researchers at the University of Leningrad determined that damage to the hypothalamus (remember our maintenance department) could impair the immune response. This led them to explore whether or not nerves were sending messages from the brain to the immune system. In Switzerland, Hugo Besedovsky led a group of scientists to determine if information was flowing in the other direction, i.e., from the immune system to the brain. He

measured the electrical activity of the hypothalamus of a rat and then injected the rat with a strong dose of antigens. As the rat's immune system went into high gear the electrical activity of the hypothalamus more than doubled. Obviously information was getting through.

You will recall that T-cells are trained in the thymus gland, an important part of the immune system. In the 1980's, Karen Bulloch, a neuroanatomist, discovered that the *vagus nerve*, which is one of a dozen nerves wired directly to the brain, has branches which are connected to the thymus gland. Subsequently, Dr. David Felten and other researchers identified nerves leading to the lymph nodes, bone marrow and the spleen. If the nerves leading to the spleen or lymph nodes are removed, the immune response is virtually stopped. They theorise that nerves may control the flow of white blood cells throughout the body and regulate the immune function.

Psychoneuroimmunology or PNI

In broad terms, PNI is a scientific study based upon the interrelationship between our mental state and our immune, endocrine and nervous systems. Lay people generally consider PNI to be Mind/Body medicine, which in actuality is a rather apt description, however, the concept of "Mind/Body medicine" is somewhat of a magnet which has attracted proponents of therapies and beliefs which are beyond the scope of PNI. In any case, PNI research takes place on a number of levels, from the macro to the micro, and involves various medical and psychological disciplines. On the macro level we have epidemiological studies which, for example, might investigate why lonely and isolated people have a mortality rate more than twice as high as their peers from the general population. Or why the immune response drops and the mortality rate increases among persons who have recently lost their spouse. These studies are often combined with studies on the micro level which involve a wide range of variables, for example, genetic factors, hormone and peptide levels, cell counts and the prevalence of antibodies.

Using sophisticated technology and the scientific method, researchers are proving many conventional wisdoms, from the dangers of exaggerated stress to the importance of getting a good night's sleep. There are, however, a number of factors which make the study of PNI difficult. First of all the mental or emotional state can be very subjective, one man's depression is another man's bad mood. Retrospective studies are also difficult when participants are asked to gauge their feelings in the past. On the micro level many studies, due to ethical considerations, can't be carried out on human beings. Blood work can be done, however, it is the blood found in the periphery and not the internal areas of the body. Animal studies overcome some of these shortcomings, but the immune system of a mouse, while very similar to that of a human, is not identical. However, researchers are employing prospective studies which concentrate on future results. In this way they are able, by means of advanced psychological tests, to better quantify the mental and emotional state and to track the outbreak of disease over a number of years. PNI researchers are also developing additional methods of experimenting with the immune response, e.g., white blood cells outside the body are exposed to substances which produce an immune reaction and the resulting cell division can be measured.

The Origins of Psychoneuroimmunology

All of the experiments and researchers outlined above are unquestionably an integral part of the history of PNI. In fact, it is a bit difficult to pinpoint any one event as the beginning of PNI; however, the coining of the term "psychoneuroimmunology" can be traced. Surprisingly, Robert Ader, the psychologist who came up with the term "psychoneuroimmunology", was carrying out a routine experiment, which by accident would prove to be one of the most important developments in PNI research.

In 1975 Robert Ader designed an experiment to test whether rats could be conditioned to have an aversion to sugar-water. First the rats were given saccharine-water. After thirty-minutes elapsed the rats were given an injection of Cytoxan (also known as cyclophosphamide) which causes nausea and a general sense of malaise. Indeed the rats developed an aversion to saccharine-water. They drank 60 per cent less when they were offered it every third day. When thirst compelled them to drink saccharine-water they became nauseous, even though they hadn't been injected with Cytoxan. Ader had proved that an aversion to saccharine-water could be conditioned.

He then decided to test how long the aversion would remain in effect. As expected, after a few days the aversion to saccharine-water subsided and things appeared to return to normal. Then after a little more than a month a number of his rats began to die and their deaths seemed to be correlated to the amount of saccharine-water they had consumed. After contemplating the unexpected deaths of his laboratory rats Ader developed an unheard of hypothesis.

Cytoxan, with which the rats had been injected, is an immune-suppressing drug used in chemotherapy for cancer treatment. Therefore, Ader reasoned that the rats' immune systems had been suppressed by conditioning. Further, he reasoned that their suppressed immune systems had failed to protect them from invading organisms, which had caused their deaths. This of course meant that the brain and the immune system had to be capable of communicating, a serious breach of the accepted medical knowledge at that time.

Ader then enlisted the assistance of Nicholas Cohen, an immunologist also working at the University of Rochester in New York, to test his hypothesis. Cohen confirmed that after drinking saccharine-water there was a significant suppression of the rats' immune system. Ader and Cohen's critics speculated that the ordeal which the rats were put through was responsible for the suppression of the immune system and not the conditioning. In response Ader and Cohen repeated the experiment using lithium chloride instead of Cytoxan. Lithium chloride caused nausea, but didn't suppress the immune system. At the end of the experiment the rat immune system was intact, proving that the ordeal of the experiment hadn't affected the rats' immune system. Later, two researchers at the University of Düsseldorf conducted a similar experiment using Cyclosporin A instead of Cytoxan. This is a medication used to suppress the immune system of organ transplant recipients and it doesn't cause nausea. Their results confirmed Ader and Cohen's original hypothesis.

In 1981, after examining various PNI research experiments, Ader edited a book containing articles by several leaders in the field of mind-body research, which he entitled *Psychoneuroimmunology*. A similar term had been used by the psychiatrist, George Solomon, who did research at Stanford University in the 1960's. Solomon became interested in the link between personality traits and emotional states to the outbreak of autoimmune diseases such as rheumatoid arthritis. Solomon sought an explanation for why two people could have the same genetic factor for rheumatoid arthritis, but only one of them might develop it. Dr. Solomon suspected that stress and personality traits might be responsible. He made a study of female patients with the disease and noted that they were significantly more likely to repress anger, to be self-sacrificing to a degree bordering on masochism, easily led and prone to depression. Dr. Solomon called this type of mind-body research *psychoimmunology*. Ader later added the element "neuro" to impart the importance of the nervous system to mind-body research. It would have been even more accurate to include "endocrine", but *Psychoneuroendocrinimmunology*, for obvious reasons, was discarded.

From Theory to Practice
More than a decade after their initial aversion conditioning experiments, Cohen and Ader came up with a practical application for their work. Cytoxan, the drug which caused the suppression of immunity and nausea, is also used in the treatment of lupus erythematosus, a severe autoimmune disorder. (Autoimmune disorders refer to conditions in which the immune system attacks the body as if it were an invading organism. Multiple sclerosis, rheumatoid arthritis and lupus erythematosus are examples of autoimmune disorders.) Since drugs like Cytoxan and other immune suppressants are toxic and often cause severe side-effects, it seems like a natural step to employ conditioning as a means of reducing the dose of Cytoxan required.

Ader and Cohen designed an experiment around a strain of New Zealand mice which suffered from lupus erythematosus.

They were able to condition the mice to survive with half of the normal dose of Cytoxan. The mice in the control group which received only half of the normal dose died. This seemed like a breakthrough; however, could humans be conditioned to suppress their immune response? They didn't have to wait long to find out.

In Cleveland, Ohio, a psychologist whose daughter was suffering from lupus erythematosus provided Ader with the opportunity to test his conditioning method on a human. She was concerned for her daughter because of the toxic nature of Cytoxan and informed her child's pediatrician, Dr. Karen Olness of Ader and Cohen's work. Olness contacted Ader and together they designed a conditioning approach specifically for the girl.

Ader and Olness rejected the idea of using saccharine-water in the case of a little girl, instead they wanted something unpleasant, unmistakable and previously unknown to the patient. They chose cod liver oil and strong rose perfume as a backup conditioning stimulus. For the first three months the girl received a monthly intravenous dose of Cytoxan as she sipped cod liver oil, smelled the rose perfume and imagined a rose in her mind. In the fourth month the procedure was repeated, except for the Cytoxan. Then every third month the drug was included again. At the end of a year she had received six doses instead of the twelve she would have normally received.

One pitfall of this regime was that the cod live oil also seemed to condition nausea. For this reason it was discontinued after the ninth month. After a year Dr. Olness concluded that the girl's progress was equal to that which could have been expected from the full dose. Eventually her disorder stabilised and she was able to attend university. When necessary she still uses the image of the rose to call up the immunosuppressive effects of Cytoxan. Although Dr. Ader cautions that a single case can't be used to draw specific conclusions, he is hopeful that this approach can benefit others suffering from lupus.

Practical Implications of Emotions and Health

We should also point out that we are using the term 'emotions' in its broadest sense, incorporating attitudes, personality traits, social support and personal relationships. Up to this point we have concentrated more on the mechanical aspects of the mind-body relationship. For a scientist it is important to understand the mechanics of the relationship of emotions to physical health; for the average person, however, the impact of emotions on his or her personal health is of greater consequence. Although in some cases scientists can't speak with absolute certainty, nevertheless, their inferences based upon PNI research and their own clinical experience enables them to offer valuable insights into the role of emotions in maintaining health.

Back in the 1950's two cardiologists, Friedman and Rosenman, coined the term "Type A personalities". Working with elite young military officers they identified many as being assertive, self-confident and tenacious. They were also quick to anger, irritable, dominating, demanding, impatient and seeking perfection from themselves and others. It was observed that they, as a group, were prone to have high serum cholesterol levels, high blood pressure and heart disease. Friedman and Rosenman eventually devised a study to quantify their observation. They studied 3500 healthy young men, half of whom had been determined to have Type A personalities. After eight and a half years had elapsed it was demonstrated that nearly 70 per cent of those who had had heart attacks were Type A personalities. The National Heart, Lung and Blood Institute reviewed their study and concluded that Type A behaviour was as good a predictor of heart disease as high blood pressure, cholesterol levels or smoking. The US Army also concluded that officers with Type A personalities sometimes have dangerous lapses in judgement and are responsible for putting inordinate stress on those around them.

Research into Type A personalities has continued and there are indications that not all traits are equally responsible for causing heart disease. Anger and hostility appear to be the most dangerous aspects of a Type A personality and the best predictors for future heart disease.

We've already looked at some of the negative impacts which prolonged stress can have on the immune system. Not only does it undermine our healing mechanisms, but it also raises our blood pressure, and stimulates the liver to produce more cholesterol and release it into the bloodstream. It also enhances our blood's ability to clot, thereby increasing the potential for heart attacks and strokes. Finally, it can cause coronary arteries to constrict. The point, if you tend toward Type A behaviour, take steps to alter your behaviour and manage your self-inflicted stress.

Emotions and the Immune System

Recall that the limbic system of the brain (which among other things regulates emotions), the hypothalamus (in extremely close contact with the pituitary gland) and the cerebral cortex (responsible for higher levels of thought) are highly interrelated. The complex interaction of these systems has a substantial impact on our immune system and our biochemistry. Well, you might rightfully ask, why can't we consciously control our immune system? Nature has wisely placed many aspects of our physiology outside of our conscious control, frankly because we simply lack the mental capacity to control either our liver, our immune system or any number of other systems. One natural barrier is that our "thinking centre" or cerebral cortex has the capacity for language, but the pituitary gland, hypothalamus and limbic system lack the ability to understand language.

Communication does take place, but not on a verbal basis. PNI research is demonstrating that although we can't consciously *control* our immune system, we can *influence* it. Constantly thoughts, attitudes and responses to the environment cause non-verbal messages to be exchanged between the cerebral cortex and areas of the brain responsible for regulating numerous physiological functions. These areas of the brain also produce various neurotransmitters and neuropeptides which not only influence the emotional state, but have an impact on the immune system as well. If you are routinely enraged by the driving skills of other motorists, the emotional centres of your brain are being informed of your rage, but they aren't necessarily aware of the source. They can't differentiate whether you are in a life-threatening situation, or rush hour traffic. It's important to be conscious of the non-verbal messages you are sending. It matters not if you are depressed because you were denied a promotion, or if you are trapped in a *truly* hopeless situation. The message, not the cause, gets through, so be aware of your non-verbal messages.

Quieting the Mind

In the next chapter we will explore the impact of spirituality on the mind and body, but here, at this juncture, we can briefly mention how spirituality and religious practices influence the non-verbal messages which affect our health. Our conscious thoughts are often agitated and chaotic, lacking focus. This sends a correspondingly distressed and jumbled message to our non-verbal emotional centres. The Buddhists have a very fitting description for this type of consciousness, they call it "monkey mind". One can easily imagine a monkey incessantly springing around a tree from limb to limb, just as an untrained mind jumps from one thought to the next. All great religious traditions have methods for overcoming "monkey mind". Prayer, meditation, yoga and elaborate rituals are all ways to quiet and focus the mind. Music, rhythm and dance are also means of quieting and focusing the mind. When our conscious mind is quieted and focused we can imagine that our non-verbal emotional centres are receiving a message equivalent to, "it's smooth sailing, things couldn't be better." In this state our healing potential is significantly enhanced.

Many people have the impression that Hinduism and Buddhism are the only religions associated with meditation. Certainly, they both place a great emphasis on the mastery of the senses and meditation, however, the other religions are also linked to meditation. Take, for example, Judaism. *The Book of Psalms* begins with these three verses:

> *Blessed is the man that walketh not in the counsel of the ungodly, nor standeth in the way of sinners, nor sitteth in the seat of the scornful. But his delight is in the law of the Lord; and in his law doth he meditate day and night. And he shall be like a tree planted by the rivers of water, that bringeth forth his fruit in his season; his leaf also shall not wither; and whatsoever he doeth shall prosper.*

Of course, we know that Jesus went into the desert for forty days to fast and commune with His spirit. Before He took up His mission it was Muhammad's custom to retire each year for the month of Ramadan to a cave in the desert on the slopes of Mount Hira to meditate. Bahá'u'lláh, the founder of the Bahá'í Faith, also retired to the wilderness before He publicly proclaimed His mission. He recounted:

We betook Ourselves to the wilderness, and there, separated and alone, led for two years a life of complete solitude.... For in Our solitude We were unaware of the harm or benefit, the health or ailment, of any soul. Alone, We communed with Our spirit, oblivious of the world and all that is therein.

Bahá'u'lláh taught that the Holy Writings are like food for the soul and He enjoined Bahá'ís to read daily from the *Sacred Writing*. He made it clear, however, that the purpose was to uplift the spirit.

Pride not yourselves on much reading of the verses or on a multitude of pious acts by night and day; for were a man to read a single verse with joy and radiance it would be better for him than to read with lassitude all the Holy Books of God, the Help in Peril, the Self-Subsisting. Read ye the sacred verses in such measure that ye be not overcome by languor and despondency. Lay not upon your souls that which will weary them and weigh them down, but rather what will lighten and uplift them, so that they may soar on the wings of Divine verses towards the Dawning-place of His manifest signs; this will draw you nearer to God, did ye but comprehend.

At any rate, whether it be a tea ceremony, prayer or meditation, if done properly the mind will be quieted and the healing centres of the brain will receive beneficial impulses from the cerebral cortex. Outside of the religious context, practitioners have developed additional techniques to quiet the mind and elicit relaxation and an improved emotional state. Autogenic Training, Guided Imagery, the Relaxation Response, Biofeedback and Aroma Therapy are examples of such techniques.

4

BODY, MIND AND SOUL

Turning the face towards God brings healing to the body, the mind and the soul.

'Abdu'l-Bahá

Enlisting God's Help

Stress, of course, can't be avoided, but we can learn to better manage stress and avoid unnecessary self-inflicted stress. Dr. Bernie Siegel, in his book *Between Office Visit*, cites a short but profound prayer by Reinhold Niebuhr:

> *God grant me serenity to accept*
> *the things I cannot change,*
> *courage to change the things I can,*
> *and wisdom to know the difference.*

If we not only apply this to major challenges, but also to our ordinary daily lives we can avoid a great deal of unnecessary self-inflicted stress. Take, for example, a simple thing like being stuck in traffic. You know you're going to be late for an important meeting, but will it help to tightly grip the steering-wheel, hold your breath and get upset about why you aren't moving? If you can serenely accept a situation which you can't change, you've learned an important stress management tool.

In this regard the German language is more accurate than English. In English one might say, "he makes me angry" or "that makes me angry." In German, "ich ärgere mich" literally (and correctly) means "I make myself angry". We may not have control of many situations and events, but with practice we can gain self-control and learn to accept circumstances which we cannot control.

Closely related to this form of acceptance is the idea of putting things you can't change in God's hands. In his book *Timeless Healing*, Herbert Benson, MD, writes of the positive impact of belief and postulates that human beings are actually "hard wired" for God, i.e., genetically predisposed to believe in God. Dr. Siegel, as well, writes of the importance of turning things over to God. In so doing you are shifting a burden from your shoulders to God's. *Acceptance, assurance* and *assistance* should be our watchwords — acceptance of things we can't change and assurance of God's assistance. 'Abdu'l-Bahá revealed a short prayer which focuses on this theme:

> *O God! Refresh and gladden my spirit. Purify my heart. Illumine my powers. I lay all my affairs in Thy hand. Thou art my Guide and my Refuge. I will no longer be sorrowful and grieved; I will be a happy and joyful being. O God! I will no longer be full of anxiety, nor will I let trouble harass me. I will not dwell on the unpleasant things of life.*
>
> *O God! Thou art more friend to me than I am to myself. I dedicate myself to Thee, O Lord.*

Research has shown that three primary attitudinal components are related to a healthy management of stress: *commitment, control* and *challenge*. Persons in a research study who were deemed to deal most effectively with stress were linked to those three traits. Commitment can be seen as doing something to the best of your ability. In so doing you derive satisfaction from your work and it helps to give purpose and meaning to your life, moreover, it focuses your thoughts. As Bahá'ís we would identify this type of commitment with the concept of work as worship.

The man who makes a piece of notepaper to the best of his ability, conscientiously, concentrating all his forces on perfecting it, is giving praise to God. Briefly, all effort and exertion put forth by man from the fulness of his heart is worship...

'ABDU'L-BAHÁ

Research also reveals that a sense of being in control is equally important to dealing effectively with stress. Stress is virtually unavoidable when one is charged with responsibility and denied an element of control. Having control over a stressful situation can actually allow it to be perceived as a stimulating challenge, rather than a debilitating factor. Commitment, control and challenge are conducive to producing an optimistic outlook, a positive attitude and a feeling of hope. All of these attitudes have been demonstrated to positively influence health. Indifference, lack of control and boredom are conducive to producing a sense of hopelessness and a state of depression — both of which impact negatively on health.

A number of studies done on rats have shown that rats in a stressful situation which is controllable are even less likely than unstressed rats to develop tumours (30% vs. 50%). However, rats in a stressful situation and deprived of control developed tumours 73 per cent of the time. Physicians need to be cognizant that when they treat conditions or diseases instead of treating patients they are undermining their patients' healing potential. Especially in today's high-tech world a hospital patient can quickly be stripped of dignity and a sense of control. Studies have shown that in these circumstances there is a decrease in the number of lymphocytes, natural killer cells and T-cells; moreover, the functionality of the lymphocytes is diminished. Added to this is the fact that being in a hospital or suffering from a major illness is, of itself, a highly stressful situation which further taxes the immune system. Involving patients in their treatment, giving them a sense of control and helping them to see their situation as a challenge, is a vital component of the art of healing.

Loneliness and a lack of social support also have been recognised as important factors responsible for diminishing health and longevity. There is, however, a difference between being alone and being lonely. It's certainly possible to be among others and feel isolated and lonely, and it is also possible to be alone without feeling lonely. Loneliness involves a sense of incompleteness and emptiness, a yearning for contact with others and general unhappiness. Loneliness has been shown to cause a reduction in the amount of natural killer cells, while those with social support and satisfying personal relationships demonstrate an enhanced immune response, an increase in natural killer cell activity and an increase in lymphocyte function. Sometimes in the course of life loneliness can strike and indeed it is difficult to bear, it's something with which we must deal. First and foremost, however, you should never lose track of the fact that when you establish an intimate relationship with God, you need never feel truly lonely again. We saw in the closing line of the above prayer:

O God! Thou art more friend to me than I am to myself. I dedicate myself to Thee, O Lord.

You might say, that's all well and good, but in reality mere words are incapable of affecting one's emotional state. Naturally, if it's a matter of mere words, proclaiming to have a personal relationship with God can't overcome loneliness, however, genuine faith is capable of affecting one's attitudes, perceptions and emotions. It's worth noting that 'Abdu'l-Bahá, who revealed that prayer, had to endure forty years of imprisonment and well knew of isolation, uncertainty, loss of control and nearly all of the harmful emotional factors which PNI research has investigated. Yet despite such hardships he was able to overcome his circumstances by turning to God. This is his personal testimony:

I myself was in prison forty years—one year alone would have been impossible to bear—nobody survived that imprisonment more than a year! But, thank God, during all those forty years I was supremely happy! Every day, on waking, it was like hearing good tidings, and every night infinite joy was mine.

Spirituality was my comfort, and turning to God was my greatest joy. If this had not been so, do you think it possible that I could have lived through those forty years in prison?

When his imprisonment was over 'Abdu'l-Bahá eventually travelled to Europe and America to spread the Bahá'í teachings. Rather than emerging from such an ordeal as a broken man, it's interesting to see the impression which he made upon non-Bahá'ís in the West. Howard Colby Ives, a Unitarian Minister, recorded his impressions:

He showed me by His voice, manner, bearing, smile, how I should be, knowing that out of the pure soil of being the good fruit of deeds and words would surely spring.

There was a strange, awe-inspiring mingling of humility and majesty, relaxation and power in His slightest word or gesture which made me long to understand its source. What made Him so different, so immeasurably superior to any other man I had ever met?

...It was my inestimable privilege to watch and talk with...the Son of Bahá'u'lláh, the Centre of His Covenant, the perfect exemplar of His Word and Life....

Here I saw a man who, outwardly, like myself, lived in the world of confusion, yet, inwardly, beyond the possibility of doubt, lived and worked in that higher and real world. All His concepts, all His motives, all His actions, derived their springs from that "World of Light".

It might surprise you to learn that research is now beginning to demonstrate the beneficial effects of belief and turning to God. For example, in 1995 researchers at Dartmouth Medical School reported that patients who were comforted by their religious beliefs were three times more likely to survive open-heart surgery than those who weren't. In a book published in 1994, *The Faith Factor: An Annotated Bibliography of Clinical Research on Spiritual Subjects*, Dr. Dale Matthews, Dr. David Larson and Ms. Constance Barry reported a number of statistically significant studies which demonstrate the influence of belief on health. Some of the factors referred to include:

Reduction in: hostility, general anxiety, death anxiety, blood pressure, alcohol use, nicotine use, drug use and depression.

Increase in: ability to cope, quality of life in cancer and heart disease patients, survival rates, self-esteem, altruism, satisfaction, marital satisfaction and general well-being.

Why haven't we heard more about this? Dr. Robert Orr and the Reverend George Isaac of the University of Chicago reviewed seven major primary care journals and found that a scant 1.1 per cent gave any assessment of spiritual or religious implications. Dr. Levin of the Eastern Virginia Medical School concluded that the mind-spirit-body question has been pushed to the fringes of the research community by most epidemiologists.

PNI and God

It should come as no surprise that those who have scientifically examined the relationship of mind and body have recognised the impact of belief and spirituality on health, moreover, many of them speak of a spiritual crisis in modern medicine.

> *To me God is psychoneuroimmunology. My definition of God is intelligent, loving energy. God is scientific. God is light. God is darkness. God is all.... Religion and science can come together. Certainly spirituality and science can come together.* Dr. Bernie Siegel, noted author, general and pediatric surgeon, founder of ECaP (Exceptional Cancer Patients).

> *In my scientific observations, I have learned that no matter what name you give the Infinite Absolute you worship, no matter what theology you ascribe to, the results of believing in God are the same.* DR. HERBERT BENSON, Associate Professor of Medicine at Harvard Medical School.

> DR. BERNIE SIEGEL
noted author......................

> *As a scientist, I believe that we're going to understand everything one day, but that this will require bringing in a realm we don't understand at all yet. We're going to have to*

*bring in that extra-energy realm, the realm of spirit and soul
that Descartes kicked out of Western scientific thought.*

*For example, there's a form of energy that appears to leave the
body when you die. If we call that another energy that just
hasn't been discovered yet, it sounds much less frightening to
me than "spirit". "Soul" is a four-letter word in our [scientific]
tradition.*

DR. CANDACE PERT, Visiting Professor at the Center for
Molecular and Behavioral Neuroscience, Rutgers
University. Former Head of Brain Biochemistry of the
Clinical Neuroscience Branch at the National Institute of
Mental Health.

*My clinical experience, as well as what we're showing in our
research, suggests that psychological, emotional, and even
spiritual factors are important, not only in terms of how they
affect our behaviors, like diet and exercise, but also in more
direct ways.*

DR. DEAN ORNISH.

Assistant Clinical Professor of Medicine and President
and Director of the Preventive Medicine Research
Institute at the School of Medicine, University of
California, San Francisco.

*We need to integrate our magnificent technological advances
with techniques that empower people to mindfulness.... The
body is a magnificent instrument. If we'll open our minds to
study how emotions influence health, then maybe we'll
eventually open our minds toward the spiritual dimensions of
health.*

DR. JOHN ZAWACKI.

Director of Clinical Services in the Division of Digestive
Diseases and Nutrition at the University of
Massachusetts Medical Center in Worcester.

PNI and Bahá'í

The recognition that healing involves the body, mind and spirit, is
fully in conformity with the Bahá'í teachings. PNI research

confirms many of the guidelines offered by the central figures of the Bahá'í Faith with respect to healing; indeed, such research should encourage many Bahá'í health care professionals to more fully integrate their beliefs and professions. Naturally, this has nothing to do with proselytising one's beliefs, which is not only unethical in a professional sense, but is also a violation of the Bahá'í teachings. Instead, it means that health care professionals should no longer feel compelled to practise a form of medicine which ignores, avoids or denies the importance of the mental and spiritual state of the patient.

The verb, *to heal*, actually means to make whole. To be *whole*, or to be of sound health, is more than the mere absence of pain, illness and symptoms. Health is a physical, mental and spiritual state of well-being. The *well* in wellness or well-being is related to *will*, i.e. "according to desire". This is a state in which the mind, body and spirit are in harmony with each other and the outside world. In this state our organic, mental and spiritual capacities are greatly enhanced, thus we are most resilient in the face of potential threats such as disease and infection, and we are better able to recover from injury. Being free of physical ailments is a condition most often found in vigorous young adults, but the kind of *wholeness* or *wellness* described above is a much rarer condition which involves wellness of mind, body and spirit. While health is certainly the desired state, we also need to be realistic and recognise that perpetual wellness is an unrealistic expectation. The most we can do is provide an optimal environment to nurture the mind, body and soul.

To achieve or to assist in maintaining a state of wellness, the physician and the individual unitedly need to strive to bring the areas of mind, body and spirit into harmony with each other. We are constantly exposed to substances, organisms, situations and events which can compromise our bodies, minds and spirits. We briefly described the stress response and its potential for weakening the immune system and causing various stress-related disorders. At the University of Wisconsin in Madison Dr. Christopher Coe, a psychologist, designed experiments to test the

effects of stress on the immune system. First, he assessed a group
of students with respect to their emotional state and the quality of
their relationships. He then took blood samples, isolated the
natural killer cells and combined them with cancer cells. Then
during the stress of final examinations the blood tests were
repeated. Dr. Coe found a consistent correlation between
examination stress and a reduced ability to lyse, or puncture,
tumour cells. Working with Dr. Richard Davidson he also
demonstrated that the emotional state had a demonstrable effect
on the immune response. By measuring the electrical patterns of
the brain related to various emotional states, they were able to
predict a decrease in the immune response of students who were
lonely, depressed, pessimistic and prone to negative thoughts and
emotions. Here we see that the youthful vitality of the students
gave them the appearance of health, but the effects of stress and
negative emotions reduced their immune response and made
them more susceptible to future illness.

This means that a *healer* can't simply treat the symptoms of a
biological entity, rather he or she has to deal with the individual as
a spiritual being with problems, fears, hopes and emotions. Again
the wisdom of Hippocrates is striking, "*it is more import to know
what sort of person has a disease than what sort of disease a person
has.*" That means taking the time to know the person's lifestyle,
nutrition, family situation, medical and life history, occupation,
etc. It also means that one should assess a patient's spiritual state.
Then the healer can employ the appropriate measures (e.g.,
medication, physical therapy, nutrition, exercise, stress reduction,
counselling and prayer) to bring the body, mind and spirit into
harmony.

Aside from the constraints of managed health care and
treatment-based fees, most of these measures pose no problem for
the modern physician, except praying with patients, or discussing
spiritual matters. These are doubtless areas with which most
physicians have little or no experience. In this area Bahá'ís have a
potential advantage. First of all, Bahá'í physicians are enjoined by
their *Sacred Writings* to enlist the help of God in treating their
patients:

O physician! In treating the sick, first mention the name of Thy God, the Possessor of the Day of Judgment, and then use what God hath destined for the healing of His creatures. By My Life! The physician who has drunk from the Wine of My Love, his visit is healing, and his breath is mercy and hope. Cling to him for the welfare of the constitution. He is confirmed by God in his treatment.

BAHÁ'U'LLÁH

Secondly, Bahá'í health care professionals should be able to relate to patients of nearly every religious affiliation, since Bahá'ís accept the validity of each of the world religions.

The holy Manifestations Who have been the Sources or Founders of the various religious systems were united and agreed in purpose and teaching. Abraham, Moses, Zoroaster, Buddha, Jesus, Muhammad, the Báb and Bahá'u'lláh are one in spirit and reality.

'ABDU'L-BAHÁ

When a patient seeks spiritual support, a Bahá'í physician who is acquainted with the Holy Writings of the various religions will be able to offer assistance based on the patient's own beliefs. Each of the Holy Books offers valuable guidance as the following passages demonstrate:

A merry heart doeth good like a medicine: but a broken spirit drieth the bones.

OLD TESTAMENT

Beloved, I wish above all things that thou mayest prosper and be in health, even as thy soul prospereth.

NEW TESTAMENT

Elevate the mind, and seek sincere faith with firm purpose...and let your happiness depend, not upon external things, but upon your own mind.

THE TEACHINGS OF BUDDHA

> *Evil is Intellect which, wrapped in gloom, looks upon wrong as right, and sees all things contrariwise of Truth...Good is the steadfastness whereby a man masters his beats of heart, his very breath of life, the action of his senses; fixed in never-shaken faith and piety.*

BHAGAVAD GITA

> *Are not, verily, the friends of God those on whom there is no fear, neither shall they be grieved?*

QU'RÁN

Finally, the Bahá'í teachings stress the need to employ both physical and spiritual means to treat patients:

> *O thou distinguished physician!...Matters related to man's spirit have a great effect on his bodily condition. For instance, thou shouldst impart gladness to thy patient, give him comfort and joy, and bring him to ecstasy and exultation.... Therefore, treat thou the sick with both powers.*

'ABDU'L-BAHÁ

> *When giving medical treatment turn to the Blessed Beauty, then follow the dictates of thy heart. Remedy the sick by means of heavenly joy and spiritual exultation, cure the sorely afflicted by imparting to them blissful glad-tidings and heal the wounded through the resplendent bestowals. When at the bedside of a patient, cheer and gladden his heart and enrapture his spirit through celestial power. Indeed, such a heavenly breath quickeneth every mouldering bone and reviveth the spirit of every sick and ailing one.*

'ABDU'L-BAHÁ

> *With regard to your question concerning spiritual healing. Such a healing constitutes, indeed, one of the most effective methods of relieving a person from either the mental or physical pains and sufferings. 'Abdu'l-Bahá has in His Paris Talks emphasized its importance by stating that it should be*

used as an essential means for effecting a complete physical cure. Spiritual healing, however, is not and cannot be a substitute for material healing, but it is a most valuable adjunct to it. Both are indeed essential and complementary.

From a letter written on behalf of **Shoghi Effendi**

Minding Your Mind

We've seen how stress, depression and a negative outlook can impair our health, yet the power of the mind is considerably more forceful than that which we've so far documented. There was a time when this was widely appreciated and incorporated into the art of healing, however, a number of scientific advances in the 19th and 20th centuries resulted in a significant shift away from this attitude.

In the mid-19th century practically every field of knowledge was undergoing revolutionary change, and the science of medicine was no exception. Louis Pasteur, a French chemist, laid the foundation for modern germ theory when he discovered that yeast was responsible for the fermentation of sugar beets into vinegar. Gradually it was accepted that we live in a world teeming with minute living organisms, which among other things are responsible for infectious disease. In the years that followed Dr. Robert Koch, a German physician, identified the specific bacteria responsible for cholera and tuberculosis. Then in 1890 it was discovered that an inoculation with a small dose of tetanus toxin would prevent the outbreak of tetanus (lockjaw) in someone who had been cut with a rusty object. In the early 20th Century penicillin was discovered, the miracle antibiotic which prevented untold masses from dying of pneumonia. Attitude, diet, willpower, expectations — none of these factors mattered, a tetanus shot or penicillin were effective regardless of the patient's lifestyle or emotions. Gradually, there was a shift away from treating patients to fighting disease. The patient was less a partner in the healing process, rather he became a passive recipient of treatments, procedures and pharmacology. Even death was no longer considered insurmountable as physicians successfully developed various reanimation techniques.

Vaccines and antibiotics, along with significant improvements in public sanitation and hygiene, resulted in a notable jump in average life expectancy. It also resulted in a considerable jump in the prestige and veneration of physicians. The public willingly entrusted their health to modern-day high priests of high-tech in white lab-coats.

In the past physicians had relied heavily upon homeostasis, which is the body's own tendency to heal itself and to maintain health by mitigating negative external factors. You'll recall that Dr. Schweitzer thought of his responsibility as, "aiding the physician within." All good healers recognised that a patient's belief in his physician was essential to optimal healing. Galen is purported to have said, "*He cures most in whom most are confident.*" Hippocrates said, "*Some patients, though conscious that their condition is perilous, recover their health simply through their contentment with the goodness of the physician.*" Research studies have confirmed that a patient's confidence in his physician is still very important, moreover, studies have shown that the physician's own confidence in a particular treatment also has a demonstrable impact upon its efficacy. That is, patients seem to be able to sense how the physician actually feels about a particular treatment. Thus it's easy to understand that when primitive people were in awe of the powers of their healers, there was always a highly favourable opportunity for homeostasis to occur, regardless of the efficacy of their treatments. Unquestionably, not only the shaman or medicine man, but all physicians and healers have profited from the fact that the body itself is capable of overcoming the vast majority of health-related problems.

The powerful healing effect which results from our confidence in physicians and their treatments is known as the placebo effect. Placebo is derived from the Latin *placere*, "to please". Once held in high regard, the placebo effect came to be viewed as a primitive trick, with little or no place in modern scientific medicine. The following dictionary definition highlights the low esteem accorded this powerful natural phenomenon, "*a harmless, unmedicated preparation given as a medicine to a patient merely to humor him, or used as a control in testing the efficacy of another, medicated substance."*

A milestone double-blind study of the placebo effect was carried out in 1955 by the Harvard physician, Henry Beecher. Around 35 per cent of Dr. Beecher's subjects were relieved of their complaints from such conditions as anxiety, common cold, headache, pain and seasickness by the placebo effect. Subsequent research has shown that several factors can enhance the effectiveness of a medication (or placebo). A medication's reputation as a "miracle drug" results in the so-called *placebo halo*. It is also known that injections and capsules are perceived as more powerful than tablets. Colors are associated with particular strengths, for example, white for analgesics, yellow and red for stimulants and antidepressants. Taking two pills is more effective than taking a single pill.

The figure of 35 per cent determined by Dr. Beecher in his study was long used as a benchmark for the effectiveness of placebos; however, when the preceding as well as various other factors are considered, the effectiveness of the placebo has been shown to be considerable higher. For instance, when a patient and physician share high expectations in the efficacy of the treatment and enjoy a relationship of confidence and trust, newer studies have shown that the placebo effect is probably more like 70 to 90 per cent effective.

Various studies have demonstrated that the overwhelming majority of visits to clinics are for complaints of unknown origin, presumably resulting from "psychosocial" factors; furthermore, somewhere between 60 to 90 per cent of visits to physicians are for stress-related complaints which are often poorly detected and inadequately treated with standard medical procedures. This would appear to be an obvious indication for reliance upon homeostasis and the placebo effect, which adhere to Hippocrates's counsel, *first do no harm*, rather than employing drugs and procedures which are often expensive and potentially result in harmful side effects.

Yet one will find few physicians willing to openly admit to the use of the placebo in their personal treatment regimes. According to surveys most physicians maintain that their peers are three times more likely to enlist the placebo effect than they are. Also, when they admit to the power of the placebo, it is almost universally in "other" specialities and not in their own. This can be traced to a number of historical precedents.

The forerunner to conventional modern medicine was known as allopathic, from the Greek, *allopatheia*, "subject to external influences". The allopathic approach was to employ treatments which produce opposite or different effects than the disease. This resulted in an essentially contrarian approach, as is evident in terms such as antidepressant, anti-inflammatory, antibiotic, antihistamine, antispasmodic, etc. An emphasis on alleviating symptoms, often without understanding their underlying cause, is frequently observable. There was a time in which allopathic, homeopathic, osteopathic and naturopathic medicine all relied upon the placebo effect. As the development of "medical science" accelerated, allopathic medicine, by the early 20th century, began licensing only physicians who had graduated from medical schools based upon "scientific medicine". In a world caught up in the magic of continual progress and scientific enlightenment, allopathic medicine was able to distinguish itself from other forms of medicine by relying upon science and insisting that each illness could be linked to a specific cause, and rejecting the concept that the mind might influence the body. Thus, the placebo effect was relegated to the sidelines, replaced by stronger, more aggressive and invasive treatments.

That, however, is somewhat misleading. Physicians and patients alike are quick to believe that medicine is a science, rather than an art, yet technology and applied chemistry don't always equal good science. Over the past decades numerous medical treatments have proved to be bogus and unsound, - e.g., bombarding children's tonsils and thyroid glands with X-rays, or treating angina pectoris by removing the thyroid or parts of the pancreas, or by injecting cobra venom. However, in the case of the treatments for angina pectoris, although there was no viable scientific justification, these techniques proved to be effective nearly 90 per cent of the time, as long as both the physician and the patient believed in them.

Since angina pectoris results from insufficient blood flow to the heart muscle, surgeons in the 1950's began a procedure which involved tying off a nearby artery to increase the blood flow to the heart muscle. Enthusiastic surgeons reported that three out of four patients were helped by the procedure, but more sceptical colleagues reported much lower success rates. So, a double-blind study was done, which today seems unthinkable. Surgeons performed phony operations in which the patients believed that their arteries were being tied off, but in reality they were only surgically opened and then closed again without any tying off of arteries! The phony surgery proved to be as effective as the "real thing", and in some trials even more effective. Thus we see that in "scientific medicine" the placebo is still at work.

Geography, culture and legal considerations also appear to influence what is viewed as good medical science. When we compare the scientific medicine practised in various countries, we can encounter significant differences. For example, American physicians are much more likely to prescribe antibiotics than their German counterparts, also bypass surgery, hysterectomies and caesarean-sections are much more prevalent in the United States than Europe. An article in the *New York Times* deemed the widespread belief that medical practice is founded upon unassailable scientific evidence as, "*so far off the mark that the term 'medical science' is practically an oxymoron.*" Dr. David Eddy, a researcher at the Jackson Hole Group, concluded that scarcely more than 15 per cent of medical treatments are based on "*reliable scientific evidence*".

'Abdu'l-Bahá once said, "*medical science is only in its infancy.*" Moreover, he also encouraged Bahá'ís to, "*develop the science of medicine to such a high degree that they will heal illnesses by means of foods.*" In spite of the relative infancy of the science of medicine, it is, as we have seen, considered the king of the sciences. Also

Bahá'ís are encouraged to, "*...invariably consult and follow the treatment of competent and conscientious physicians...*" and, "*...doctors who have studied a scientific system of medicine.*" The Universal House of Justice gave a further clarification, "*thus the obligation to consult physicians and to distinguish between doctors who are well trained in medical sciences and those who are not is clear, but the Faith should not be associated with any particular school of medical theory or practice.*" If we accept Dr. Eddy's conclusions, currently it might not be as easy as we once thought to identify a truly scientific system of medicine.

Thankfully, the House of Justice has given Bahá'ís ample latitude in this regard, "*it is left to each believer to decide for himself which doctors he should consult, bearing in mind the principles enunciated above.*" Personally, in cases of acute illness and trauma I would turn to conventional medicine, but for chronic conditions and "civilised" diseases I might also consult a licensed naturopathic physician. Naturopathic physicians, N.D.s, are trained in acupuncture, clinical nutrition, lifestyle modification counselling, herbal medicine, homeopathy, hydrotherapy and physical medicine (e.g., massage, mobilisation), as well as a standard medical and scientific curriculum. It's essential to keep in mind that *science* and *technology* are not synonymous terms. After all, the word physician is derived from the Greek word for nature, *physike*. An approach which recognises and seeks to enhance the process of homeostasis and respects the wisdom of nature can also be scientifically sound.

In Germany, where I've lived since 1984, there appears to be a welcome synthesis at work. A growing number of physicians who have studied conventional medicine are starting to augment their skills by taking electives in naturopathy. American medical schools are also beginning to offer electives in alternative medicine. The University of Arizona in Tuscon has employed Andrew Weil, M.D., as director of its programme of integrative medicine. In many areas of life Bahá'ís have demonstrated an uncanny ability to reconcile disparate groups by finding areas of common ground. Perhaps a new generation of Bahá'í physicians will help unify the *science of medicine* and the *art of healing* by rejecting all forms of professional bias and diligently and openly searching for the most effective and least harmful treatments available, regardless of which particular school of medicine they represent. Bahá'u'lláh enjoined man to, *"free himself from idle fancy and imitation, discern with the eye of oneness His glorious handiwork, and look into all things with a searching eye." "By its aid* [justice] *thou shalt see with thine own eyes and not through the eyes of others, and shalth know of thine own knowledge and not through the knowledge of thy neighbour." "Lay fast hold on whatever will profit you, and profit the peoples of the world."*

It's precisely because of the power of the mind to influence results that it is sometimes difficult to draw universal and absolutely irrefutable conclusions. In any case, one thing is clear, it would be a serious error to overlook the ability of the mind to affect the healing process. Tucked away in the notes of a study on effectiveness of various chemotherapies published in the 1983 *World Journal of Surgery,* was a staggering bit of information. As is widely known, chemotherapy often results in the loss of scalp hair. In a typical double-blind study one group of patients only received a placebo, yet 30 per cent of these patients actually lost their hair! We still don't understand how the placebo effect works, but in the area of pain reduction there have been experiments which demonstrate that placebos do result in measurable physiological changes. Some 40 per cent of subjects who were given a placebo for pain from dental surgery reported a reduction in pain. They were then given naloxone, a drug which blocks the endorphin receptors at the pain site. There was then an immediate reoccurrence of pain, which demonstrated that the placebo had resulted in the release of endorphins, our natural painkillers. In another study on post-operative pain, 40 per cent of patients responded as well to placebo injections as to morphine, and placebos have been shown to be 60 per cent effective in reducing headaches. (Interestingly, in especially susceptible persons, hypnosis can reduce pain, but there is *no* release of endorphins.) Subsequent research, however, indicates that the function of placebos in pain reduction is more complicated than the above experiment might indicate.

Physicians familiar with PNI research have much fewer qualms about the role of the placebo in the practice of medicine. Admittedly, the contemporary practice of informed consent, the fast-paced stream of patients and the litigious climate in some societies makes it more difficult, but not impossible, for physicians to take full advantage of the placebo effect. Thomas Delbanco, M.D., is a director of general medicine and primary care at Beth Israel Hospital, and an associate professor of medicine at Harvard Medical School. His comments reflect the importance of the placebo effect in the art of healing:

> *The placebo effect is wonderful medicine.... The placebo is one of the most powerful medicines we have. It's very hard to tell sometimes whether what we're doing is more than the placebo effect....Uncertainty is the worst illness. The fear of the unknown can really be disabling. Even if the news is bad, people feel better if the uncertainty is dispelled.... I was in Germany recently, visiting a hospital where they were treating people homeopathically. In the U.S. medical world, we don't believe in homeopathy.... Eighty-five percent of the pneumonias in that German hospital were treated with homeopathic medicines, and only fifteen percent were treated with the antibiotics that I've been trained to use.... Maybe homeopathy has nothing to do with this, maybe it's all placebo. But whatever it is, it's powerful medicine because their patients with pneumonia get better...Well, we should be more open about an awful lot of different kinds of healing. What we do is still much more art than science, although we glory in the science of what we do....Our science is progressing at a fantastic clip...but our art also has to progress.*

The use of alternative medicine is growing continuously. Lecture material presented at Harvard University on the implications of alternative therapies on clinical practice revealed some startling facts:

A national survey of alternative medicine prevalence, costs, and patterns of use showed:

1) One-third of the respondents used one or more alternative therapies for some medical problem during the course of a year.

2) Of these, 70 per cent did not inform their medical doctors of their use of alternative therapies.

3) Alternative therapies are used primarily for chronic rather than life-threatening medical conditions.

4) In 1990 Americans made an estimated 425 million visits to alternative medical providers, well above the 338 million visits to US primary care physicians during the same period.

5) Out-of-pocket expenditures associated with alternative therapy use in the United States in 1990 was $10.3 billion, nearly equal to the $12.8 billion out-of-pocket expenses incurred that same year for all US hospitalisations.

The study concluded that the use of alternative medicine is considerably higher than previously anticipated and physicians were urged to ask their patients about their use of alternative therapies when obtaining a medical history. Today in the United States nearly 30 medical schools offer courses in alternative or complementary medicine. Among them is Harvard Medical School which has a course which has the objective of giving physicians sufficient knowledge to responsibly advise patients who use or request alternative medical therapies. Although there is no research available, it is probably safe to conclude that physicians who are acquainted with nutritional, natural and alternative therapies and, when appropriate, use them, probably have patients who speak with them openly about their use of alternative therapies.

The Power of Words

Actually it's important for a physician to know when a patient is simultaneously receiving alternative therapies, since, for example, certain herbs and vitamins can react with some medications. Yet the patient, by remaining silent, is protecting, perhaps unconsciously, the placebo effect. Only a short time ago many physicians scoffed at the notion of taking vitamins, warning their patients of the potential health dangers, citing them as a waste of money and insuring that a typical diet supplied all the necessary vitamins. Now that has been shown to be patently incorrect. In a recent survey of 181 American cardiologists, 44 per cent admitted taking vitamin E, vitamin C or beta carotene supplements alone or in combination for their potential beneficial effects. The most common dose of vitamin E was 400 units daily; vitamin C, 500 milligrams daily; and beta carotene, 20,000 units daily, well above the levels advocated by the American Medical Association only a short time ago.

We've already seen that if a physician is perceived as being equivocal about a treatment this will have a detrimental effect on the placebo effect. We can no doubt surmise that the placebo effect of vitamins, herbs, tonics and various alternative therapies would be greatly diminished when a trusted physician dismisses or ridicules their use. Even a facial expression, or a shaking of the head, can convey the same message. It's obvious that patients, through experience, have intuitively learned to guard their trust in alternative therapies from someone whom they perceive as negatively predisposed. Also it appears clear that patients are seeking something which is often missing from conventional medicine: a sense of control and involvement in the healing process, being treated with dignity by someone who is prepared to listen and understand, and a belief in the inherent healing ability of nature.

These are qualities which are generally present in healers, but not necessarily found in all modern physicians. Dr. Herbert Benson wrote, "*But as naturally as faith and remembered wellness occur in us, they will not come as naturally to a medical system that has denied their validity.*" In particular it seems that physicians could be more attuned to the power of words and their impact on patients. A good healer will dispense words as carefully as he or she dispenses drugs. All of us, but especially health care professionals, need to understand that words can act like medicine (or poison) and actually trigger physiological responses. Confucius said, "*Without knowing the force of words, it is impossible to know men.*" In the *Old Testament* we read, "*Pleasant words are as a honeycomb, sweet to the soul, and health to the bones.*" In the *Bhagavad Gita* we find "*Words causing no man woe, words ever true, gentle and pleasing words... these make the true religiousness of Speech.*" The Bahá'í teachings also pay particular attention to the power of words:

> *Follow thou the way of thy Lord, and say not that which the ears cannot bear to hear, for such speech is like luscious food given to small children. However palatable, rare and rich the food may be, it cannot be assimilated by the digestive organs of a suckling child. Therefore unto every one who hath a right, let his settled measure be given.*
>
> *Not everything that a man knoweth can be disclosed, nor can everything that he can disclose be regarded as timely, nor can every timely utterance be considered as suited to the capacity of those who hear it. Such is the consummate wisdom to be observed in thy pursuits.*

'ABDU'L-BAHÁ

> *Every word is endowed with a spirit, therefore the speaker or expounder should carefully deliver his words at the appropriate time and place, for the impression which each word maketh is clearly evident and perceptible.... One word may be likened unto fire, another unto light, and the influence which both exert is manifest in the world....Therefore an enlightened man of wisdom should primarily speak with words as mild as milk, that the children of men may be nurtured and edified thereby and may attain the ultimate goal of human existence which is the station of true understanding and nobility.... It behoveth a prudent man of wisdom to speak with utmost leniency and forbearance so that the sweetness of his words may induce everyone to attain that which befitteth man's station.*

BAHÁ'U'LLÁH

> ...*Human utterance is an essence which aspireth to exert its influence and needeth moderation. As to its influence, this is conditional upon refinement, which in turn is dependent upon hearts which are detached and pure. As to its moderation, this hath to be combined with tact and wisdom as prescribed in the Holy Scriptures and Tablets.*
>
> *O My Name! Utterance must needs possess penetrating power. For if bereft of this quality it would fail to exert influence. And this penetrating influence dependeth on the spirit being pure and the heart stainless. Likewise it needeth moderation, without which the hearer would be unable to bear it, rather he would manifest opposition from the very outset. And moderation will be obtained by blending utterance with the tokens of divine wisdom which are recorded in the sacred Books and Tablets. Thus when the essence of one's utterance is endowed with these two requisites it will prove highly effective and will be the prime in transforming the souls of men.*

BAHÁ'U'LLÁH

Many people can recount incidents in which physicians have coldly blurted out a diagnosis or prognosis which in an instant shattered someone's world. Health care professionals need to understand the power and malleability of words, tempering the desire to be scientific, accurate and honest with the knowledge that words can inspire minds, uplift spirits and provide hope — which in turn can result in an improvement of condition. Of course, words wrongly used can also destroy hope, spur resignation and lead to depression. Some physicians mistakenly want to avoid giving false hope. Clearly, there is no such thing as false hope, as Cicero said, "*to the sick, while there is life there is hope.*" Goethe wisely observed, "*in all things it is better to hope than to despair.*"

'Abdu'l-Bahá removed any moral considerations for Bahá'í physicians in this regard:

> *...If a doctor consoles a sick man by saying: 'Thank God you are better, and there is hope of your recovery,' though these words are contrary to the truth, yet they may become the consolation of the patient and the turning-point of the illness. This is not blameworthy.*

If, for example, a patient wants to know his or her particular chances for survival a physician needs to exercise extreme caution. By simply saying that there is a 60 per cent survival rate, a physician is also saying the patient has a 40 per cent chance of dying. Instead of a cold detached statement of statistical probability, a healer might say something like this when a patient asks about the chances of survival:

> *Well that's really a difficult thing to say for a number of reasons. First, no two people are alike, statistics don't tell us a number of important factors which have an impact upon recovery. There are so many cases of people with conditions much more serious than yours, who have been given a short time to live and have gone on to outlive their physicians. Don't ever forget that no two people are alike, and no two people react exactly the same way to a particular disease. Secondly, statistics are of necessity historical while medical research is continually making great advances at an exponential rate. You're going to be receiving the very latest in medical treatment which I believe can heal you; moreover, if you carefully follow the treatment regime which we'll develop together, we will greatly enhance your natural healing ability. If you take your medication, watch your nutrition, manage stress and get in touch with your body you can meet this challenge. Even without all your advantages, in the past 60 per cent of people with this condition, many much worse off than you, recovered. I'm confident that you'll put your faith in God and do all in your power to help me to help you. Don't worry about averages, together we're going to do everything possible to restore your health, I'm confident and you should be too.*

Patients on the other hand, shouldn't confuse such encouragement with meaningless platitudes. There is always hope, dramatically demonstrated in documented cases of spontaneous remission of diseases — cases which baffle medical experts and defy explanation. The human body, mind and spirit have powerful potentialities which we can't as yet begin to completely understand, but we can tap into them. When faced with serious illness or life-threatening injuries one needs the care of a skilled and *trusted* physician. In addition one must be willing to follow the physician's counsel, have faith in God, belief in the body's inherent ability to heal itself, and a determination to meet the challenge mentally, spiritually and physically. In addition, we can employ such things as nutrition, prayer, visualisation, stress management, exercise and breathing to provide our bodies with an optimal environment for recovery.

5

SPIRITUAL HEALING

Men should hold in their souls the vision of celestial perfection, and there prepare a dwelling-place for the inexhaustible bounty of the Divine Spirit.

'Abdu'l-Bahá

If we'll open our minds to study how emotions influence health, then maybe
we'll eventually open our minds toward the spiritual dimensions of health.

John Zawacki, M.D.,

Professor of Medicine, University of Massachusetts Medical School

'Abdu'l-Bahá describes four types of healing which don't involve medicine, two of which are spiritual in nature.

1. According to 'Abdu'l-Bahá, health-like disease is contagious. *The contagion of disease is violent and rapid, while that of health is extremely weak and slow.... That is to say, the contagion of disease is violent and has a rapid effect while that of health is very slow and has a small effect, and it is only in very slight diseases that it has even this small effect.... This is one kind of healing.*

2. *The other kind of healing without medicine is through the magnetic force which acts from one body to another, and becomes the cause of cure. This force also has only a slight effect. Sometimes one can benefit a sick person by placing one's hand upon his head and upon his heart. Why? Because of the effect of the magnetism, and of the mental impression made upon the sick person which causes the disease to vanish. But this effect is also very slight and weak.*

3. *Of the two other kinds of healing which are spiritual, that is to say, where the means of cure is a spiritual power, one results from the entire concentration of the mind of a strong person upon a sick person, when the latter expects with all his concentrated faith that a cure will be effected from the spiritual power of the strong person, to such an extent that there will be a cordial connection between the strong person and the invalid. The strong person makes every effort to cure the sick patient, and the sick patient is sure of receiving a cure. From the effect of these mental impressions an excitement of the nerves is produced, and this impression and this excitement of the nerves will become the cause of the recovery of the sick person. So when a sick person has a strong desire and intense hope for something, and hears suddenly of the tidings of its realization, a nervous excitement is produced, which will make the malady entirely disappear.... But all this has effect only to a certain extent, and that not always. For if someone is afflicted with a very violent disease, or is wounded, these means will not remove the disease or close and heal the wound. This is to say, these means have no power in severe maladies, unless the constitution helps, because a strong constitution often overcomes disease. This is the third kind of healing.*

4. *But the fourth kind of healing is produced through the power of the Holy Spirit. This does not depend on contact, nor on sight, nor upon presence; it is not dependent upon any condition. Whether the disease be slight or severe, whether there be a contact of bodies or not, whether a personal connection be established between the sick person and the healer or not, this healing takes place through the power of the Holy Spirit.*

It is the "*inexhaustible bounty of the Divine Spirit*" which 'Abdu'l-Bahá associates with the strongest form of spiritual healing. Indeed, as 'Abdu'l-Bahá taught, the effect of this spiritual power isn't limited to healing, rather, "*it will show its effect in every condition in the world of existence.*" Specifically, this spiritual healing, "*consists in praying to God and in turning to Him*" to receive, "*healing from His Divine bounty.*"

'Abdu'l-Bahá explained that physical diseases, "*are cured by medicine*", while "*diseases which are caused by the emotions of the mind are cured by the power of the spirit of man.*" Notice that He speaks of the spirit of man rather than the Divine Spirit. Thus we see that conditions which are caused by the emotional state of the individual (psychosomatic illnesses) can be overcome by the power of the human spirit or mind. The Divine Spirit, however, can potentially heal all diseases, for it "*dominates all the bodily ailments and those of the mind.*"

The questions of spiritual healing and faith healers are fraught with controversy and are themes which need to be handled with wisdom by Bahá'ís. The Guardian of the Bahá'í Faith, Shoghi Effendi, was careful that the teachings not be associated with controversial subjects which might convey a misleading representation of the Faith, or lead to its exploitation. Consequently, he made it explicitly clear that there is, "*no such thing as BAHÁ'Í HEALERS*". The Guardian emphasized that the Book of Laws instructs the sick to seek competent medical help as well as assistance through prayer. A Bahá'í who claimed to have healing powers was cautioned:

1. not to, "*...try and take the place of a regular doctor in trying to heal others, but only give them your kind help through constructive suggestion....*"

2. and not to, "*...associate this help with being a channel of the direct grace of Bahá'u'lláh....*"

Nevertheless, while recognising the wisdom of not sanctioning the existence of Bahá'í Healers, or associating the Faith with Faith Healers, we still can understand how individuals can potentially heal with the assistance of the Holy Spirit.

'Abdu'l-Bahá wrote:

> *He who is filled with the love of Bahá, and forgets all things,*
> *the Holy Spirit will be heard from his lips and the spirit of life*
> *will fill his heart, the lights of the sign will shine forth from his*
> *face, words will issue from his mouth in strands and pearls,*
> *and all sickness and disease will be healed by the laying on of*
> *the hands.*

In any case, we see that both the Divine Spirit and the human spirit can have a positive impact upon health. Interestingly, even the act of seeking assistance from God has a positive impact on the human body and spirit. Thus prayer is a two-edged sword. The patient has the potential of receiving the bounty of Divine assistance, but in addition, the patient's emotional state is enhanced through the process of sincere reflection and prayer. Moreover, while there are no qualitative studies to document this specific assertion, it is highly likely that believing in Divine healing can result in a powerful placebo effect. If, for example, we know that a patient's firm belief in a physician can produce a placebo effect, one could readily expect that a belief in the Divine Cure might well produce a powerful placebo effect.

Thus, when we consider the effects of prayer and belief on health, there is a blending of several positive effects at work. Among other things, prayer quiets the mind and reduces stress and anxiety. This, as we have seen, strengthens the immune system and our recuperative powers. In addition, through the act of praying the patient is involved in the healing process and gains a sense of control, two more factors which enhance the immune response. Also the patient is given a sense of hope and positive expectation, again factors which have been demonstrated to improve the immune response. There is also the potential of a placebo effect and most importantly, the possibility of having one's prayers answered.

Many of the studies dealing with the effects of faith, belief, and prayer on health don't differentiate between these factors, notwithstanding, there are studies which confirm their positive influence. For example, after reviewing over two hundred epidemiological studies Dr. J.S. Levin of the Eastern Virginia Medical School reached the conclusion that belief in God increases health and lowers death rates. In a very dramatic study done at the Dartmouth Medical School, Dr. Thomas Oxman reported that patients who were consoled and comforted by their religious beliefs were three times more likely to survive open-heart surgery.

Another study of coronary care patients in San Francisco by Dr. Randolf Byrd sought to measure the influence of outside group prayer on patients' progress. Nearly 400 patients were divided into two groups. One group was prayed for while the other was not. Neither the patients nor their care-givers knew which patients were being prayed for. Dr. Byrd then analysed the patients' progress and concluded that 84 per cent of the prayed-for group had a good treatment response as opposed to 73 per cent of the not-prayed-for group. Although the results were not phenomenal, they were considered statistically significant. While interesting, we don't know two pieces of important information, namely, how many of the two groups were prayed for by family and friends, or how many prayed for themselves. A study combining the Oxman and Byrd studies might be even more revealing, i.e., find a group which doesn't employ prayer and belief and separate them into two groups, one of which would be prayed for by an outside group.

In an experiment to measure the effect of spiritual qualities on health, Dr. David McClelland, Harvard psychologist, measured the amount of salivary IgA in students before and after viewing a film on Mother Teresa and her work with the poor in Calcutta. IgA is an immunoglobulin which protects against colds and respiratory infections. All the students showed an increased secretion of IgA, even those who questioned Mother Teresa's motives. After viewing a film on Attila the Hun everyone's IgA levels dropped.

As we have seen, the mind possesses enormous capacity to influence the healing potential. The spontaneous remission of diseases which customarily have fatal outcomes are often deemed miracles. A miracle is defined as "*an event or action that apparently contradicts known scientific laws and is hence thought to be due to supernatural causes, especially to an act of God.*" Saint Augustine understood quite well how important the word *apparently* is to the pervious definition. He taught:

> *Miracles do not happen in contradiction of nature, but in contradiction of what we know about nature.*

Of all the miracles attributed to the various Prophets, I find none easier to believe than the miracles associated with spontaneous healing, especially as we learn more about the healing power of the mind and spirit. Jesus taught:

> *Have faith in God. Truly, I say to you, whoever says to this mountain, 'Be taken up and cast into the sea,' and does not doubt in his heart, but believes that what he says will come to pass, it will be done for him. Therefore I tell you, whatever you ask in prayer, believe that you receive it, and you will.*

Imagine someone who comes into the presence of a person, whom many believe to be a messenger of God on earth. They have heard wondrous accounts of His powers and witnessed people willing to sacrifice their lives and property to follow Him. He will obviously have a radiant and commanding presence, much like the description by 'Abdu'l-Bahá quoted above:

> *Holy Spirit will be heard from his lips and the spirit of life will fill his heart, the lights of the sign will shine forth from his face, words will issue from his mouth in strands and pearls, and all sickness and disease will be healed by the laying on of the hands.*

Even if we discount the involvement of supernatural power, none the less, one can readily acknowledge that an encounter with such an individual by a person seeking healing would constitute the most powerful placebo effect imaginable.

Try to imagine this scene from the Gospel of St. Luke, which describes an incident which occurred nearly two thousand years ago. Jesus and His twelve disciples had been travelling continuously from village to village, preaching and ministering to the people. The rumours which preceded Jesus were told and retold and, if human nature hasn't changed too much, they were greatly embellished, only heightening the sense of expectation. When He finally arrived at a certain rural village, suddenly the quiet monotonous village life gave way to pandemonium as all the villagers and people from near and far gathered to witness such a momentous event. At one point in the middle of a throng of curious thrill-seekers Jesus cried out, "*Who touched me?*" All of His disciples denied touching Him, but Jesus maintained that He felt power leaving Him as someone touched Him.

> *And when the woman saw that she was not hid, she came trembling, and falling down before him, she declared unto him before all the people for what causes she had touched him, and how she was healed immediately.*
> *And he said unto her, 'Daughter, be of good comfort: thy faith hath made thee whole; go in peace'.*

Under such circumstances one might not find it difficult to believe that many people were made whole through their faith in the power of the Holy Spirit. Admittedly, when we acknowledge that such stories were first recorded decades after the death of Jesus based on second-and third- hand accounts, there is a possibility that the exact nature of the events might not be historically accurate. Nevertheless, as we see in this instance, it was, according to Jesus, her faith which healed her, even though He acted as a conduit of the Holy Spirit in this case.

As we consider the two types of spiritual healing described by 'Abdu'l-Bahá, how would one categorise such examples of healing? Perhaps there is a combination of both types of healing at work — a sense of expectation and an excitation of the nervous system, but also the power of the Holy Spirit. In any case, what matters most is that spiritual healing is possible, moreover, as we will see, cases of medical miracles and spontaneous remission of disease have been documented.

For example, two physicians, Dr. Tilden Everson and Dr. Warren Cole, critically reviewed medical journals dating back sixty years for cases of spontaneous remission of cancer. They set strenuous standards for cases deemed worthy of reporting. First, since leukemias and lymphomas (forms of blood cancer) often go into remission, they were excluded from the review. Secondly, they eliminated any cases which exhibited any degree of diagnostic uncertainty. In spite of such rigorous standards, they still found 176 cases of spontaneous remission of cancer documented in medical journals — cases in which there was either no treatment, or treatment which should not have effected a cure.

In 1993 the Institute of Noetic Sciences undertook an even more exhaustive review of medical literature, covering over 800 medical journals published in more than twenty languages. Their resulting collection of over 3,500 cases of spontaneous remission was published under the title, *Spontaneous Remission — An Annotated Bibliography*. There were spontaneous remissions of every form of cancer and nearly every disease. In 15 per cent of the cases remission occurred without any drugs or treatment, while the rest took place after palliative surgeries or treatments which should not have produced a cure.

Each year more than five million people visit the Roman Catholic shrine in Lourdes, France. Many are pilgrims seeking a miracle cure for ailments deemed incurable by conventional medicine. Over 6,000/- people have claimed cures since 1858, but the Roman Catholic Church has only recognised 65 as authentic miracle cures. The Church has its own medical bureau which initially examines the cases. If it is considered significant, a case is then passed on to a 25 member international committee of medical specialists for rigorous review. First, they must be satisfied that the disease was serious and properly diagnosed, and did not result from psychological causes. Then, in contrast to many known cases of spontaneous remission, the recovery must also demonstrate unusual swiftness to be assessed a miracle cure.

One can certainly question whether spiritual healing has anything to do with the miracle cures at Lourdes, or any documented case of spontaneous remission. Be that as it may, we must accept that there is yet much to learn about the healing potentialities latent in our own selves. The door is still open with respect to the possibility of miracle cures, thus belief remains an important and viable factor in healing.

> *Miracles aren't a basis for belief,*
> *but belief is a basis for miracles.*

The Relaxation Response

In 1975 Dr. Herbert Benson, Associate Professor of Medicine at the Harvard Medical School, wrote an insightful book entitled, *The Relaxation Response*. Dr. Benson identified the Relaxation Response as a hypometabolic state, a state which we also reach during sleep. For example, after several hours of sleep one's oxygen consumption will decrease on average by 8 per cent compared to a resting wakeful state. Also our metabolism, blood pressure, heart rate, rate of breathing and muscle tension will decrease, while our slow brain waves will increase in a hypometabolic state. In effect, this hypometabolic state is the complete opposite of a stressful state.

In contrast to the hypometabolic state which is reached after several hours of sleep, an individual can elicit the relaxation response within minutes and achieve very dramatic results. For instance, within three minutes subjects show a dramatic drop in oxygen consumption, from 10 to 17 per cent, and an increase in slow brain wave activity. The relaxation response, without any side-effects, mimics drugs known as alpha- and beta-blockers, by suppressing the action of the hormone noradrenaline which increases heart rate and blood pressure. Consequently, the body is better able to cope with mildly stressful situations without eliciting a stress response. Dr. Benson is also the President of the Mind/Body Medical Institute, which has identified a number of positive long-term effects associated with the relaxation response:

1. A significant reduction of blood pressure in patient suffering from hypertension.

2. A reduction in pain severity, anxiety, depression and anger in patients suffering from chronic pain.
3. A seventy-five per cent cure rate of patients suffering from sleep-onset insomnia.
4. Thirty-six per cent of women with unexplained infertility conceived within six months.
5. Reduction in cardiac arrhythmias.
6. Reduction in the frequency and severity of migraine and cluster headaches.
7. A fifty per cent reduction in office visits by patients who frequently visited their physicians and exhibited psychosomatic symptoms.

Dr. Benson is careful to stress that there is no "Benson technique" for eliciting the relaxation response. He has found any number of techniques which are capable of bringing about the relaxation response, including, but not limited to: meditation, prayer, autogenic training, jogging, swimming, Lamaze breathing exercises, yoga, tai chi chuan, and qigong. What is particularly interesting is that tapping into one's deepest religious beliefs is an especially effective way to induce the relaxation response.

Although there is no "Benson technique", Dr. Benson does provide a universal method to help patients elicit the relaxation response.

1. You should select a word or short phrase which is deeply-seated in your faith.
2. While sitting comfortably, close your eyes and relax your muscles.
3. Breathe deeply and naturally, while repeating your selected phrase or word.
4. Quiet your mind by taking a passive attitude. When thoughts come to mind, merely discard them with an "Oh, well".
5. Once or twice a day repeat this exercise for ten to twenty minutes. After you finish, remain seated for a minute or two, serenely allowing your thoughts to return. Then open your eyes and remain seated for a bit before rising.

A Christian might use the phrase, "Our Father who art in heaven", a Hindu, "Om", a Jew, "The Lord is my shepherd", a Muslim, "Bismi'lláh Ar-Rahman Ar-Rahim" (In the Name of God, the compassionate, the Merciful), and a Buddhist , "The Law be your isle, The Law be your refuge, Look for no other refuge!". If a Bahá'í chooses to follow Dr. Benson's generic technique, there are any number of short verses from the Bahá'í writings which could be employed to elicit the relaxation response. Here is a short sample:

1. *"Alláh-u-Abhá"* (Arabic phrase meaning, "God the All-Glorious"). Bahá'u'lláh enjoins Bahá'ís to repeat the Greatest Name (Alláh-u-Abhá) 95 times each day after performing the ablutions of washing the hands and face. This of course is an ideal choice for Bahá'ís to elicit the relaxation response. This should take about ten minutes if, while breathing slowly and deeply, you repeat the Greatest Name as you inhale and exhale.

2. *"I bear witness to Thy unity and Thy oneness, and that Thou art God, and that there is none other God beside Thee."* Bahá'u'lláh: Alternative verse for the Medium Obligatory Prayer.

3. *"...The healer of all thine ills is remembrance of Me, forget it not..."* Bahá'u'lláh: From A Selection of Bahá'í Prayers and Holy Writings

4. *"Thy Name is my healing, O my God, and remembrance of Thee is my remedy."* Bahá'u'lláh: From the Short Healing Prayer

5. *"Glorified be God, the Lord of Splendour and Beauty"*. Or, *"Glorified be God, the Lord of Might and Majesty, of Grace and Bounty"*. Or simply, *"Glorified be God"*. Bahá'u'lláh: Alternative verses for the Obligatory Prayer (see *The Kitáb-I-Aqdas*, 13 & 14)

Dr. Benson not only suggests using religious phrases, but also informs patients that secular focus words like *calm, love, ocean, one* and *relax*, work equally well. Interestingly, he reports that 80 per cent of his patients select prayers as the focus of their elicitation. Irrespective of the word or phrase used, about a quarter of all patients report becoming more spiritual as a result of evoking the relaxation response. As a result, the Mind/Body Medical Institute began to look more closely at the reported claims of feeling more *spiritual.*

First the researchers developed a questionnaire to identify and quantify the sense of spirituality which occurs with the relaxation response. It's worth noting that women as a group, for reason the researchers couldn't identify, scored higher on the spirituality scale than men. It also turns out that the relaxation response, like physical exercise, brings cumulative rewards, i.e., the longer and more routinely one does it, the more pronounced is the positive effect.

As they began to examine the results they found two recurring themes from the group which registered an increase in spirituality after invoking the relaxation response. First, they felt the presence of God, or a force or higher power that was beyond themselves. Secondly, they felt a warm intimate relationship or sense of closeness with this presence. Those who experienced these sensations — a pleasant force in and around them — demonstrated the greatest health benefits from the relaxation response.

Some have undoubtedly, perhaps understandably, questioned the reason for Bahá'ís being enjoined to repeat the Greatest Name 95 times each day. Now, however, it's clear that this ritual, if done with a sense of mindfulness, can increase our spirituality and also have a positive impact upon our health. As Bahá'u'lláh taught, prayer *"will lighten and uplift"* and by keeping God's commandments we shall *"attain everlasting felicity"*.

When I first encountered the Bahá'í Faith I was particularly taken with the emphasis on unity, but beyond that one of the aspects of the teachings which appealed to me in particular was the rational approach to religion. For that reason the following statement by the Guardian was particularly appealing to me.

It [the Bahá'í Faith] *is free from any form of ecclesiasticism, has neither priesthood nor rituals, and is supported exclusively by voluntary contributions made by its avowed adherents.*

In other instances the Guardian, through a secretary, clarified that there are indeed a few simple rites and ceremonies in the Bahá'í Faith, but, "*its teachings warn against developing them into a system of uniform and rigid rituals incorporating man-made forms and practices, such as exist in other religions where rituals usually consist of elaborate ceremonial practices performed by a member of the clergy.*"

The Obligatory Daily Prayer

One of the first rituals which one encounters in the Bahá'í teachings is the obligatory daily prayer. Actually Bahá'ís have three prayers to choose from: short, medium and long. The long obligatory prayer is, like the repetition of the Greatest Name, a very effective way to effect the relaxation response. The prayer is indeed long and it is to be said in private. It involves genuflections such as standing, raising one's arms above one's head, kneeling, squatting and sitting. The short prayer on the other hand can be said in less than a minute. Bahá'ís are free to pick any one of the three.

Even before I actually signed a card and declared myself a Bahá'í I tried as best I could to follow the Bahá'í laws. The short obligatory prayer is to be said at noon, so coming out of a strict Protestant Christian background I took it to mean that it had to be said exactly at noon. As you can imagine I rarely managed to note the time, which meant that I ended up saying the long prayer nearly all of the time. The result was that unbeknownst to me I was eliciting the relaxation response routinely for the first time in my life. Like Dr. Benson's patients, I definitely came to feel more spiritual.

Later I learned that the short obligatory prayer could be said from noon until sunset, so to save time I gradually began to replace the long prayer with the short prayer. It was more convenient, though I did notice a gradual but perceptible change in my spiritual state. Yet, I must admit that the idea of rituals, regardless of how few, was something difficult for me to embrace. Rather than engaging in the lengthy ritual of saying the long prayer, I would use the time to read from the scriptures instead.

Obviously I was not alone in my difficulty with rituals. Before my birth and long before I became a Bahá'í, a believer wrote to the Guardian and expressed difficulty with the wisdom of having any rituals. The Guardian, through his secretary, gave the following response:

> *Bahá'u'lláh has reduced all ritual and form to an absolute minimum in His Faith. The few forms that there are — like those associated with the two longer obligatory daily prayers — are only symbols of the inner attitude. There is a wisdom in them, and a great blessing but we cannot force ourselves to understand or feel these things, that is why He gave us also the very short and simple prayer, for those who did not feel the desire to perform the acts associated with the other two.*

Now I've come to understand that there is truly a wisdom in these particular rituals. Lately, I've begun incorporating the repetition of the Greatest Name and the long daily prayer into the conclusion of my yoga exercises. It's a wonderful way to start the day!

The Obligatory Prayer for the Departed

Stress researchers have categorised a number of life events and evaluated them as to their stressfulness. Very high on the list is the loss of a loved one. Again it's especially interesting that this is a situation which is associated with one of the few Bahá'í rituals. Once more, to be perfectly honest, I initially had difficulty understanding the wisdom of this ritual.

Part of my difficulty was surely cultural in origin. The Bahá'í scriptures were revealed in the Persian and Arabic languages. By tradition the prayers and scriptures aren't simply read aloud in these languages, rather children are taught at an early age to sing or chant prayers in a beautiful and melodious fashion. Through years of practice Bahá'ís from a Persian or Arabic background often develop an ability to create a stirring experience by combining the scriptures with a moving musical melody and a beautiful voice.

The obligatory prayer for the departed consists of two short paragraphs, then the Greatest Name is repeated six times. Then each of the following verses is repeated a total of 19 times:

> *We all, verily, worship God.*
> *We all, verily, bow down before God.*
> *We all, verily, are devoted unto God.*
> *We all, verily, give praise unto God.*
> *We all, verily, yield thanks unto God.*
> *We all, verily, are patient in God.*

Each verse can be repeated 19 times, or the stanza can be repeated 19 times. Either way, 114 verses are spoken or chanted. One person sings, chants or reads the prayer while those present stand in a show of respect. This is the only obligatory prayer to be said in congregation.

Chanted in the original language the prayer becomes a soothing dirge, hypnotically repetitious and moving. One can easily get caught up in a sense of comforting calm. This is obviously how the prayer was intended. Unfortunately, those of us who are the product of Western culture don't often possess the ability to sing a monody. If one can imagine it being sung as a slow Gregorian chant, then it is possible to picture how calming and comforting it can be. In any case, anyone in this situation should use this prayer, however it might be sung or spoken, as an opportunity to evoke the relaxation response in order to better deal with grief. This, in my opinion, is not only a prayer for the departed, but it is also a powerful prayer to comfort those left behind.

The Healing Prayer

Praising God and contemplating the grandeur of God has long been recognised in all mystical traditions as a means of achieving inner peace and happiness. Contemplating the attributes of God is also one of the most effective ways to allow the power of the Holy Spirit to reach us. It is also a potent means of invigorating one's faith, and, as Jesus said, it is thy faith which will heal thee.

We live in a world in which we are bombarded with negative thoughts and images. Alzheimer's, flesh eating bacteria, skin cancer, breast cancer and so on — daily we are made aware of our vulnerability. If we develop a cough the potential causes and dangers are firmly planted in our minds: bronchitis, asthma, TB, etc. Even without any symptoms, family history can lead some to feel they are a ticking timebomb. Through modern medical knowledge we often learn with alarming exactness how our bodies are failing to function properly when we visit the doctor. Even when you receive medicine you are made aware of a number of potentially harmful side-effects.

Rarely, however, do we reflect on the tremendous potential for self- healing which we examined in the preceding chapters. We will deal with diet and nutrition later, but at this point one short comment is in order. Every bite you take of fresh fruit, vegetables, whole grains and legumes is loaded with thousands of different phytochemicals which fight cancer, high cholesterol and a huge number of potential health hazards. So every time you eat have a pleasant mental image of taking a powerful medicine which is allowing your body to remain healthy. Try occasionally to visualise how your various cells are eagerly utilising the supplies you have just delivered — in short, try to counteract the flood of negative information.

Praising God is also a powerful antidote to the constant flood of negative information. Knowing that there is a limitless source of goodness into which one can tap is an intensely calming thought. Knowing that you have an intimate relationship with an All-Powerful, All-Knowing, All-Loving God is the most comforting thought conceivable. These thoughts, combined with a technique to elicit the relaxation response, are a powerful means to assist our bodies in the healing process.

There are a number of Bahá'í healing prayers, but two revealed by Bahá'u'lláh are particularly important. They are known among the Bahá'ís as the long and short healing prayers. Neither one of these prayers is obligatory, but they are frequently used by Bahá'ís when confronted with illness. The long healing prayer is very effective in invoking the relaxation response. It is a masterful collection of the attributes of God, combined with a hypnotically repetitive refrain.

There are over forty verses, each contains different attributes and names of God, followed by the same or similar refrain. For example:

> *I call on Thee O Lord of Bounty, O Most Compassionate,*
> *O Most Merciful One! Thou the Sufficing, Thou the Healing,*
> *Thou the Abiding, O Thou Abiding One!*
> *I call on Thee O Constant One, O Life-giving One, O Source*
> *of all Being! Thou the Sufficing, Thou the Healing, Thou the*
> *Abiding, O Thou Abiding One!*

Dealing with a serious illness is unquestionably one of life's most difficult challenges. The long healing prayer, if said sincerely and mindfully, can open one up to the power of the Holy Spirit, quiet the mind and calm the body. Shoghi Effendi pointed out that the healing prayer is invested with a special powers:

> *The daily obligatory prayers, together with a few other specific*
> *ones, such as the Healing Prayer, the Tablet of Ahmad, have*
> *been invested by Bahá'u'lláh with a special potency and*
> *significance, and should therefore be accepted as such and be*
> *recited by the believers with unquestioning faith and*
> *confidence, that through them they may enter into a much*
> *closer communion with God, and identify themselves more*
> *fully with His laws and precepts.*

6

THE VIRTUE FACTOR

> The greatest bestowal of God to man is the capacity
> to attain human virtues.
>
> 'Abdu'l-Bahá

Through the behavioural sciences we've learned a great deal about the psychology of the individual and the dynamics of group behaviour. Within the scope of this chapter, however, it might be helpful to take a more basic approach to understanding human behaviour. When we observe the animal kingdom we find many shared drives and behaviours which we've come to recognise as necessary for the survival of the fittest within each species. The selfishness evident in animals isn't viewed as inherently evil, rather we understand it is an innate quality necessary for their self-preservation. The aggressiveness of the predator, or the violence of the dominant male, is also something natural which we consider vital to survival and evolution.

According to the Bahá'í teachings, the humans species developed over the vastness of time and assumed varying forms in the process. Just as a developing foetus passes through various developmental stages, the human species on a macro level has passed through a number of developmental stages. Obviously there were stages in our development in which selfishness, aggressiveness, dominance and violence were necessary for our survival and development. At some level we could say that our brutish ancestors lived as innocents in paradise. They weren't brooding about the past or fretting about the future. Guided primarily by their instincts they lived in the "here and now". As we developed into conscious thinking beings, we gradually acquired a sense of right and wrong, a measure of free will and an ability to remember the past and plan for the future. Also we became pointedly aware of our own identity and conscious of our inevitable mortality.

We can debate why, but in any case the human species eventually recognised its spiritual nature and came to understand that a higher power created and sustained the world. With the development of the human intellect and the awakening of the spirit within us, human behaviour, while still greatly influenced by the forces which shaped our developmental past, began to evolve into something which often violated many of the patterns of behaviour which we had once shared with animals.

> *In man there are two natures; his spiritual or higher nature and his material or lower nature. In one he approaches God, in the other he lives for the world alone. Signs of both these natures are to be found in men. In his material aspect he expresses untruth, cruelty and injustice; all these are the outcome of his lower nature. The attributes of his Divine nature are shown forth in love, mercy, kindness, truth and justice, one and all being expressions of his higher nature. Every good habit, every noble quality belongs to man's spiritual nature, whereas all his imperfections and sinful actions are born of his material nature. If a man's Divine nature dominates his human nature, we have a saint.*

> ´ABDU´L-BAHÁ

We might think of *virtues* as those qualities and traits which separate us from the aggression, selfishness and violence of our savage past. Contrary to the innocence of the animal, our primal urges and tendencies (the id), when fused with the self (the ego) can result in behaviour which we've come to view as evil. Animals kill to eat, to protect their young, or to defend their territory. Humans, on the other hand, kill for sadistic pleasure, for sexual gratification, to take material goods, to enhance their macho image, or because of blind rage, jealousy or any number of reasons. Greed, rancour, spite and many such negative traits, as well as altruism, compassion, selflessness and goodwill are the things which separate humans from animals. Sheer brute force no longer dominates most individual interaction, but money, status, power and influence are often wielded as powerful substitutes for violence and intimidation in our modern world. The conquest and subjugation associated with dominant males can now take much more subtle forms. While animals live in comparative innocence, the light of virtue and the darkness of vice demarcate our world.

> *How lofty is the station which man, if he but choose to fulfil his high destiny, can attain! To what depths of degradation he can sink, depths which the meanest of creatures have never reached! Seize, O friends, the chance which this Day offereth you, and deprive not yourselves of the liberal effusions of His grace.*
>
> BAHÁ'U'LLÁH

If you reflect upon it, you will see that a great deal of negative or pernicious behaviour results from an exaggerated or warped sense of ego combined with our baser animalistic tendencies. For that reason you will find *self-knowledge* and *self-control* at the heart of all religions. You will also readily discover that the primary goal of all religions is cultivating our spirits by instilling virtues, while containing our animalistic tendencies by helping us to overcome vices. Gradually, it's becoming evident that our individual and collective well-being is directly connected to our ability to awaken our virtuous and spiritual nature.

In his book, *Earth in the Balance*, Al Gore reached this conclusion:

> *The more deeply I search for the roots of the global environmental crisis, the more I am convinced that it is an*

*outer manifestation of an inner crisis that is, for lack of a
better word, spiritual.*

Of course our individual and collective health is influenced by
our collective spiritual state. War, environmental destruction and
contamination, climate changes, starvation and universal medical
assistance are impacted by mankind's collective spiritual state. In a
world inhabited by virtuous spiritual people most of our collective
problems would vanish. That may seem unattainable, but on an
individual level we are indeed able to greatly affect our own
spiritual state. Anger, greed, hate, resentment, gluttony, fear,
anxiety and selfishness, which have been shown to be deleterious
to health, can be overcome. Traits such as altruism, sympathy,
caring and sharing can be cultivated, and these positive traits have
been shown to have a positive impact upon personal health.

The point, however, should be made that repressing
emotions, e.g., putting on a happy face while you are raging on the
inside because of someone's actions, is neither virtuous nor
healthy. Similarly, it isn't virtuous for a coward to become a
pacifist, rather when a courageous and powerful individual
eschews violence we find virtue. True virtue isn't simply role
playing, rather it involves internalising spiritual teachings to a
degree that they become the core of our behaviour and character.
We can learn to remain serene and avoid anger rather than simply
repressing it. To do this we need to be conscious of the dangers of
egotism and aware of the source of negative human behaviour.
The absence of negative emotions is a healthy and virtuous state,
but the repression of emotions is neither healthy nor necessarily
virtuous. 'Abdu'l-Baha taught:

> *Recognise your enemies as friends, and consider those who
> wish you evil as the wishers of good. You must not see evil as
> evil and then compromise with your opinion, for to treat in a
> smooth, kindly way one whom you consider evil or an enemy is
> hypocrisy, and this is not worthy or allowable. You must
> consider your enemies as your friends, look upon your evil-
> wishers as your well-wishers and treat them accordingly. Act*

*in such a way that your heart may be free from hatred. Let not
your heart be offended with anyone.*

Another trap is that we often confuse excessive kindness and
extreme submissiveness with virtuous behaviour. To meekly suffer
an injustice is neither fair to the victim nor the perpetrator. We
need to be fair to all, ourselves included. Again to quote 'Abdu'l-
Bahá:

*The foundation of the Kingdom of God is laid upon justice,
fairness, mercy, sympathy and kindness to every soul. Then
strive ye with heart and soul to practise love and kindness to
the world of humanity at large, except to those souls who are
selfish and insincere. It is not advisable to show kindness to a
person who is a tyrant, a traitor or a thief because kindness
encourages him to become worse and does not awaken him.
The more kindness you show to a liar the more he is apt to lie,
for he thinks that you know not, while you do know, but
extreme kindness keeps you from revealing your knowledge.*

Since the basic human character is formed at an early age, it's
essential that character training begin at a very young age. The
Bahá'í teachings make the analogy of the individual character as
being like a tree. While the tree is young, its trunk and branches
are green and pliable. Whatever is crooked can generally be made
straight, however, once the tree approaches maturity change is
exceedingly difficult. A parent or teacher, in the Bahá'í view, is
equivalent to a physician for the soul and character of the child.
'Abdu'l-Bahá taught:

*If a child be trained from his infancy, he will...drink in the
crystal waters of the spirit and of knowledge, like a young tree
amid the rilling brooks. And certainly he will gather to himself
the bright rays of the Sun of Truth, and through its light and
heat will grow ever fresh and fair in the garden of life.
Therefore must the mentor be a doctor as well: that is, he must,
in instructing the child, remedy its faults; must give him
learning, and at the same time rear him to have a spiritual
nature. Let the teacher be a doctor to the character of the child,*

*thus will he heal the spiritual ailments of the children of men.
If, in this momentous task, a mighty effort be exerted, the
world of humanity will shine out with other adornings, and
shed the fairest light.*

Unfortunately, we generally forget the influence which our
animal nature has upon our thoughts and actions. All of us need
to work diligently on improving our character, and we must
ultimately accept responsibility for our actions. However, we also
need to be cognisant of the enormity of the task. Since the bulk of
our character was formed in childhood, we need to accept
limitations in our own selves and in those around us, set attainable
goals for ourselves, and be careful not to fix our expectations too
high for our fellow human beings.

There is a Gospel song recorded by the Five Blind Boys of
Alabama which has some sound advice which could serve as a
guide for most people:

*I'm not what I ought to be, but I'm better than I used to be,
and I'm getting better all the time.*

God's forgiveness and magnanimity are boundless, so don't
punish yourself for the past, you can seek forgiveness, but you
can't erase the past. You can, however, shape the present and the
future one day at a time.

*Let each morn be better than its eve and each morrow richer
than its yesterday.*

BAHÁ'U'LLÁH

You can also spare yourself lots of useless negative feelings by
recognising that judgment is ultimately in God's hands. You can
only be responsible for your own actions, if you suffer an injustice
you can certainly stand up for your rights, but afterwards leave the
judgment to God, don't allow yourself to be consumed with
negative emotions.

Remember that a crooked tree isn't easy to bend, it requires
great effort and patience. The best medicine is to follow the great
spiritual teachings and try to consciously apply them to one's daily

life. In all the religions of the world we find that humility and selflessness are the foundation of all virtue. Here are some particularly pointed examples from the teachings of Bahá'u'lláh, Buddha, Krishna and Muhammad.

> *Thine eye is My trust, suffer not the dust of vain desires to becloud its lustre. Thine ear is a sign of My bounty, let not the tumult of unseemly motives turn it away from My Word that encompasseth all creation. Thine heart is My treasury, allow not the treacherous hand of self to rob thee of the pearls which I have treasured therein. Thine hand is a symbol of My loving-kindness, hinder it not from holding fast unto My guarded and hidden Tablets.... Be as resigned and submissive as the earth, that from the soil of your being there may blossom the fragrant, the holy and multicolored hyacinths of My knowledge. Be ablaze as the fire, that ye may burn away the veils of heedlessness and set aglow, through the quickening energies of the love of God, the chilled and wayward heart. Be light and untrammeled as the breeze, that ye may obtain admittance into the precincts of My court, My inviolable Sanctuary.*

> BAHÁ'U'LLÁH

> *Behold, all the people are imprisoned within the tomb of self, and lie buried beneath the nethermost depths of worldly desire! Wert thou to attain to but a dewdrop of the crystal waters of divine knowledge, thou wouldst readily realize that true life is not the life of the flesh but the life of the spirit. For the life of the flesh is common to both men and animals, whereas the life of the spirit is possessed only by the pure in heart who have quaffed from the ocean of faith and partaken of the fruit of certitude. This life knoweth no death, and this existence is crowned by immortality.*

> BAHÁ'U'LLÁH

> *Learn to distinguish between Self and Truth. Self is the cause of selfishness and the source of evil; Truth cleaves to no self; it is*

universal and leads to justice and righteousness. Self, that which seems to those who love their self as their being, is not the eternal, the everlasting, the imperishable. Seek not self, but seek the truth. If we liberate our souls from our petty selves, wish no ill to others, and become clear as a crystal diamond reflecting the light of truth, what a radiant picture will appear in us mirroring things as they are, without the admixture of burning desires, without the distortion of erroneous illusion, without the agitation of clinging and unrest.

Yet you love self and will not abandon self-love. So be it, but then, verily, you should learn to distinguish between the false self and the true self. The ego with all its egotism is the false self. It is an unreal illusion and a perishable combination. He only who identifies his self with the truth will attain Nirvana; and he who has entered Nirvana has attained Buddhahood; he has acquired the highest good; he has become eternal and immortal.

FROM THE TEACHINGS OF BUDDHA

Who hateth nought of all which lives, living himself benign, compassionate, from arrogance exempt, exempt from love of self, unchangeable by good or ill; patient, contented, firm in faith, mastering himself, true to his word, seeking Me, heart and soul; vowed unto Me, that man I love! Who troubleth not his kind, and is not troubled by them; clear of wrath, living too high for gladness, grief, or fear, That man I love! Who, dwelling quiet-eyed, stainless, serene, well-balanced, unperplexed, working with Me, yet from all works detached, That man I love! Who, fixed in faith on Me, dotes upon none, scorns none; rejoices not, and grieves not, letting good or evil happen, light when it will, and when it will depart, that man I love! Who, unto friend and foe keeping an equal heart, with equal mind bears shame and glory; with an equal peace takes heat and cold, pleasure and pain; abides quit of desires, hears praise or calumny in passionless restraint, unmoved by each;

*linked by no ties to earth, steadfast in Me, that man I love!
But most of all I love those happy ones to whom 'tis life to live
in single fervid faith and love unseeing, drinking the blessed
Amrit of my Being!*

FROM THE TEACHINGS OF KRISHNA

*Clothe not truth with vanity, nor hide the truth the while ye
know. Be steadfast in prayer, give the alms, and bow down
with those who bow. Will ye order men to do piety and forget
yourselves? Ye read the Book, do ye not then understand? Seek
aid with patience and prayer, though it is a hard thing save for
the humble, who think that they will meet their Lord, and
that to Him will they return.*

FROM THE QU'RÁN

Conclusion

It's rather ironic that leading a virtuous life is portrayed in our
modern global civilisation as a renunciation of happiness and the
"good life". In reality a virtuous life is the only path to happiness,
although we often mistakenly treat pleasure and happiness as
synonyms. Wealth, consumption and fame are considered the
keys to true happiness and our civilisation is built upon attaining
them. Interestingly, the social sciences are beginning to show the
deleterious effects of materialism.

In February 1999 a very provocative article appeared in the
International Herald Tribune under the title, "Dark Side of
American Dream: Money Can't Buy Well-Being", by Alfie Kohn.
He writes:

*Over the last few years, however, psychological researchers
have been amassing an impressive body of data suggesting
that satisfaction simply is not for sale. Not only does having
more things prove to be unfulfilling, but people for whom
affluence is a priority in life tend to experience an unusual
degree of anxiety and depression as well as a lower overall
level of well-being.*

Likewise, those would like nothing more than to be famous or attractive do not fare as well, psychologically speaking, as those who primarily want to develop close relationships, become more self-aware, or contribute to the community.

The article quotes a prominent researcher, Richard Ryan, Professor of Psychology at the University of Rochester, as stating that recent studies expose:

...the dark side of the American dream. The more we seek satisfaction in material goods, the less we find them there. The satisfaction has a short half-life; it's very fleeting.

People who seek happiness and satisfaction through material goals are more prone to have behavioral problems and physical discomfort. They also score lower on measures of vitality and self-actualisation. These detrimental effects hold true regardless of age, or level of income. Finally, it is not just an American phenomenon. Research in cultures around the globe yields the same results, leading a life which focuses on materialism ends in unhappiness and dissatisfaction.

O people of the world! Forsake all evil, hold fast that which is good. Strive to be shining examples unto all mankind, and true reminders of the virtues of God amidst men. He that riseth to serve My Cause should manifest My wisdom, and bend every effort to banish ignorance from the earth. Be united in counsel, be one in thought. Let each morn be better than its eve and each morrow richer than its yesterday. Man's merit lieth in service and virtue and not in the pageantry of wealth and riches. Take heed that your words be purged from idle fancies and worldly desires and your deeds be cleansed from craftiness and suspicion. Dissipate not the wealth of your precious lives in the pursuit of evil and corrupt affection, nor let your endeavours be spent in promoting your personal interest. Be generous in your days of plenty, and be patient in the hour of loss. Adversity is followed by success and rejoicings follow woe. Guard against idleness and sloth, and cling unto that which profiteth mankind, whether young or old, whether high or low. Beware lest ye sow tares of dissension among men or plant thorns of doubt in pure and radiant hearts.

O ye beloved of the Lord! Commit not that which defileth the limpid stream of love or destroyeth the sweet fragrance of friendship. By the righteousness of the Lord! Ye were created to show love one to another and not perversity and rancour. Take pride not in love for yourselves but in love for all mankind. Let your eye be chaste, your hand faithful, your tongue truthful and your heart enlightened.

BAHÁ'U'LLÁH

7

NUTRITION: THE FOUNDATION OF HEALTH

The Báb hath said that the people of Bahá must develop the science of medicine to such a high degree that they will heal illnesses by means of foods...

At whatever time highly-skilled physicians shall have developed the healing of illnesses by means of foods... it is certain that the incidence of chronic and diversified illnesses will abate, and the general health of all mankind will be much improved.

'Abdu'l-Bahá

The ancients recognised the importance of diet as a means of restoring and maintaining health. Hippocrates taught, "*Let thy food be thy medicine and thy medicine be thy food.*" The prominent 12th century physician, Moses Maimonides, also saw nutrition as the primary therapy of choice, "*No illness which can be treated by diet should be treated by any other means.*" With the discovery of vitamins and the rise of allopathic medicine, the idea of food as medicine was gradually relegated to the field of folk medicine, certainly not to be placed on the same level as X-rays, pharmaceuticals and surgery.

At a time in which antibiotics and inoculations were transforming modern medicine, 'Abdu'l-Bahá's view that science would eventually confirm the prodigious role of nutrition in matters of health seemed rather unlikely. After all, a patient's diet and attitude were generally deemed inconsequential with respect to the effectiveness of drug therapy. Although the field of clinical nutrition made tremendous strides in the 20th century, it's worth noting that at a time in which America was on its way to the moon not a single medical school in the United States had a required course in nutrition. Even today, if a medical student doesn't elect to study nutrition the chances are that he or she will only have a smattering of nutrition in biochemistry and clinical medicine courses. In the true allopathic tradition, if one gets advice from a physician about diet, it often concerns which foods to avoid after a trend or an illness has been diagnosed. Rarely will a physician counsel an otherwise healthy patient about nutrition in order to avoid future health problems.

There is, however, a growing body of physicians who appreciate the importance of diet and there are literally thousands of studies in clinical nutrition published by medical researchers every year. Heart associations, cancer institutes and foundations for the prevention of various illnesses have also contributed a great deal to public awareness concerning the importance of nutrition. A wealth of information is already available, but the science of medicine will remain flawed until nutrition is more fully integrated into medical schools and primary care.

It is therefore evident that it is possible to cure by foods, aliments, and fruits; but as today the science of medicine is imperfect, this fact is not yet fully grasped. When the science of medicine reaches perfection, treatment will be given by foods, aliments, fragrant fruits, and vegetables, and by various waters, hot and cold in temperature.

                                                    'ABDU'L-BAHÁ

Today you can hardly pick up a newspaper or magazine without reading about how nutrition has been shown to have a newly discovered impact on health. Admittédly, the public has grown sceptical as nutrition experts disagree and flip-flop on questions of diet. It seems at times as though the only advice which has remained constant is Grandma's adage, "eat your fruits and vegetables."

In the middle of the 20th century it appeared that by taking a multi-vitamin which contained all the minimum daily requirements a person could eliminate any potential dietary risks. That gave many a false sense of confidence that they could substitute desserts and snacks for well-balanced meals as long as they took a vitamin pill. Some even entertained the idea that eating would eventually be replaced by a pill, just as Tang, the instant breakfast drink, replaced orange juice for the astronauts. Yet, it would seem that the importance of nutrition would be obvious.

Our bodies are made up of trillions of cells, each of which is an unimaginably tiny and highly complex chemical factory. They work unceasingly to sustain an optimal living environment. When we fill up our automobiles we are careful about which fuel we put in our tanks. We would never pour a soft-drink into a steam iron, or pour vodka on a houseplant. Yet for some reason we are very cavalier about the fuel we put in our own bodies.

Food has the ability to dramatically reduce the incidence and severity of a vast range of illnesses. Cancer, heart disease, strokes, high blood pressure, blood clots, arthritis, diabetes and osteoporosis are examples of problems which potentially can be averted or alleviated through diet. It's logical that if these trillions of cells can be supplied with the proper nutrients, there is a greater opportunity for them to function optimally. If, however, they are confronted with toxic substances and insufficient or unbalanced supplies, then it is clear that they cannot function ideally. Often they are thrown into an emergency situation to counteract what we ingest. Unlike your car which will fail after it's had a cup of sugar, our bodies are able to adapt to any number of extreme situations, but we do increase the likelihood that eventually something will go wrong when we consume poison and junk.

Jean Carper, the award-winning onetime medical correspondent for CNN and author of *Food, Your Miracle Medicine*, wrote: "*Food is the breakthrough drug of the twenty-first century.*" Nutrition will enable people to live longer and, more importantly, healthier lives. In the 21st century we will surely learn a great deal more about our individual genetic predisposition to disease and our personal physician, perhaps in conjunction with a nutritionist, will guide us in shaping a diet which will be especially tailored to our individual needs. Until the science of medicine reaches that stage, it is a good idea to have a thorough working knowledge of nutrition, and, if possible, to find a personal physician who is well-versed in this area. Because of the rapid and continual developments in the field of nutrition it's advisable, in addition to finding a physician whom you trust, to subscribe to a periodical about nutrition or check in regularly at a website in which you have confidence.

Finding a physician who incorporates nutrition into the practice of medicine is not always an easy matter. You might ask at a health food store, check the referral section at a website like Dr. Weil's, or simply ask friends and colleagues. Dr. Weil and the University of Arizona have begun a programme of integrative medicine whose graduates should be well-versed in nutrition, and perhaps other medical schools will follow. In addition to the conventional allopathic practitioners, there is also the possibility in some states in the United States of finding a licensed naturopathic physician. Some states don't have a licensing procedure for NPs and therefore there are some people who use the title of NP, although they studied via correspondence school.

Orthomolecular medicine and nutrition is another interesting possibility. The two-time Nobel prize winner, Dr. Linaus Pauling, coined the term Orthomolecular Nutrition. Dr. Pauling postulated that by providing cells with the proper molecules in the appropriate concentration, diseases could be avoided and abated. Literally orthomolecular means, "pertaining to the right molecule", be they amino acids, enzymes, hormones, materials, phytochemicals, trace elements, vitamins, etc. Those who adopt the orthomolecular approach to nutrition perceive each individual as unique. Optimal nutrition and health require much greater care than simply avoiding the diseases associated with vitamin and mineral deficiencies, thus the orthomolecular approach seeks to attain or restore ideal health by understanding each patient's biochemical uniqueness and corresponding nutritional needs.

In the orthomolecular view, one's sex, age, emotional and spiritual state, genetic predisposition, degree of physical activity, living and working environment, the soil in which one's food is grown, one's drinking water and stress levels are some of the primary factors used to determine an individual's optimal nutritional needs. This is considerably different than the RDA (recommended daily allowance) approach. Orthomolecular medicine's proponents see it as a paradigm shift in medicine. Conventional medicine, in their view, is toximolecular, which involves administering drugs at sub-lethal levels to mask the outward manifestation of disease, without addressing the root cause. The patient is exposed to lethal reactions, dangerous side-effects and in some cases dependency.

A study which appeared in the *Journal of the American Medical Association* in 1998 and was reported in the *Washington Post* lends credence to the orthomolecular contention. It was reported that yearly two million patients in American hospitals become seriously ill because of toxic reactions to drugs which were correctly prescribed and properly administered. Of these patients, over one hundred thousand died from a toxic reaction to prescribed drugs. Only a fourth of the deaths could be attributed to allergic reactions, which potentially could have been avoided. Thus toxic side effects to drugs is at least the sixth leading cause of death in the United States, possibly even the fourth leading cause of death. What is particularly important in this study is that the drugs were correctly prescribed and taken; cases of prescription error, overdose and uncertain bad reactions were not included in the study. The study did not, however, determine how many lives were saved by the drugs in question, which is, of course, an important consideration. None the less, the fact that 6.7 per cent of patients suffered serious adverse reactions to properly prescribed drugs should cause us to reconsider the advantages of nutritional therapy, especially in the area of preventive medicine.

It would seem that cultural bias also plays a role in how drugs are prescribed and how diet and optimal nutrition are assessed. For instance, a major epidemiological study of diet and disease in China (which we will revisit later) was carried out by Cornell University, the Chinese Academy of Preventive Medicine and Oxford University. The Chinese diet in general is low in fat and high in fibre. For example, as a per centage of calories a typical American diet has ten times more animal protein than a typical Chinese diet. Fat intake in China is about 15 per cent of total calories, while the figure in the United States is about 38 per cent. An average Chinese diet contains 33 grams of fibre, compared to only about 11 grams in an average American diet. Not surprisingly, the cholesterol levels in China range from 88 to 165, while the range in the United States is from about 155 to 274. Thus a Chinese person at the high end of the range would be in the healthiest range in the United States. This result, as we will see later, is directly correlated to diet.

That being the case, one would expect American physicians to bang the drums very loudly for a re-examination of the normal range of cholesterol in particular and the American diet in general; however, according to an Associated Press article they appear to be taking a much different approach. Americans drug researchers have suggested that up to six million Americans with "slightly elevated" cholesterol levels (around 220) should also be considered as candidates for the drug lovastatin, one of five similar "statin" cholesterol lowering drugs. The drugs, which must be taken for life, cost between $900 to $1,800 per year, so we are considering at least a $6,000,000,000 annual medical cost for a problem which in a majority of cases could be controlled by nutrition. Moreover, such drugs have also been linked to cancer in laboratory rats and mice, although as yet a human link has not been established.

We should never neglect medical treatment when it is necessary, but also remember that by taking a proactive approach to nutrition we can significantly reduce the likelihood of being afflicted by a number of illnesses, or of having to rely upon pharmaceuticals to restore our health.

Before getting to know the basics, a few facts need to he studied.

Phytochemicals

Phytochemicals are a recent and particularly interesting development in the field of nutrition. As we mentioned above, not too long ago it seemed that by taking a vitamin pill, a few spoonfuls of commercially packaged fibre, and eating enough protein we could more or less eat as we pleased. After all, just think of how many pounds of fruits and vegetables one would have to eat to get all the vitamins which are in a single high-potency tablet. Yet with the discovery of phytochemicals, the wisdom of Grandma's command to "eat your vegetables" became strikingly apparent.

The term phytochemical is based on the Greek word for plant, "phyto". Only a short time ago these powerful compounds weren't even known to exist, yet they appear to be an extremely important shield in our natural defence against cancer. A single piece of fruit or a vegetable can have thousands of different phytochemicals. It is thought that they evolved to protect plants from sunlight, but it turns out that they serve a number of protective functions in humans. Among other things they can remove carcinogens from cells, disrupt the binding of molecules in cells which can produce carcinogens, prevent carcinogens from attaching to DNA, help cause a precursor to estrogen to take a benign rather than a carcinogenic form, and prevent cancer-causing hormones from attaching to cells.

In the United States the National Cancer Institute has begun a major research project to isolate and study phytochemicals. One of the first phytochemicals to receive media attention was sulforaphane, which is present in broccoli, cauliflower, brussel sprouts, turnips and kale. A diet rich in sulforaphane is believed to be effective in reducing the incidence of breast cancer. A research team from John Hopkins Medical Institutions reported in the Proceeding of the National Academy of Sciences that rats in a control group which were injected with a carcinogen (DMBA) developed mammary tumours 68 per cent of the time. Rats who were also given a high dose of sulforaphane developed tumours only 26 per cent of the time. Sulforaphane is believed to work by increasing a natural substance known as a "phase 2 enzyme". If a cell has been invaded by a carcinogen, the presence of sulforaphane will activate the release of the phase 2 enzymes which will remove the cancer-causing agent from the cell by binding it with another molecule.

Sometimes it's really quite difficult to picture what is going on at the microscopic level. For instance, just imagine that tomatoes alone have an estimated 10,000 different phytochemicals! The appearance of cancer in the human body is a long process with myriad steps which are routinely thwarted by the body's defence mechanisms. Fortunately, numerous phytochemicals assist the body at various stages in the prevention of cancer. In the *Journal of the American Medical Association (JAMA)* the head of the Fred Hutchinson Cancer Research Center, John Potter, MD, said, "not all of them do it equally, but the overall effects of these compounds is to reverse or slow the process [of cancer].... The weight of the evidence is very much in favour of reduced risk of cancer with higher consumption of these products. What we need to do is to understand why vegetables and fruits lower the risk. Of course, from the public health viewpoint, it doesn't matter.... But knowing strengthens the argument and may make for some very useful science."

As we have seen, sulforaphane helps remove carcinogenic substances from cells once they have been exposed. P-coumaric acid and chlorogenic acid, two of a tomato's thousands of phytochemicals, help the body to prevent even the formation of carcinogenic substances known as nitrosamines.

Another phytochemical, phenethyl isothiocyanate (PEITC), found in cabbage and turnips, attaches to enzymes in cells known as P450s. This prevents the cell's DNA from being damaged by carcinogens. Grapes and berries also protect cells in a similar fashion.

Even if a tumour manages to form, phytochemicals are also believed to help in the containment of tumours. German medical researchers isolated a compound in soyabeans, genistein, which inhibits the formation of capillaries in tumours, thus robbing the tumour of its supply of blood and oxygen. The high levels of soya in Asian diets is believed to be part of the explanation for their low incidence of breast and prostate cancer.

All fruits and vegetables have vitally important phytochemicals, so a diet rich in a variety of them is particularly significant. Even a vegetable like a cucumber, which was once deemed to be of minimal nutritional value, has important flavonoids, compounds which bind with cells at the expense of potentially harmful hormones.

Later we will explore some of the important healing attributes of specific foods, but to finish this brief look at some of what is known about phytochemicals, have a look at this table:

Category	Potential Sources	Health Functions
Phytoestrogens	Soya, alfalfa sprouts, licorice	Aids menopausal systems, may suppress certain cancers.
Phenols	1. Carrots, alfalfa sprouts 2. Cabbage, citrus, broccoli	Reduce blood clots, may suppress cancer. Antioxidant, block some hormone receptor sites peppers, cucumbers, tomatoes.

	3. Grape seeds	Antioxidant, block destructive enzymes.
	4. Green & black tea	Cancer suppresser.
	5. Grape skins	Antimutagen, antioxidant, may suppress cancer, enhances detoxification enzymes.
	6. Squash	Tumour inhibitor.
Sulfur compounds	Onions, garlic	Elevate production of enzymes which guard the liver, reduce triglycerides, anti-inflammatory, lower blood pressure, antibiotic, antimicrobial, antifungal, antiparasitic, inhibit cholesterol synthesis
	Broccoli, cauliflower, Brussel sprouts, cabbage, mustard, radish	Enhance production of protective enzymes
Organic acids	1. Most fruits & vegetables	Bind iron-preventing carcinogenic oxidants.
	2. Cabbage, kale	May help prevent colon cancer.
	3. Tomatoes, peppers	Inhibit carcinogenic nitrosamines.
	4. Rice, grain, tea	Inhibit tumour growth.
Protease inhibitors	Soya, potatoes, cereals	Suppress the activation of certain genes known to cause cancer, protect against free radicals and radiation.

Terpenes	1. Carrots, yams, apricots cantaloupes	Antioxidants, reduce DNA damage caused by free radicals.
	2. Spinach, kale, turnips	Protect vision by suppressing macular degeneration.
	3. Chile peppers	Protect DNA from binding with carcinogens.
	4. Tomatoes	Protect against UVA & UVB rays.
Phytosterols	Plant oils, soya, corn, sesame, wheat pumpkin	Inhibit uptake of dietary cholesterol, block hormones which promote cancer.
Saponins	Yams, beets, soya, nuts	Possibly suppress reproduction of cancer cells.

Certain phytochemicals have already been synthesised and marketed in tablet form. Without passing judgment on this, it would be a shame if, as was the case with vitamins, people felt they could eliminate broccoli or other vegetables from their diet by taking a pill. If you do decide to take them, then take them as a supplement, not as a replacement. Remember, each vegetable has thousands of phytochemicals and we do not have a complete understanding of how they interact and function. Fruit and vegetable juices also supply phytochemicals, so if you are on the go they offer a handy and nutritious alternative to soft drinks.

There is also the distinct possibility that medical researchers will develop medicines from phytochemicals which can't be obtained from diet alone. For example, monoterpenes, found in citrus peel oil have been shown to regulate malignant cell proliferation by inhibiting growth-enhancing RAS proteins. Indeed, monoterpenes and perillyl alcohol, found in cherries, are being clinically tested for this reason. In mice they have been shown to prevent breast, lung, liver and skin cancer. Dr. Pamela Crowell, assistant professor of biology at the Indiana School of Medicine, said in *JAMA*, "These compounds should be considered as drugs even though they are present in the diet. It would be impossible to achieve therapeutic levels by altering the diet. For example, limonene is present only in orange peel, not in the rest of the fruit or juice. We worked out how many oranges you would have to eat [daily] in order to get the needed therapeutic levels of limonene. The answer came out to about 400."

In any case, phytochemicals are an exciting and highly promising field of scientific research. Until we know more, the best course of action is to eat a diet rich in a wide variety of fruits and vegetables.

Fat or Fiction?

There was a silent fat revolution which began in the 20th century. The types and amounts of fat consumed today reflects the rapid rise of technology and industrialisation, and perhaps no other area of basic nutrition is as fraught with confusion by the general population, or contradictory advice by experts. This is another area where you will have to make up your mind as to which expert opinion to believe. First it might be helpful to briefly explain the types of fat and then sketch the history of fat in the human diet.

Fat has come to be regarded as an unhealthy substance to be avoided whenever possible. For example, a fat-free cookie made with bleached flour, refined sugar and artificial flavours would be considered by many to be nutritionally superior to a cookie containing fat, but which was made with wholegrain flour, raw canesugar and natural flavours. Fat is not our enemy, it is an essential component in healthy nutrition. Surely you've heard the term "essential fatty acids" and indeed our bodies cannot function properly without them. Fat is a basic building block for cell membranes, it is required for the absorption of fat-soluble vitamins such as A, D, E, and K; it cushions our vital organs to protect them from trauma, protects our nerve cells; it's a source of energy; it's necessary for soft and supple skin, and we need fat for healthy hair.

So we've established that fat is indispensable, but a major aspect of remaining healthy consists of knowing which type of fat is helpful, and limiting our overall intake of fat. Most people have heard that saturated fat is bad for one's health. For decades people switched from butter, which is high in saturated fat, to margarine to be on the safe side. Now many believe that such a switch was ill-advised. Before we get into why, we need to understand the structure of fat. You may have often heard the terms, saturated, monounsaturated and polyunsaturated and not quite understood what they mean. It sounds terribly complicated, but it is possible to glean a basic understanding of what is involved, even without a degree in chemistry.

There are three types of fatty acids:
1. Saturated
2. Monounsaturated
3. Polyunsaturated.

A fatty acid is a chain of carbon with a group of molecules (carboxyl) at one end which enables it to combine (react) with other molecules. The chains can be as long as 24 carbons, or as short as 3 carbons. In oils and fats, groups of three fatty acids join with one glycerol molecule to form triglycerides — another term you've probably heard.

1. *Saturated Fat*

If a fat is chemically stable, it is "saturated" with hydrogen atoms. Because saturated fats are chemically stable they can withstand high cooking temperatures, and they are also less prone to becoming rancid. Saturated fatty acid chains are straight in structure, thus at room temperature they can pack together tightly and solidify.

Saturated fats are primarily found in meat and dairy products, although amounts can be found in plant-based oils, especially tropical oils such as palm and coconut.

2. *Monounsaturated Fat*

Monounsaturated fat doesn't possess all necessary hydrogen atoms, thus it is chemically unstable. Monounsaturated fatty acids are missing 2 hydrogens, so the adjacent carbon atoms "double" bond with each other. This gives the molecule a curved "cis" shape. Because of the curved structure of the fatty acid, at room temperature the molecules can't pack together tightly enough to turn solid. Thus olive oil remains fluid at ambient temperatures.

Olive, almond, avocado, pecan and canola oils are rich in monounsaturated fat. Monounsaturated fats are generally considered the healthiest form of fat, partially because they are relatively stable, yet have no cholesterol.

3. *Polyunsaturated Fat*

Polyunsaturated fat, which is missing from 4 to 6 hydrogens, is considerably more unstable than monounsaturated fat. Although polyunsaturated fat is prone to turn rancid, we can't do without it since it contains the essential fatty acids which are needed for proper metabolism.

Because polyunsaturated fat is unstable, it is important not to overheat it. It should also be stored in the refrigerator, never exposed to light, and the expiration date should be taken seriously, even if you don't smell anything unusual.

There are two groups of essential fatty acids found in polyunsaturated fat: omega-6 linoleic acid and omega-3 linolenic acid.

Omega-6 helps our blood to clot and our blood vessels to constrict when we are injured.

Omega-3 inhibits harmful clotting, relaxes smooth vascular muscles, and helps prevent heart arrhythmia — it basically reduces the risk of heart disease.

During the 20th century, for reasons we will see shortly, the ratio of omega-6 to omega-3 went from about 1:1 to as high as 20:1 in some American diets. Many nutritionists see this imbalance as a root cause of heart disease and other civilised disorders.

In order to counter this imbalance you can include flaxseed oil in your diet, which is rich in omega-3. Pumpkin seed oil also has omega-3 and it is an especially fine tasting oil with a warm nutty taste. Cold water fish is also an excellent source of omega-3. Flaxseeds, rich in omega-3, are very tasty and a nice addition sprinkled on salads, or any number of dishes. Beans and walnuts also are a good source of omega-3.

It would be nice if that were the end of the story, unfortunately there are a few other important considerations concerning fat. If you have been using supermarket type oils, then cold-pressed olive oil, flaxseed oil, etc. will have a noticeable taste, which can be traced back to the seeds, nuts or fruit from which they were extracted. Supermarket type oils are processed at high temperatures (500 ° F, 260° C), treated with toxic chemical solvents and caustic soda, deodorised and bleached, thus they are colourless, odourless, tasteless, and, unfortunately, nearly worthless. The processing destroys natural antioxidants, essential fatty acids and forms free radicals. Thus when you are shopping for oils, be sure to select unrefined oils which were mechanically cold pressed.

Trans Fatty Acids (TFAs)

There were virtually non-existent in the human diet until the 20th century. What are they? Well, as we saw above most monounsaturated or polyunsaturated fats remain liquid at room temperature because of the molecular shape resulting from the missing hydrogen atoms. With the rise of technology and industrialisation manufacturers discovered a process of "hydrogenating" vegetable oils. This made margarine, shortening and similar products possible by altering the molecular structure of the fat so that it could solidify at room temperature. At the time there was a surplus of liquid oils, so the process of hydrogenating oil seemed a perfect match for the burgeoning snack food industry. Unfortunately, during this hydrogenation process TFAs are formed.

By 1911 the well-known Crisco shortening was on store shelves. By the 1940's margarine comprised 90 per cent hydrogenated oils. Based on statistics from the US Department of Agriculture, by 1985 the consumption of margarine had increased by nearly 750 per cent and the use of refined oils had increased by over 1,500 per cent. During this time total fat consumption increased by 35 per cent, while vegetable fat in particular increased by 270 per cent. Interestingly, although most people believe that the consumption of animal fat increased during the 20th century, it actually decreased, although the incidence of heart disease increased dramatically during the 20th century.

According to Dr. Mary Enig, a long-time researcher and expert on trans fatty acids, the molecular shape of the TFAs is such that they can't be properly metabolised by cells. The utilisation of essential fatty acids is impeded, the prostaglandin function is disturbed, and the cell membrane is adversely affected by TFAs. She also maintains that TFAs lower "good" HDL cholesterol, increase "bad" LDL cholesterol, increase blood insulin levels, compromise the body's ability to expel carcinogens and toxins, lower the immune response of B cells, are associated with reproduction problems, and increase lipoprotein (a) which is associated with heart disease. She also notes a positive correlation between TFAs and cancer and TFAs and heart disease.

It is estimated that Americans consume between 11 per cent and 20 per cent of their total fat as trans fatty acids. This is easy to understand when you consider that french fried potatoes, commercial cookies and crackers, doughnuts, and chips contain around 40 per cent TFAs. Unless you live in a place like Canada where food labels are required to specify the amount of TFAs, you may never have given them much thought. If you want to reduce the amount of TFAs in your diet, watch for the term "hydrogenated vegetable fat" or "partially hydrogenated fat" on labels; avoid fried fast foods and snacks like doughnuts. You'll even find TFAs in candy bars, so if you don't want to give up chocolate, then look for chocolate with cocoa butter instead of hydrogenated fat.

Right now the danger of TFAs isn't widely known or universally accepted. Physicians such as Dr. Andrew Weil who take a holistic approach to medicine advise their patients to avoid TFAs, while others concentrate on reducing total fat, yet others continue to view saturated fat as the enemy to be avoided. You're going to have to decide which experts to believe on this issue.

A case can certainly be made that nature and evolution have given us the ability to metabolise naturally occurring fat. The amount of fat in the human diet has varied greatly based on climate and geography, exceeding 60 per cent of total calories in Eskimos and being as low as 10 per cent among some African tribes. Yet, historical evidence indicates that traditional diets, regardless of fat consumption, protected against the diseases of affluence such as heart disease, high blood pressure, cancer and diabetes. According to the non-profit Price-Pottenger Nutrition Foundation, which gathers data on traditional diets, our ancestors incorporated fats into their diets which were easy to extract. For thousands of years butter, various other animal fats, palm oil, coconut oil, olive oil, peanut oil, fish oil, flaxseed oil and sesame oil have been part of a healthy human diet.

Many of us have the impression that people nowadays live much longer than in any previous time in history. Because the average life expectancy might have been 40 years at another point in time, one gets the mistaken impression that anyone who lived to be 55 was elderly "back then". Mark Twain once said, "statistics don't lie, liars use statistics." Actually, the average life expectancy is greatly influenced by infant mortality and the incidence of infectious disease. In reality, someone in the 19th century who managed to survive to the age of 50 had a life expectancy which varied only slightly from our current life expectancy.

Personally I've been a vegetarian for about 12 years. I occasionally eat eggs in baked goods, moderate amounts of cheese, and low-fat milk and yogurt, so I don't have a vested interest in defending saturated fat. None the less, I believe it is just as important to eliminate TFAs from the diet as it is saturated fat. Dr. Enig's views on the danger of TFAs and the relative safety of saturated fat are supported by some personal anecdotal evidence.

My ancestors lived in the mountains of North Carolina. I remember my maternal grandparents' eating habits very well, and by most current thinking they should have died early with cardiovascular disease. A typical day's diet might have been something like this:

Breakfast: two fried eggs, bacon, biscuits with butter, grits with butter, buttermilk, coffee with real cream.

Dinner (mid-day): fried chicken, fried potatoes and cabbage with onions, corn, string-beans cooked in salt-pork, cole-slaw, cornbread and butter, pound-cake loaded with butter and eggs, tea.

Supper: leftovers from dinner, perhaps with a bit of fried ham, some squash, fresh cucumbers and tomatoes, tea.

They used lard (hog fat), bacon grease, and primarily home-grown vegetables. They rarely ate processed foods and eschewed margarine, even when everyone was telling them how healthy it was. They never drank alcohol, or red wine. They also had plenty of home-grown fruits: apples, cherries, peaches, pears, berries and grapes. Most of their kin ate a similar diet. Of course genetics play a role, but my grandfather and his brothers lived to their 90s, and my grandmother and her sisters lived into their 80s and 90s. Looking back at my family tree, my ancestors and many of their neighbours lived long, healthy lives on a diet loaded with saturated fat.

This was always a puzzling contradiction for me until I learned of the impact of TFAs. Although my ancestors had a diet brimming with saturated fats, they had minimal TFAs in their diet, but plenty of roughage, vegetables and fruit. I suspect that had they used olive oil in place of butter, lard and grease they probably would have lived longer, but to me on a personal level it makes a strong case for watching out for TFAs.

However, to be objective it has to be noted that many mainstream medical and nutritional authorities don't view TFAs with particular suspicion. One particular expert who downplays the importance of TFAs estimated that TFAs make up only 2 to 3 per cent of daily fat intake. Yet a recent study published by the Nutrition Research Division of Health Canada found that TFAs made up 7 per cent of average total fatty acids in mothers' milk.

Some mothers had TFA per centages as high as 17 per cent. In the *Mayo Clinic Health Letter*, March 1996, the question on the danger of TFAs was answered in this way:

> *Trans fatty acids don't pose as much of a health concern as saturated fats... To control blood cholesterol, your goal is to limit total fat. When you do add fat to food, the American Heart Association recommends margarine instead of butter because butter is high in saturated fats and cholesterol. The more liquid the margarine, such as tub or squeeze-bottle varieties, the less hydrogenated it is and the fewer trans fatty acids it contains.*

Interestingly, in 1991 researchers in a Mayo Clinic study of normal pregnant mothers found that all tested subjects were deficient in omega-3 essential fatty acids. The researchers recommended that omega-3 fatty acids be supplemented during pregnancy and that refined and hydrogenated fats be avoided.

In the May 5, 1996 volume of the *American Journal of Clinical Nutrition*, the following position was taken:

> *...Epidemiologic data are conflicting with respect to cardiovascular disease outcomes. We cannot conclude that the intake of trans fatty acids is a risk factor for coronary heart disease nor can we expect that substituting trans- for cis-containing fats will reduce the risk of coronary heart disease. Few rigorous studies have dealt with biomedical effects of trans fatty acids and possible mechanisms relevant to human health and diseases.*

Finally, lest you be tempted to ignore the potential health risk of TFAs, there was a major study on the impact on TFAs on breast cancer which was reported by the news service of the University of North Carolina at Chapel Hill in September of 1997. The study was funded by the European Commission and took place in Finland, Germany, the Netherlands, Northern Ireland, Spain, Switzerland and the United States. The study appeared in the September issue of the journal *Cancer Epidemiology, Biomarkers & Prevention*. The lead author was Dr. Lenore Kohlmeier, professor of epidemiology and nutrition at UNC and member of the UNC Lineberger Comprehensive Cancer Center.

Rather than asking the nearly 700 research subjects to recall what they had eaten, minute fat samples were analysed and the presence of TFAs was quantified. The study was designed to statistically control the impact of smoking, drinking, degree of obesity, age at first childbirth, family history of breast cancer, age at menarche and menopause and other factors which could potentially influence the results.

The study showed a significant association between TFAs and breast cancer. Women with high intake of TFAs and low intakes of polyunsaturated fats had a risk factor 3.5 times as high as women who consumed significant amounts of polyunsaturated fats. According to Dr. Kohlmeier:

> *Another interesting finding was that among our subjects, women who reported low intakes of polyunsaturated fats while showing the highest levels of trans fatty acids had the greatest risk of breast cancer. That suggests there might be an interaction between the two types of fat such as competition at the molecular level resulting in polyunsaturated fats having a protective effect.*
>
> *Since trans fatty acids already have been associated with cardiovascular disease, the preference is, of course, to reduce trans fatty acid intake. If you do reduce that intake, it would take a year or two to show a reduction of the acids in stored body fat.*
>
> *This work, because it is the first to show a significant association between breast cancer and trans fatty acids, needs to be confirmed with other studies. Still, we think it is important because so many women are at risk of breast cancer, and there are so few factors, especially dietary factors, known to reduce the risk.*

According to Dr. Kohlmeier, some European food manufacturers have already begun a search for a way to eliminate TFAs from margarine. Scientists from the Danish Nutrition

Council counselled that research indicates that TFAs are as harmful in the development of arteriosclerosis as saturated fats, perhaps even more so. They advised that the TFA level of Danish margarine be reduced to maximal five per cent.

One final consideration, metals, generally aluminium and nickel, are used as catalysts in the manufacture of hydrogenated fats. Thus there is also the potential danger of toxic metal residue in hydrogenated fats. I recall a margarine brand which used the marketing slogan, "it's not nice to fool Mother Nature", meaning that their product tasted like butter. Now it appears that the slogan may have unwittingly foreshadowed the impact of hydrogenated fat on health.

Some Free Radical Advice

Oxygen, you can't live with it, and you can't live without it. Surely you've heard the buzzword, antioxidant. So why are we against oxidants? An oxidant is an agent to oxidation, the process of uniting with oxygen such as in burning or rusting. Like a car we need to burn fuel, so oxygen is vital to our existence. Our cells contain enzymes and catalysts which use oxygen to convert food into energy and water. The "normal" oxygen molecule is made up of two oxygen atoms and is relatively harmless to the human body. However, oxygen can assume other forms which are highly reactive and are believed to contribute to the development of a number of diseases. Similarly, the deterioration of organ tissue and DNA through the effects of certain types of oxygen is recognised as part of the aging process.

When you slice an apple and leave it exposed to the air you will notice that it quickly turns brown. This is oxidation at work, as is the development of age-spots on our skin as we grow older. But the effects of oxidation are more than skin-deep. Cataracts, certain cancers, heart disease, strokes and various other conditions are all associated with the effects of oxidation. Researchers are narrowing in on how certain types of oxygen, known as free radicals, interact with our bodies to cause various diseases. This is very important research which allows us to use nutrition to counter the deleterious effects of these free radicals.

Simply defined, a free radical is a molecule or atom with at least one unpaired or "free" electron. Such an atom or molecule is, figuratively speaking, like a magnet looking to latch on to something. Actually the body takes advantage of these free radicals to boost our immune system to kill bacteria and control inflammation. They are also useful in the control of smooth muscle tone and help regulate blood vessels. Our bodies manufacture so-called *endogenous antioxidants* which help keep the supply of the potentially dangerous free radicals in check.

When, however, excess free radicals do manage to react they can inflict damage and set off a chain reaction of destructive events. To illustrate, let's look at how some scientists believe free radicals can bring about atherosclerosis, a blockage of the coronary arteries and a principal cause of heart attacks. When LDL cholesterol in a blood vessel is exposed to a free radical it can become oxidised. At that point a white blood cell on the artery wall called a *macrophage* will engulf the oxidised fat particle to eliminate it. So far so good, but the white cell can't purge the LDL cholesterol and becomes engorged and begins to swell. Gradually as this process is repeated the artery walls become thicker and the volume of blood is correspondingly reduced. As if that weren't enough, researchers believe that free radicals may also oxidise *nitric oxide* which is the body's own nitroglycerin, which is used to dilate the arteries and allow more blood flow.

Of course the engorged white blood cells are also no longer able to attack invading viruses, bacteria or cancer cells, so our health is further compromised. The peroxidised fats in atherosclerotic plaque pose even more health dangers. Our bodies produce a hormone called PGI which protects us against abnormal blood clots. Peroxidised fats inhibit the production of this important hormone, which increases the likelihood that a clot can form. Once it forms, iron and copper can leak from the clot's red blood cells and set off additional free radical reactions in other fat molecules. The end result can be a clot which can break loose and cause a stroke or heart attack.

With respect to cancer, when free radicals penetrate a cell's membrane they can harm its nucleus and damage the genetic code. When this happens there is a potential for cells to mutate and begin growing out of control.

Lysosome is a substance found in the cytoplasm of cells and it contains very powerful enzymes which are capable of breaking down almost any form of living matter. When free radicals damage cell membranes, lysosome can be released and break down surrounding healthy tissue. Some researchers believe this can cause some forms of rheumatoid arthritis.

Our overall strategy should be to reduce our exposure to free radicals and provide our bodies with the necessary stores of antioxidants to neutralise their harmful effects.

Avoiding Free Radicals
Unfortunately, with every breath we take we are breathing in perhaps hundreds of millions of free radicals. If you live in an area with heavy air pollution then the potential is correspondingly higher. If you smoke or live with a smoker, it is equivalent to living next to a toxic, free radical producing smokestack. Radiation (sunlight included), chlorinated water, some pesticides and toxins can all produce free radicals. Even the normal metabolising of our food can produce free radicals.

There is also a growing body of evidence which indicates that exhaustive physical exercise can greatly increase the level of free radicals in the body. During exhaustive exercise our total oxygen consumption can increase ten to twentyfold, and individual muscles may increase their oxygen consumption by factors above one hundred. All this time tremendous numbers of free radicals are produced. Another related process, known as *ischemia reperfusion*, produces excessive amounts free radicals. In order to supply muscles with blood during exercise, blood is diverted from internal organs (e.g., kidneys, intestines, liver). During the period of exercise these areas will experience hypoxia (lack of oxygen), but when the exercise is over blood will surge back to them. In the process great numbers of free radicals will be released. Obviously, ignoring air pollution warning and engaging in strenuous exercise during a pollution alert would even compound the danger of free radicals.

As we saw in the previous sections, heating unstable polyunsaturated oils will produce free radicals. So commercial cornoil, safflower oils, sunflower oil, etc. which have been heated to 500° F will have high levels of free radicals. If you fry with otherwise healthy cold-pressed polyunsaturated oils you will also create free radicals. Remember, keep such oils in a cool dark place, use them for salad etc., but not for cooking. Think twice about free radicals when you are tempted to eat french fries, or any other fried or deep fried food.

So basically we can't avoid free radicals, but we can reduce our exposure. Avoid cigarette smoke, excessive exposure to sunlight, extremely exhaustive exercise, chlorinated drinking water, and food prepared with processed or over-heated polyunsaturated fats and oils.

Protecting against free radicals

Fortunately, in addition to avoiding unnecessary exposure to free radicals we can also assist our bodies in the fight against free radical damage. Our bodies produce two enzymes without which death by free radical damage would be swift in coming. These two antioxidants are SOD (superoxide dismutase) and GSH (glutathione peroxidase). Thankfully our bodies are able to increase their production to cope with increased free radical exposure. Furthermore, there is an ingenious synergy which takes place among these naturally produced enzymes, antioxidant phytochemicals and vitamins.

For example, the body engages in a game of chemical tag and the molecule which is "it" becomes a radical. Once a fat molecule is tagged by a free radical it becomes a radical, but when vitamin E engages the fat radical it becomes a "radical" in the process. Vitamin E, however, is less reactive, so it survives longer and poses less of a threat to the body than oxidised fat. When a vitamin E molecule in its radical form is tagged by vitamin C, then the vitamin E reverts back to its old healthy antioxidant self. Now the vitamin C molecule is a radical, but when it comes in contact with our naturally produced GSH it returns to its healthy state. (Every molecule of GSH has to have four atoms of selenium, thus the presence of selenium in our diet is an essential factor in our antioxidant protection.) Finally, vitamin E also lends another hand by restoring vitamin A to its healthful state.

So we see that nature has provided us with an excellent shield against free radical damage, but when sudden and extreme exposure happens, then damage can and does occur. Nowadays we live in a world with diminished protection from ultraviolet rays, polluted air and water, processed foods of questionable value, and vegetables grown in nutrient poor soils with pesticides. Is it really so difficult to believe that our natural defences might need to be augmented? You can find a wealth of studies which verify the importance of antioxidants, for example:

One can readily follow why a study by Dr. Fred Gey of the University of Bern, sponsored by the World Health Organization, found that low vitamin E blood levels were more important than blood cholesterol or high blood pressure in predicting death from heart disease.

In the *American Journal of Clinical Nutrition* it was reported that individuals who took at least 100 IU of vitamin E for at least two years have around 40 per cent less coronary heart disease. A study reported in the *Journal of Lipid Research* demonstrated that subjects who took 800 IU of vitamin E cut LDL (Low Density Lipoproteins) oxidation in half.

Researchers at Boston University found that vitamin C can prevent the oxidation of nitric oxide (mentioned above) so that arteries are better able to dilate. They remarked that their results could help, "explain the association between increased uptake of antioxidants vitamins and reduced risk of coronary artery disease." Researchers at the University of Freiburg found a similar improvement in artery dilation due to the antioxidant properties of vitamin C.

In a study entitled, "Genetic susceptibility to head and neck cancer: interaction between nutrition and mutagen sensitivity", researchers concluded: "Low intake of vitamins C and E was also associated with an increased risk of disease and was interactive with mutagen sensitivity in risk estimates. This study supports the concept that the risk of head and neck cancer is determined by a balance of factors that either enhance or protect against free radical oxygen damage."

According to a study by the United States' National Institute of Aging, published in the *American Journal of Clinical Nutrition*, the elderly who took vitamin E supplements had an overall 27 per cent lower death rate, a 22 per cent reduction in cancer, and a 41 per cent reduction in heart disease. The study followed over 11,000 seniors from 1984 to 1993. The primary benefit in vitamin E was seen in its ability to combat the destructive action of oxygen free radicals.

Another study by the National Institute of Aging, reported in the *New England Journal of Medicine*, showed that vitamin E in high doses slowed the rate of disability of patients with moderately severe Alzheimer's disease. Researchers now want to give vitamin E to patients with the early stages of the disease in order to retard its onset.

In a study on the age-related degradation of the brain, researchers at the University of Arizona College of Medicine and the Veterans Affairs Medical Center concluded, "antioxidants may play an important role in preventing free radical damage associated with aging by interfering directly in the generation of radicals or by scavenging them."

Dr. Jeffery Blumberg, professor of nutrition at Tufts University published research in the journal *Advanced Nutrition* which demonstrates that vitamin E significantly reduces muscle damage from radicals produced during strenuous physical exercise. According to Dr. Blumberg, "the potential benefit is great, data are consistent and compelling, and the risk of side-effects is essentially nil. It makes a clear case for recommending supplements. A dose of 400 international units (IU) of vitamin E is associated with a reduced risk of chronic diseases such as cancer and heart disease, and can also enhance immunity and protect against infection." (Current RDA for men is only 15 IU units and 12 IU for women.)

In a study on prostate cancer, researchers surmised that vitamin C actually uses free radicals to inhibit cancer cell growth. Their conclusion, "vitamin C inhibits cell division and growth through production of hydrogen peroxide, which damages the cells probably through an as yet unidentified free radical generation mechanism. Our results also suggest that ascorbic acid is a potent anticancer agent for prostate cancer cells."

Antioxidant Vitamin Supplements

This is another area where we are forced to choose our experts and act accordingly. While many experts maintained for decades that a typical Western diet supplied all necessary vitamins, some are now beginning to acknowledge the potential benefits of antioxidant supplements. Yet many in the medical establishment continue to take a wait-and-see position on vitamins until there is irrefutable and conclusive evidence. However, even among those nutritionists and nutritionally minded physicians who recommend vitamin supplements, all would advise that vitamins should be seen as supplements and not as substitutes for a well-balanced diet.

If you consume multiple portions of foods from the following list daily, then you have the basis of an antioxidant diet:

spinach, squash, broccoli, yams, carrots, tomatoes, citrus fruit, berries, kiwi, cantaloupe, peppers, onions, garlic, cabbage, kale, peaches, nuts, seeds, wholegrains and apricots.

If you aren't eating such foods daily, you should be, regardless of whether you take antioxidant vitamins.

Anyone who is taking blood-thinning medications should *not* take vitamin E or a multi-vitamin which contains vitamin K without consulting a physician. Since one's age, sex, family history, stress levels and many other factors should be evaluated, I don't want to offer any universal advice with respect to vitamins. Actually everyone should discuss vitamin supplements with a physician. If you are informed about nutrition, broaching this subject is a good opportunity to explore your physician's attitudes and knowledge of nutrition. Dr. Weil's books and website offer a great deal of useful information about vitamins and nutrition and his website even has a vitamin planner which takes several factors into consideration before recommending vitamins.

Before we leave this subject there was recently a news items which appeared worldwide in newspapers and magazines about a study published in *Nature* which showed a potential danger of genetic damage when taking vitamin C. British researchers at the University of Leicester gave 30 men and women a daily 500mg supplement of vitamin C and measured the oxidation of DNA. One portion of DNA, the guanine bases, were, as had been previously demonstrated, protected, however, another indicator of DNA oxidation, oxoadenine, increased. According to one of the researchers, Joseph Lunec, at this level vitamin C's, "protective effect dominated, but there was also a damaging effect."

Dr. Victor Herbert, professor of medicine at the Mt. Sinai School of Medicine, has been a longtime campaigner against supplements of vitamin C which he believes interact with iron in the body to produce free radicals. According to Dr. Herbert vitamin C which is naturally present in foods is an antioxidant, however, he maintains that supplemental vitamin C can also produce oxidant effects (as the above study indicated). On the other hand, Dr. Balz Frei, Director of the Linus Pauling Institute at Oregon State University, argues that the Leicester study focused too closely on a single biological marker which hasn't yet been demonstrated to be useful as an indicator for cell damage through oxidative stress. He maintains that vitamin C should be considered in its totality with respect to lowering the risks for cancer, heart disease and other major illnesses. Dr. Weil continues to recommend supplemental vitamin C, but taken in smaller doses throughout the day. Finally, Dr. Lester Packer, Professor of Molecular Biology at the University of California at Berkeley and a foremost expert on free radicals, has openly admitted to taking a number of antioxidant supplements.

Fibrer to the Rescue

Fibre is another buzzword, but it's important to *really* understand its usefulness. In the past typical diets were much higher in fibre than today, yet the importance of fibre was not understood. Conditions such a diverticulitis were virtually unknown then thanks to diets rich in fibre. The German word for fibre is Ballaststoff, literally "*burden material*", because it was believed that since it wasn't digested it was a burden or load for the body. During much of the 20th century patients suffering from a number of digestive ailments were stirred away from "*burden material*" the very thing which would have helped, and given instead Schonkost, literally "*gentle food*"!

Fibre in a roundabout way helps us in the battle against free radical damage. Fibre such as barley or oat bran pass through the small intestine undigested. But once in the large intestine they are broken down by useful bacteria which convert them to tiny molecules which attach to water and increase the stool volume. The good news which scientists have only recently discovered is that these tiny molecules also bind with cholesterol. The bacteria in the large intestine continue to break down the fibre molecules, but the cholesterol remains and is eventually whisked along down the colon and excreted.

But there's more. One of the ways in which cholesterol is used by the body is for the production of bile by the liver. Bile is transported to the small intestine to help break down fat and when it is no longer needed it is returned to the liver. Fibre also attaches to bile which, instead of being returned to the liver, will be excreted. The body then requires more bile, so it extracts cholesterol from the blood to produce it. The good part is that the body primarily uses LDL cholesterol for this purpose. You will recall that LDL cholesterol is the so-called *bad* cholesterol which reacts with free radicals and blocks blood vessels.

Fibre has another important function which is regularity. Our bodies eliminate many toxins through the intestines. The longer the cells in the colon are exposed to toxic substances, the greater the risk that mutations can occur, thus regularity is important in preventing cancer of the digestive tract. There is ample evidence that diets which are high in fat and low in fibre present an elevated risk of cancer.

When we compare the colon cancer rates of nations with their fibre consumption, the results are dramatic. The Japanese, with a low fat / high fibre diet, have only one-fifth the American rate of colon cancer. Although the Finns have high fat diets, they also eat lots of wholegrains and fibre. The result is that their colon cancer rate is only one-third of the American rate. India too has a very low rate of colon cancer. None the less, a recent study published in the *New England Journal of Medicine* has caused a great deal of uncertainty by claiming that there is no relationship between dietary fibre and colon cancer. In the same issue (January 21, 1999 — Volume 340, Number 3) John D. Potter, M.D., Ph.D., of the Fred Hutchinson Cancer Research Center, offered these preliminary insights:

> *Since 1970, a large number of case-control studies have explored the role of dietary fibre in colorectal cancer, with relatively consistent results suggesting a reduced risk with higher consumption. A recent meta-analysis of a series of such studies showed both an inverse association and a dose-response relation. On the other hand, the cohort studies have been much less convincing.*
>
> *In this issue of the Journal, Fuchs et al. report no association between fibre consumption and colorectal carcinoma or adenoma in women.*
>
> *... In contrast with these findings, the earlier literature shows an inverse association between the incidence of colorectal neoplasia and the intake of plant foods (as opposed to nutrients), whether vegetables, fruit, or cereals. Such an inverse relation has been found with many other cancers.*
>
> *How are we to resolve this paradox? There are numerous technical issues that bear on the question, many involving the translation of dietary data collected by means of food-frequency questionnaires into nutrients. How accurate is the measurement of the foods? How well do we determine the fibre content of foods? How appropriate is the data base to the place and time of the study? How accurate and detailed is the*

data base, both in its catalogue of relevant foods and in its imputation of fibre content? Should we be looking at specific kinds of fibre rather than treating a very heterogeneous mixture as a single variable?

The story of fat and heart disease became clear as a result of a program of research that involved both epidemiology and experiments in human nutrition — feeding studies in which subjects were fed known amounts of relevant foods and biologic responses were measured. If fat is a dietary constituent that lacks uniform characteristics, the same is even more true of fibre. In order to take the next steps in understanding the roles of fibre (and its components), plant foods (and their constituents), complex carbohydrates, and sugar in colorectal cancer, we need a greater focus on experimental human biology and better data bases for nutritional epidemiology. With fat and heart disease, the ability to subdivide fat into structural groups and to measure lipids and lipid subfractions in plasma made the task easier. For plant foods and colorectal cancer, we need a biologically relevant classification scheme for components and a systematic approach to understanding the relevant intermediate biology. We have barely begun.

Despite this study, keep in mind a simple fact. A typical person in Japan is five times less likely to develop colon cancer than an American, yet if that person moves to the United States and adopts an American diet, he or she is just as likely as an American to develop colon cancer. This certainly isn't rocket science. Additionally, regardless of its role in preventing colon cancer, fibre is also beneficial for gastrointestinal, gastric, gallbladder, cholesterol, constipation, obesity, and diabetic conditions.

It's important to remember, fibre is only present in grains, fruits and vegetables. Meat and dairy products, rich in fats and protein, have zero fibre. There are some excellent natural sources of fibre. For example:

Wheat bran: 50 per cent fibre, 15 per cent protein, rich in folic
               acid (especially important for preventing colon

	cancer and heart disease), niacin, potassium and magnesium.
Wheat germ:	18 per cent fibre, 27 per cent protein, rich in vitamin E, magnesium, potassium, folic acid, and zinc.
Linseeds:	39 per cent fibre, 24 per cent protein, and rich in omega-3 fatty acids.

If you currently have a low fibre diet, don't increase your intake drastically. You should gradually increase your consumption of fibre and allow your metabolism time to adjust. Also it is important to drink fluids copiously when you have a high fibre diet, otherwise you can suffer from constipation or even blockage. Finally, if you have an excessively high level of fibre in your diet there is a potential that your digestive track won't have time to absorb sufficient nutrients, especially if you take fibre in pill form. But generally, if you use nutrient-rich fibre sources like wheat bran you are getting plenty of nutrients along with fibre. If you are concerned about this, dried fruits are also rich in important nutrients, minerals and fibre and a safe way to augment your fibre intake.

Cholesterol

This is another area where expert opinions vary greatly. Cholesterol is a primary building material used by our cells and organs for a variety of purposes. Our bodies produce much more cholesterol than we consume through our diets, in fact, even people who strictly avoid all animal products are capable of making adequate amounts of cholesterol. Just how much we produce, and the impact of dietary cholesterol has on our *serum* or blood levels of cholesterol appears to be a highly individualised matter.

Generally, the less cholesterol we consume, the lower our serum cholesterol. In some people, however, the liver seems to react quickly to dietary cholesterol and reduce production correspondingly. If you are one of those lucky people then you probably won't have to pay such special attention to saturated fat and cholesterol in your diet. In fact, in some people low fat diets don't result in significant reductions of serum cholesterol levels, and in some people high fat diets don't significantly increase cholesterol levels.

Then there are those who are genetically predisposed to high serum cholesterol levels. Our cells have receptors for LDL (Low Density Lipoproteins), the so-called bad cholesterol, which they require for cell metabolism. So LDL will be removed from the blood by the cells and used by them as necessary. Any excess is broken down by lysosome, powerful enzymes which can break down nearly all living matter (see Some Free Radical Advice discussed earlier). Some individuals lack adequate LDL cell receptors, so regardless of diet they will be prone to heart diseases and high serum cholesterol levels. Fortunately, in these cases drugs can truly save lives.

Some researchers maintain that high cholesterol levels aren't in and of themselves necessarily dangerous or a good predictor of heart diseases. Cholesterol becomes dangerous when it is oxidised, thus again it is understandable that low serum levels of the antioxidant vitamin E can be an even better predictor of heart diseases.

Other researchers believe that cholesterol also functions as a natural antioxidant. They speculate that while oxidised fat poses long-term risks, it is less harmful than the free radical damage which would otherwise occur. Thus in some instances a high level of cholesterol could be indicative of the presence of excessive free radicals and oxidative stress. If they are indeed correct, then replacing stable saturated fats with highly unstable polyunsaturated fats loaded with free radicals might not be the wisest course of action. A more expedient approach might be to replace saturated fats with relatively stable monounsaturated fat, reduce free radical exposure and eat a diet rich in antioxidants and fibre. Interestingly, there are numerous studies which indicate that high blood levels of antioxidants result in reductions of serum cholesterol levels. This would seem to support the notion that the body might indeed use cholesterol as an antioxidant.

In any case, most researchers would agree that it is beneficial to limit the intake of dietary saturated fats and cholesterol. Perhaps more significant than the total level of serum cholesterol is the ratio of HDL (High Density Lipoprotein) to LDL cholesterol. For our purposes we will call HDL and LDL cholesterol, although they are actually lipoproteins (cholesterol attached to complexes of compounds used as transporters). For clarity we can think of LDL as a delivery system of cholesterol for the cells. HDL is the reverse, i.e., a pick-up and return system for cholesterol. Cells also have HDL receptors, and when a HDL particle docks with a cell, the cell can fill the HDL particle with cholesterol like an empty sack. Once filled the HDL will dislodge and make its way back to the liver to deliver the excess cholesterol. The liver will throttle its production of cholesterol when it is supplied with returned excess cholesterol.

Thus if the ratio of HDL to total cholesterol is good then the overall cholesterol level isn't necessarily of great import, especially if an individual has a diet rich in antioxidants. For example, if your total cholesterol is 200 and your HDL cholesterol is 80, then you have a ratio of 200/80 or 2.5, which is excellent. For men aged 40 and above a ratio of 4.0 should be the upper limit, for women it would be around 3.2. Thus if your total cholesterol is 200 then your HDL should be at least 63 for a woman, or 50 for a man.

As a rule of thumb people are advised to keep their total cholesterol under 200, but a level of 200 with an excellent HDL ratio would probably be preferable to a cholesterol level of 150 with a HDL ratio above four. In general the HDL for women should be 55 mg/dl or higher, and 45 mg/dl for men. A few limited and somewhat controversial studies have associated very low cholesterol levels with increased risks of colon cancer, strokes, depression and even suicide. Such results are totally at odds with the information gleaned from the major epidemiology study in China which was previously mentioned. Dr. T. Colin Campbell, a nutritional biochemist from Cornell University and one of the primary designers of the China study confirmed that cholesterol is positively linked to a number of diseases. According to Dr. Campbell, "so far we've seen that plasma cholesterol is a good predictor of the kinds of diseases people are going to get. Those with higher cholesterol levels are prone to the diseases of affluence — cancer, heart disease and diabetes." Moreover, as far as the question of colon cancer is concerned, the areas in China with the highest cholesterol levels also have the highest rates of colon cancer.

Although Japan is, like most highly industrialised nations, affected by pollution, stress and cigarette smoking, nevertheless, it has the longest life-expectancy of any nation. Japan also has the highest number of centenarians in the world. The Japanese have very low rates of breast cancer, colon cancer, prostate cancer, lung cancer, and heart disease. They also have low cholesterol levels, which are positively associated with diet. Studies have demonstrated that Japanese who immigrated to the United States and adopted a typical American high fat diet also suffered the same risk of disease as the average American.

Now as the Japanese diet is becoming more Western things may be changing. The traditional Japanese diet prior to 1960's was high in carbohydrates (79%), extremely low in fat (9%), and modest in protein (13%). Soya products were the primary source of protein fortified with seafood, a little poultry and sparse consumption of meat. Their diet also included rice, millet, barley, sweet potatoes, taro, vegetables, seaweed and fruit. Their high rates of elevated blood pressure and strokes might be the result of excessively high salt intake.

In the next chapter we will explore dietary ways to avoid heart disease, but one final word to the controversy about low cholesterol levels. Someone who tries to lower cholesterol by consuming refined polyunsaturated fats, highly processed low-fat and fat-free products at the expense of a well-balanced diet of wholegrains, fresh fruits and vegetables may well run the risk of exchanging high cholesterol for other health problems. Drs. Siguel and Lerman of the Boston University Medical Center are experts on dietary fats. In a study published in the journal *Metabolism* they maintain that diets deficient in healthy fats pose a dangerous risk to human health. Thus it is possible that the problems associated with low cholesterol levels are actually the result of a low-fat, nutritionally poor diet. According to Dr. Siguel, "essential fatty-acid deficiency is perhaps the most important health problem in America." But as you might expect, other experts disagree with Dr. Siguel and Dr. Lerman. So again, one is left to choose.

Some Primitive Advice

If we consider mankind's entire timeline, the portion representing civilisation is minuscule. Over millions of years our bodies adapted to a diet which was considerably different than the diet of the ancient civilisations, and vastly different than our modern diet. Certainly cooking and baking were probably the first major changes to the human diet. Even until recent times the Eskimos ate much of their meat raw which was ideal because of their limited access to vegetables and fruits. This insured their survival because they didn't lose essential nutrients through the process of cooking.

The types and abundance of food in the industrial nations have resulted in enormous changes in our diets. On a positive note, fresh fruits and vegetables are available throughout the year, as are once exotic foods and spices. On the other hand, our processed and refined foods are loaded with salt, sugar and stripped of nutrients. For example, a slice of white bread has less than one-fourth the fibre of a slice of whole-wheat bread. Three and one-half ounces of raw potato only has 7mg of salt, but that amount of potato chips has over 450mg. Cooking spinach destroys 60 per cent of its vitamin C. Grilling meat alters the proteins and makes absorption difficult. Finally, as we saw above, the ratio of omega-6 fatty acids in our diets has increased enormously in modern times and many nutritionists are very concerned about deficiencies of omega-3 essential fatty-acids.

Basically over millions of years we adapted to a diet of roots, berries, nuts, fruits, grains, bugs and occasionally meat and fish. Today the empty calories of refined sugar and an overabundance of salt defines much of our modern diet. Although salt is essential to the proper functioning of our cells, it was very scarce for primitive humans. Thus our bodies evolved so that we could retain salt. That served us well for millions of years, but today the average American eats about 15 pounds of salt each year. That is equivalent to eating a bowling ball made of salt every year!

As we saw in a previous chapter our cells use salt (sodium) and potassium as a kind of biological yin and yang. Since the raw roots, berries, vegetables and fruits in our ancestors' diets were so rich in potassium the body didn't have to be concerned with storing it. Now, however, there is a terrible imbalance because we eat much too much salt and too little potassium. This imbalance has been linked to civilised diseases such as heart attacks, strokes and cancer.

So when you consider your diet it is important to consider your primitive roots, limit your salt intake, avoid refined and processed foods, and try to eat plenty of nuts, legumes, grains, vegetables and fruits.

Potassium

The chances are that even if you manage to cut back your consumption of salt, you will probably go from a bowling ball down to a cantaloupe. Salt is hidden everywhere, even things like diet sodas have salt added to them. Cookies and sweets usually have salt added to them too. Manufacturers take advantage of the fact that salt is an inexpensive way to give foods a familiar and appealing taste. I remember years ago reading about anthropologists who made contact with a stone-aged tribe deep in the jungle of the Philippines. As I recall they showed them a mirror and then gave them some cookies to eat. They reported that after eating the cookies they went to the edge of the jungle and vomited. It's too bad that we've lost that natural reaction to processed foods, but if we can't realistically give up salt, then we at least need to make sure that we have a diet rich in potassium.

Some researchers consider a diet rich in potassium more important than a diet low in salt. A high potassium diet is a very effective way to combat hypertension, and reduce the likelihood of stroke. As you know salt causes us to retain water, so the volume of blood increases as does the pressure on our arteries in the heart, brain, and kidneys. For reasons which aren't yet completely understood, potassium helps the body to counter the effects of salt. Also in some studies potassium has been shown to reduce cholesterol levels. Researchers have also discovered that potassium retards the growth of abnormal cells which can become cancerous.

HOW MUCH? You should try to have at least 3000mg of potassium in your diet daily.

GOOD SOURCES:

One banana	450mg
A slice of watermelon	600mg
One avocado	1200mg
Baked potato	840mg
One cup raisins	1090mg
One cup yogurt	580mg
One cup orange juice	500mg
One cup of grapefruit juice	400mg
One cup navy beans	720mg

THE GOOD NEWS is that nearly all fresh fruits and vegetables are good sources of potassium.

Folic Acid

Imagine a wonder drug which cost virtually nothing, can cut the rate of birth defects in half, fight cancer, eliminate between 15 to 40 per cent of heart attacks and strokes, and has no side-effects when taken as prescribed. The wonder drug is folic acid, one of the B vitamins.

Low levels of dietary folic acid have been associated with a wide range of health problems including increased risk of strokes, heart disease, birth defects (*spina bifida* or incomplete closure of the spine, *anencephaly* or missing brain, and *encephalocele* or hernia of the brain), and cancer (cervical, lung, esophagus, breast, rectum and colon).

Experts report a trend of mild folic acid deficiency, which isn't severe enough to cause anemia, but which can lead to the above-mentioned health problems. A study published in the April, 1998 edition of the *New England Journal of Medicine* found that there is, "strong evidence that increased consumption of folic acid will prevent cardiovascular disease...and that we should recommend consumption of at least 400 micrograms of folic acid daily." Some researchers suggest that governments should require that foods be fortified with folic acids, just as was done with iodine in salt, and vitamin D in milk.

The big surprise with folic acid was its role in mitigating the dangerous effects of homocysteine. Homocysteine is an amino acid which is formed as a by-product of the digestion of protein. There is conclusive evidence that high levels of homocysteine can cause coronary heart disease. A 1995 article in *JAMA* estimated that in the United States alone 56,000 lives could be saved annually simply by reducing homocysteine levels through daily consumption of 0.4mg of folic acid. The United States Food and Drug Administration (FDA) has required that beginning in 1998 cereals be fortified with 0.14mg per 100 grams of cereal, much too low in the opinion of many researchers. Still that is a big step for the FDA, since as late as the 1960s the FDA required a prescription for folic acid supplements above 0.1mg!

Women of child-bearing age should be especially careful to consume adequate folic acid, even before they become pregnant. This is due to the fact that most of the birth defects which result from low folic acid levels occur very early in the pregnancy, often before the mother realises that she is pregnant. The same issue of *JAMA* estimated that nearly half of all neural tube defects could be avoided if women consumed sufficient amounts of folic acid.

GOOD SOURCES include:

Chicken livers (1/2 cup)	0.54mg
Orange juice (1 cup)	0.13mg
Beans	
Wheat germ	
Soyabeans	
Broccoli	

Thus three cups of orange juice daily could save your life, or protect your future child from birth defects. It would also supply you with half of your daily requirement of potassium, natural vitamin C and powerful phytochemicals which fight cancer (carotenoids, flavonoids and terpenes).

The Most Basic Nutrient

It may seem rather banal, but water is our most basic nutrient and surprisingly few people drink enough water. There's nothing softer or smoother than a newly born baby and there's a good reason. A newborn baby is about 80 per cent water. By the time we reach old age we are literally dried out, having lost 30 per cent of our initial proportion of water. Although the elderly require less fluids, still they are often prone to dehydration because they no longer have a strong urge to drink. That is a good reason to develop the early habit of drinking water routinely throughout the day.

The amount of water we require is influenced by our physical activity, heat, humidity, and even what we drink. But since we lose about two quarts (1.89 litres) daily primarily through urination, respiration and perspiration, experts recommend that we at least drink that amount daily. That, however, is a minimum. It's better to base a recommendation on body weight and physical activity. As a general approach, you can use ½ ounce of water per pound of body weight for an adult with little physical activity. For the active it should be a factor of 2/3 ounce of water per pound of body fat. Thus, if you weigh 180 lbs you need more than 11 glasses of water daily, or 15 glasses if you are active.

Our foods also supply us with some water, for example, watermelon isn't a misnomer since it is over 90 per cent water, as is lettuce. During the burning of food the body produces energy and water as a useful by-product, still our primary source of water comes from what we drink. Coffee, tea and alcohol are diuretics which generally increase our fluid requirements, so pure water should be our main fluid of choice.

Our blood is primarily composed of water which our kidneys filter at a rate of about 15 quarts (14 litres) per hour. Waste products, toxins and excess water are filtered out and move on to the bladder; however, if we don't have sufficient water in our systems our bodies can't afford to pass water on to the bladder. Thus we have waste circulating in our blood and collecting in our tissues. Drinking water is like taking a shower on the inside, it is a cleansing operation. If you are rinsing yourself out thoroughly then your urine should look nearly clear, if it isn't then the chances are that you aren't getting enough water. One major exception is that taking vitamin supplements can cause urine to become bright yellow.

The quality of the water you drink should be a principal consideration. In some places buying bottled water might be necessary, but before you simply purchase bottled water you should have your home water tested. Often public health officials can be of assistance. Remember too, not all bottled water is equal. In the United States, for example, many municipalities simply bottle tap water and sell it as bottled water, although a somewhat higher quality testing is required. So it would be wise to check labels. Also there are various filter systems available, but it is difficult to give a blanket recommendation. Start with your local public health officials and your public librarian.

The Basics

For reasons of space it's not possible to review the individual vitamins and minerals, but I would encourage you to pursue the study of nutrition with one of the many excellent books available. In the next chapter we will explore specific food strategies for avoiding major diseases, but before we do that we should briefly look at two basic components of nutrition, protein and carbohydrates. Fat, the third basic component, has already been mentioned.

Protein is composed of amino acids which themselves are composed of carbon, hydrogen, nitrogen and oxygen. We produce a great number of amino acids ourselves, but there are nine *essential* amino acids which we can only derive from food. Meat, eggs, dairy products and fish contain most of the essential amino acids, but plant sources generally are missing some amino acids. Thus vegetarians need to understand amino acids and mix their plant sources so they obtain all nine. For example, beans and rice complement each other very well. There are some excellent non-animal protein sources which should be part of every vegetarian's diet: soya, wheat-germ, brewers yeast and nuts.

For much of the 20th century there was great concern about adequate dietary protein. Indeed, for that reason many well-meaning physicians and nutritionists cautioned against a vegetarian diet. Even today many people are concerned about getting enough protein. Times have changed and nowadays nutritionists generally believe that modern diets contain too much protein, essentially because most meals are centred around meat.

In general men need more protein than women, but current thinking is that protein should account for only about 15 per cent of the total calories, which if you will recall is close to what the Japanese had in the mid-1950's. Adequate protein, like every aspect of diet, is essential, but an overabundance should be avoided for a number of reasons.

Meat, the main source of protein in Western diets, is high in calories, high in saturated fats, and high in protein. When we eat carbohydrates we start digesting them with enzymes as soon as we begin chewing. Meat, however, requires a great deal of energy to digest. After sloshing around in a bath of hydrochloric acid in your stomach, fatty meat moves on to the small intestine to be soaked in bile acids, and complete digestion of meat can take days. All of this costs energy which the body could use for more productive purposes.

Another problem with the digestion of protein is that it emits toxic substances. Protein, unlike fats and carbohydrates, contains nitrogen and these residues have to be taken care of by the liver. The liver converts them into urea, also toxic, which the kidneys must then eliminate. (High-protein diets rich in meat are also recognised as one of the major causes of kidney stones.) These nitrogenous residues can also wreak havoc with the immune system and bring about allergies and autoimmune reactions.

Carbohydrates at the beginning of the 20th century accounted for about 70 per cent of calories in an American diet, today they only make up around 45 per cent of calories. Unlike protein, few people are concerned about getting adequate carbohydrates, but they should be. Carbohydrates are very efficient fuels which burn quickly and cleanly, leaving only water as a by-product.

Carbohydrates are starches and sugars and for that reason many people associate them with foods which lead to obesity. If you are ever in Hawaii where Japanese tourists abound, it's instructive to compare them to tourists from the US mainland. The Japanese still consume around 70 per cent of their calories as carbohydrates, compared to 45 per cent for the Americans, but obesity is rare among Japanese. A similar comparison can be made with China. Proportionally, the Chinese have as many calories in their diet as Americans, and as many carbohydrates as the Japanese, but they too are not burdened with obesity. Remember, meat, while high in calories, protein and fat, has no fibre. But potatoes, pasta, rice and grains, in addition to being highly efficient fuels, are rich in fibre and low in fat.

Of the carbohydrates present in the Western diet, too many of them (around 50 per cent in an American diet) are simple carbohydrates. Simple carbohydrates are basically sugars:

Sucrose   -   from cane or beets
Fructose   -   from fruit
Glucose   -   from grapes
Lactose   -   from milk

We need SOME simple sugars for energy. They are excellent in this regard because they are already broken down into simple molecules. Of course, the obvious problems caused by sugar is tooth decay, and, in excess, obesity. But obesity is more complicated than simply consuming more calories, and there are other unwanted consequences from consuming too much sugar.

Insulin is a hormone which the pancreas produces to metabolise simple carbohydrates and sugar. When we eat a great deal of sugar at one time, our pancreas goes into overdrive to produce sufficient insulin. Long after the glucose is metabolised the insulin remains in the blood-stream. The presence of insulin also stimulates the production of LDL (bad-cholesterol) and retards its breakdown. Excessive sugar intake also increases triglyceride levels which further increases the risk of heart disease. Insulin can also result in hypoglycaemia and cravings for more simple carbohydrates, which exacerbates the initial problem.

It is also suspected that excessive sugar consumption can contribute to glucose intolerance. When this happens insulin no longer works as efficiently and an individual may feel compelled to continue eating although the body would normally suppress the appetite. Then in a vicious cycle the more obese a person becomes the less efficiently sugar is burned. The sugars continue to stimulate the release of insulin, but it no longer functions properly, perhaps because of blocked insulin receptors on cells.

Because the obese person's cells aren't receiving sufficient glucose to produce energy, he frequently feels tired and is prone to physical inactivity. Unfortunately, excessive insulin can also interfere with thyroxine (a thyroid hormone) and lower the rate of metabolism, leading to even greater obesity.

Finally, insulin also retards the production of growth hormone, which in adults plays an important role in the proper functioning of the immune system. Growth hormone is released during sleep, so if you are going to indulge your sweet-tooth, do it during the day when you are active and not in the evening. (Carrots, potatoes and cornflakes should also be avoided as late night snacks because they produce sharp rises in blood sugar.) Otherwise insulin will remain in circulation long after you go to bed. Moreover, insulin can interfere with neurotransmitters and result in a sleep disorder.

If this situation continues, the pancreas can become so exhausted that diabetes can result. (Equally unsettling, one recent study found that only 3 per cent of diabetics consumed the recommended 50 to 60 per cent of calories as carbohydrates.) So as you can see, simple carbohydrates can result in some very complex disorders!

Fruits provide us with the sugar we need for energy, plus they supply important antioxidant vitamins, phytochemicals, minerals and fibre. As we have seen, three cups of orange juice is rich in folic acid, potassium and vitamin C, but fruit juice also has lots of natural sugar. The same is true for dried fruits. If you are going to partake of these treats, you really don't have much room left in a healthy diet for sweets, so you need to be very sensible in your selection of sweets.

For example, an 8oz cola can have as much as 6 teaspoons of refined sugar, a handful of jelly beans can have up to 8 teaspoons of sugar, as can a cup of fruit yogurt! Imagine someone drinking a supersized cola and taking in 12 teaspoons of sugar. We need to visualise the surge of insulin coursing through our veins to deal with such a senseless act. Tasteful desserts are one of the treats in life, but don't waste your precious sugar intake on meaningless calories. Incidentally, colas (diet too) have the added disadvantage of robbing the body of calcium because of their high phosphorus content.

One often hears that sugar is sugar and there is no advantage to using honey or raw canesugar. The sugar may be the same, but raw canesugar and honey still have measurable amounts of minerals, vitamins, important trace elements, and in the case of honey antibacterial properties. Honey, for example, also has boron, an obscure but very important trace mineral. Women with low boron diets have difficulty retaining calcium and magnesium, thus increasing the risk of osteoporosis and other ailments. In fact, studies have shown that a boron- rich diet can curb calcium losses by as much as 40 per cent. Dr. Forrest Nielsen of the US Dept. of Agriculture's Human Nutrition Research Center in North Dakota found that adequate boron can be nearly as effective as estrogen replacement therapy in stimulating estrogen (estradiol 17B) levels. Besides honey, boron is also found in fruits, legumes, nuts and soya. It is estimated that Americans generally have less than half of the necessary boron in their diet. That might explain why Chinese women who consume minimal amounts of dairy products (and colas) still have far less problems with calcium absorption and osteoporosis than American women.

But let us leave the complicated subject of simple carbohydrates and move on to complex carbohydrates. The molecules in complex carbohydrates in fruits, vegetables, legumes and grains are, as the name implies, complex. It takes time to break them down, so that means that there isn't an instant "sugar rush" which is particularly important for diabetics. This is the primary fuel our bodies evolved to burn. In the typical American diet the amount of complex carbohydrates is much too low. You should be consuming more than 50 per cent of your calories as carbohydrates and concentrating on complex carbohydrates. Also if you begin a meal with some complex carbohydrates and give them about a quarter of an hour, it will help still your appetite for fatty foods.

Summary: Eat more fruits, vegetables, legumes, wholegrains, and nuts. Drink more water and eat more fibre. Avoid unnecessary free radical exposure, discuss antioxidant supplements with your physician. Avoid refined foods, fats and oils. Reduce your overall fat intake, especially trans fatty acids and saturated fats. Cook with monounsaturated oils, not with polyunsaturated oils. Cold-pressed oils such as flaxseed, pumpkin and walnut should be used for salad dressings — never heated. Eat less protein in the form of meat, eat less simple carbohydrates and more complex carbohydrates.

8

FOOD STRATEGIES

Do not neglect medical treatment when it is necessary, but leave it off when health has been restored. Treat disease through diet, by preference, refraining from the use of drugs...

Bahá'u'lláh

In many ways food literally shapes our future. Imagine if everyone could glimpse into the future and see themselves as they would be at age fifty, sixty or seventy. The man frail and bedridden by heart disease might cry out, "Why me, what did I do to deserve this"? Surely, if given another chance this man would do everything in his power to avoid this outcome. But most of us live in denial, believing that somehow we are impervious to the risks that our lifestyles entail. Lung cancer, heart disease, osteoporosis, diabetes — those things happens to other people.

Yet we shouldn't be preoccupied with our health, or constantly live in fear of disease. Healthy habits simply need to be internalised — become second nature if you will. Yes, you can have a piece of cake loaded with whipped cream, but that should be an exception, something which you savour because it doesn't happen every day. Good nutrition and physical activity need to become a natural part of your daily routine. Just as we develop our spirits by communing daily with God, we need to recognise that eating responsibly is actually a means of preserving the temple of our spirits.

The ancient Greeks marvelled at the instinctive wisdom in nature which guides animals to eat what they need. We too possess a degree of this same inherent capacity, however, inner harmony and the ability to live mindfully in the present are prerequisites for recognising this natural wisdom. Moreover, by sticking primarily to wholesome natural foods it's much easier to follow that silent inner voice. On the other hand, if eating involves giving in to impulse cravings which spring out of clever advertising, then you are heading down fool's river without a paddle, and it may turn out to be a perilous journey which leads to a tragic destination.

Spiritual sustenance goes hand in glove with our physical well-being. Wholesome natural foods, fragrant and appealing to the senses, are the material counterpart of the words of God which sustain our spirits. Think of fruits, vegetables, grains and spices as God's gift to life, placed here for a reason. The more we tamper with these special gifts, the more we whittle away at their intrinsic value. If we feed our spirits gossip tabloids, adventure stories and fashion magazines and ignore prayer, reflection and sacred literature, then we allow our spirits to wither. In the same manner, greasy food, soft drinks, etc., can gradually tear away at the temple of the soul.

Preparing tasty nutritious meals for loved ones and guests can impart a sense of the sacred. The good news is that nutrition is an extremely powerful tool. If you are the family cook and you know that your spouse's family has a history of a particular disease, then you can quietly do a great deal to prevent your loved ones from suffering the same fate. What we eat and what we avoid will, statistically speaking, add years to our collective lives. Individually, there is no guarantee, but there is always a potential for premature death and needless suffering if one ignores the benefits of nutritional research.

The author, Jean Carper, has done a wonderful service for ordinary people. She has consulted over 10,000 published studies on clinical nutrition, done extensive interviews with experts at the forefront of nutritional research, and consolidated this information in a highly useful and very readable book. *Food — Your Miracle Medicine* should have a place in every personal library, and this international bestseller has no doubt improved the health of countless people. Much of the material presented in this chapter can be found in her book, along with a great deal of additional information about specific illnesses and foods.

Cancer

Cancer is a word anyone dreads hearing from a physician, both the disease and its treatment arouse frightening visions. Imagine if a simple lifestyle change could cut your risks of developing cancer by 30 or even 60 per cent. Those are the kind of numbers that researchers are using to describe the potential of food in preventing cancer. Of course lifestyle also plays a significant role in reducing the risks of cancer. For example, researchers at the International Agency for Research on Cancer in Lyon, France, found that someone who is a heavy drinker and smoker is over 135 times more likely to develop nasal cancer, and 43 times more apt to develop throat cancer.

Controlled human studies of diet and cancer are particularly difficult to design because of the huge numbers of variables involved. Could an obscure trance element deficiency, exposure to some environmental toxins, passive smoking, noise pollution or any of the thousands of possibilities have skewed the results? Do nutrient amounts which produce no results in a six-month study have a significant impact when eaten over a lifetime?

Of course not all studies involving mice or rats are applicable to humans. For example, many promising cancer therapies which are effective for rodents, aren't nearly as useful in fighting human cancers. Yet animal studies, because of rodents' shorter lifespan and the ability of researchers to more rigorously control variables, offer obvious advantages. And metabolically we do have a great deal in common with mice. Personally, research which demonstrates that a specific diet is linked to disease or its prevention in animals is something which I don't lightly dismiss.

Medical researchers are beginning to better understand cancer, but, regardless of their more complete understanding, aggressive and toxic therapies often remain the most viable treatment options. That being the case, the most sensible thing to do is to use the wealth of knowledge at our disposal to prevent the development of cancer.

Cancer is often decades in the making. Genetics, smoking, exposure to radiation, environmental toxins, free radical damage, diet, physical activity and a host of factors can contribute to the eventual development of cancer. Even if you do everything possible to avoid it, you can only reduce your risk, not eliminate it. It is not a disease of the spirit and no one who is diagnosed with cancer should feel guilty. Indeed, many people who have recovered from cancer consider it a wake-up call which positively changed their lives forever. Cancer forces a person to take stock of his life and to understand how precious our time on earth is. Often they become more spiritual and reflective, and they frequently begin to make dramatic lifestyle changes. Smoking, junk food, inactivity and negative attitudes are discarded in favour of living each day to the fullest, seeing the beauty in life and relationships, and eating responsibly.

These are wonderful developments, but we shouldn't wait for something to happen which forces us to change our lifestyle. When cancer is diagnosed that essentially means that our immune system wasn't capable of keeping it in check. Our treatment for much of the 20th century, highly simplified, was to surgically remove the tumour, bombard the area with radiation, and try to kill any remaining cancer cells with toxins. Then with the help of drugs, we gave the body a chance to try again. However, during this time the immune system was highly compromised, and there was always the potential for other problems to develop during the treatment period. Newer approaches are changing the way we treat cancer, and gene therapies offer the potential for revolutionary treatments in the coming decades, but right now prevention is our best treatment. (Refer to the chapter Future Medicine for more information about modern cancer treatments.)

It is sometimes difficult to imagine how minute amounts of nutrients in foods can play such an important role in our health. We need to think of what is happening at the cellular level in order to envision, for example, how a free radical oxygen molecule can penetrate a cell's membrane and damage the DNA. To enlarge a photo of a cell to the size of a computer screen you would need to magnify it around 30,000 times! Hidden inside every microscopic cell you can find the entire genetic code for your body. This chemical chain is super-coiled so that 2 metres (6.6ft) of DNA can fit into each cell. These estimated 3 billion building blocks make up the approximately 100,000 human genes. These genes basically make protein molecules which either become part of the body or become enzymes which promote a specific chemical reaction. As we saw in chapter 2 the body has a fantastic quality control system to avoid mistakes when DNA is replicated, but as mentioned above, several factors can cause mutations in our DNA. When this occurs the protein which a gene produces no longer functions properly. For example, enzymes necessary to regulate growth activity may suddenly allow a cell to begin growing uncontrollably. Fortunately, because the body has many backup controls, usually several mistakes must occur before cancer can result.

While foods help to prevent cancer, they are not a substitute for medical treatment, although many of the most modern biological therapies for cancer mimic the anticancer action of some phytochemicals. Phytochemicals can be thought of as mild anticancer agents which, as we will see, assist the body in eliminating myriad processes which can lead to cancer. They can help to eliminate or neutralise enzymes and carcinogenic agents, and sometimes even allow cells to revert back to normalcy. Some foods have been shown to neutralise up to 50 different carcinogens. Foods have various chemical properties which assist us in warding off cancer. The trick is to eat a wide variety of fruits, vegetables and grains and keep antioxidants and phytochemicals circulating in your body and available for your cells as they are needed.

Once cancer strikes, food can certainly be employed as an adjunct to conventional therapies. If you (or a loved one) have cancer you might want to check out the American Institute for Cancer Research — Online at http://www.aicr.org/aicr.htm. AICR is a non-profit charity which funds nutritional research on cancer and provides useful information in this regard as well as links to other helpful sites.

The National Cancer Institute of the United States has begun research on a number of fruits and vegetables because of their expected anticancer possibilities including: berries, broccoli, brussel sprouts, cabbage, cauliflower, cantaloupe, cucumbers, carrots, celery, citrus fruits, eggplant, flax, ginger, garlic, licorice, oats, onions, peppers, potatoes, soyabeans, tea, tomatoes, various spices, and wheat. You would do well to make them a part of your diet, remembering that virtually all fruits and vegetables, not just those listed, are useful in preventing cancer.

Let's have a look at some of what scientists have discovered.

Yogurt : In particular it protects against colon and endometrial cancer, but yogurt boosts the immune system and thus fights infection and tumour development in general. Researchers in Italy and California have documented that yogurt with active live cultures dramatically increases the production of gamma interferon and the activity of natural killer cells. Natural killer cells, you will recall, attack cells which have been invaded by viruses and also tumour cells. A study at the University of California School of Medicine at Davis found that yogurt eaters had five times as much gamma interferon in their blood as non-yogurt eaters.

Yogurt is also rich in calcium which suppresses enzymes in the colon which promote tumour growth. Also the lactobacillus acidophilus cultures disrupt enzyme activity in the colon which encourages tumour growth. Yogurt is also rich in potassium which can retard the growth of abnormal cells.

If you are lactose intolerant (missing the enzymes which digests milk sugar) you can probably tolerate yogurt made with live cultures because the bacteria break down the lactose for you.

Wheat Bran is especially effective in protecting against colon and breast cancer. A low-fat, high-wheat fibre diet slashed the rate of breast tumour development by half in animal studies. In human studies eating wheat bran reduced the serum level of cancer enhancing estrogen by nearly twenty per cent (control groups on other fibre sources showed no such reduction).

Researchers aren't sure exactly why, but wheat bran significantly inhibits cancer enhancing activity in the colon. Perhaps by reducing bile acid concentrations, bacterial enzymes in the stool, or perhaps pentose (wheat sugar) suppresses polyp growth. In any case, wheat bran works.

Wheat bran is high in fibre and complex carbohydrates, low in fat, and supplies protein, minerals (calcium, iron, magnesium, potassium, zinc, copper, manganese, selenium) and B vitamins. An excellent food, which unfortunately in some people may cause allergies.

Watermelon is red because of a pigment lycopene, which researchers believe may be twice as powerful as beta carotene at neutralising the effects of oxygen free radical damage. People with high serum levels of lycopene have reduced risks of a variety of cancers including cancer of the digestive tract and prostate. Watermelon is also particularly high in the powerful antioxidant glutathione (see separate heading).

Tomatoes are also loaded with lycopene, the same powerful antioxidant found in watermelon. Independent researchers at the USDA and the University of Dusseldorf confirmed that lycopene is more easily absorbed by the body when it has been heated with oil. Fortunately, heating a tomato sauce doesn't adversely affect the concentration of lycopene.

Researchers have detected extremely low serum levels of lycopene in patients with pancreatic cancer. Low levels have also been observed in patients with bladder cancer and rectal cancer, and a precancerous condition associated with cervical cancer.

Turmeric (*Curcuma longa*) is a spice used to give mustard and curry their characteristic yellow color. Turmeric or *curcumin* is a very important spice with numerous purported health claims and used widely in herbal medicine. It is thought to shield the liver from toxins, neutralise several carcinogenic substances, and inhibit cancer . It also is a powerful anti-inflammatory agent, reduces blood clotting and aids cholesterol metabolism. It tastes great too.

Tea : Great news for Bahá'ís and other prodigious tea drinkers around the world — tea fights cancer. Although some epidemiological studies which seek to link eating patterns with disease rates have delivered contradictory results with respect to the effects of tea; controlled laboratory experiments with animals and live cells have consistently demonstrated powerful antioxidant cancer inhibiting properties in tea. Moreover, Dr. Chung Yang of Rutgers University, a prominent phytochemical researcher, says, "Some newer, more powerful studies using computer calculations of populations data, however, do show a protective factor in tea polyphenols."

Camellia sinensis is the plant whose leaves are used to make both green, oolong and black tea. Green tea undergoes a fermentation process to become black tea and this may account for the fact that green tea has considerably higher antioxidant properties than black tea.

Chemicals in tea called catechins which belong to the phenols classification of phytochemicals have been shown to protect against cancer (skin, colon, lung, prostate, esophageal and liver). Epigallocatechin gallate (EGCG) in particular has been shown to be an especially powerful antioxidant. In studies on genetic mutations in bacteria EGCG was shown to be nearly 100 times more potent than vitamin C and around 25 times more powerful than vitamin E in shielding DNA from damage.

Researchers from the Medical College of Ohio and the University of Toledo reported in the June 1997 issue *of Nature* that they may have discovered why green tea protects against cancer. At the cellular level enzymes called urokinase break down proteins and thereby make room for tumours and the blood vessels that will sustain them. They began to devise a synthetic molecule which would interfere with this process, but then

realised that there was already a naturally occurring molecule —
EGCG found in green tea.

The M.D. Anderson Cancer Center in Houston, Texas, has
begun trials on cancer patients to determine if green tea
supplements can shrink existing tumours. You might want to give
serious consideration to drinking a bit of green tea regularly. I
must admit that I don't particularly enjoy it as a plain hot tea, but
I do find that it makes a delicious cool drink, or a nice hot spice
tea with fresh ginger, cloves, cinnamon, nutmeg and milk.

The antioxidants in tea also contribute to an improved
metabolism of cholesterol. And if that weren't enough, researchers
at the University of California Berkeley discovered that hexane, a
chemical also found in green tea, protects against cavities.

Soya — could easily fill an entire chapter itself. It's difficult to
imagine a more versatile and nutritious food than soya. As
mentioned previously researchers have long been intrigued with
the low cancer rates in Japan vs. the United States. Genetics has
been ruled out because Japanese who live in American and adopt
the typical diet lose their health advantage. For every 100,000
women in America around 22 will develop breast cancer, vs. 6 in
Japan. Thus an average American woman is nearly four times
more likely to develop breast cancer. For every 100,000 American
men, around 16 will develop prostate cancer, vs. only 3.5 in Japan,
making Americans more than four times more likely to develop
prostate cancer.

Researchers have zeroed in on some factors which they
believe contribute to the Japanese advantage: low levels of dietary
fat, high intake of soya protein and green tea. Within Japan,
women who consume the most soya have the lowest breast cancer
rates. In any case, we see that diet plays an extremely important
role in the development of cancer. Researchers have already
identified several ways in which soya inhibits the development of
cancer.

Isoflavones can be thought of as plant-estrogen, although
they are extremely weak compared to human estrogen. None the
less, these plant-estrogens can block human estrogen and inhibit

certain cancer processes by docking at estrogen receptors on cells and depriving cancer cells of estrogen needed for growth. Isoflavones function somewhat like tamoxifen, a promising cancer inhibiting drug, but without its side-effects. The blood level of isoflavones in Japanese women is between 5 and 20 times higher than American women. This may explain why Asian women's menstrual cycle is generally two to three days longer than American women. In an English study, women given two ounces of soya daily had a delay in ovulation. Some researchers theorise that this lengthening of the menstrual cycle may also be partly responsible for lower breast cancer rates. That is, because of the longer cycle there are fewer surges of estrogen and a lower total lifetime exposure to estrogen.

Parenthetically, lifelong consumption of soya seems to account for the lower incidence of menopausal symptoms in Asian women. One study found that over half of American women complained of menopausal symptoms, compared to less than ten per cent of Asian women. Thus in some women a diet rich in soya could possibly supersede hormone replacement therapy.

Rats exposed to carcinogens which produce breast cancer and feed a diet of soyabeans developed mammary tumours from 40 to 65 per cent less than a control group. When rats were fed soya with the isoflavones removed there was no reduction in tumours.

Paradoxically, soya's plant-estrogens may also account for its ability to inhibit prostate cancer. Actually human female estrogen is currently used as a treatment for prostate cancer. Estrogen interferes with the production of testosterone, which can feed prostate tumours. Estrogen has a downside in men, it can impair male sexual function, and cause breast development. Plant-estrogens, however, have none of estrogen's side-effects. Asian men do develop prostate cancer, but, perhaps because of soya, it advances more slowly and thus they often die of other causes.

Genistein, unique to soya, is the primary isoflavones compound found in soya and it appears to have a number of functions beyond mimicking human estrogen. Genistein is known to interfere with a number of enzymes which are involved in the development of cancer. A German study reported in the April 1993 Proceedings of the National Academy of Sciences found that genistein blocks the growth and development of blood vessels (angiogenesis) required to nourish tumours. Genistein is also an effective antioxidant and it has even been shown to cause some aberrant cells to revert to normalcy.

In a study done at Michigan State University and presented in Belgium at the Second International Symposium on the Role of Soya in Preventing and Treating Chronic Disease looked at the role of soya in preventing colon cancer. Researchers measured a precursor of colon cancer (Aberrant Crypt Foci or ACF) in rats fed on a soya diet. The measure of ACF formation is frequently used for assessing anticancer drugs. While rats in the control group developed an average of 5 tumours, rats in the group given soya flour developed around 30 per cent less ACF and no tumours.

Phytosterols (plant cholesterol) found in soya is known to inhibit colon cancer by protecting against the harmful effects of bile acid. Studies have shown that *saponins* from soya inhibit the DNA synthesis of tumour cells and kill Sarcoma 37 cells. *Protease Inhibitors* present in soy appear to protect against cancer by inhibiting the activation of certain cancer-producing genes and also by protecting against the effects of free radicals. *Phytate* in soya has also been shown to stimulate natural killer cells.

Of course, for our purposes we needn't be concerned with isolated properties of soya, but rather begin to integrate soya into our diets. As we will see in the next section, even if soya didn't offer any protection against cancer, its role in protecting against cardiovascular disease would warrant its inclusion in a healthy diet.

Tip : Soya flour is an easy way to increase your soya intake. It can be used in soups, sauces, and blended with fruit juice. In most recipes calling for a cup of wheat flour a couple of tablespoons of soya flour can be mixed to replace an equal amount of wheat flour. Soya substitutes for meat, milk and cheese are available (see www.galaxyfoods.com). Soyabeans are another easy option, and of course there is tofu. Ask at an Asian grocery store about soya products and you'll probably be surprised at the number and variety available.

Red Meat : *AVOID IT*. Several international studies have linked consumption of red meat to increased risks of colon and pancreatic cancer. A study of 90,000 women done by the Harvard School of Public Health found that women who ate a dish of red meat daily had a 250 per cent increased risk of colon cancer, compared to a group which ate meat less than once a month. A Japanese study found that eating meat once a day increased the risk of pancreatic cancer by 50 per cent.

If you don't want to give up red meat, then you should avoid cooking it at high temperatures (frying, grilling, broiling or barbecuing) because this, according to Dr. Richard Anderson of the National Cancer Institute, produces heterocyclic aromatic amines (HAA's) which cause cancer. Stew, boil or poach meats to reduce the amounts of HAA's.

Pectin, according to a University of Texas study, was shown to cut the rate of colon cancer in rats in half and it also reduced cholesterol levels by 30 per cent. Although insoluble fibre is generally associated with preventing colon cancer, pectin, a soluble fibre found especially in apples, is also very effective. In lesser quantities it can be found in apricots, carrots, citrus fruit, pears, prunes, and dried beans.

Onions : contain quercetin which is a powerful antioxidant. Quercetin, a flavonoid, possesses a number of demonstrated beneficial properties. Dr. Terrance Leighton, professor of biochemistry and molecular biology at the University of California Berkeley, commented, "Quercetin is one of the most potent anticancer agents ever discovered." Beyond protecting cells from DNA damage it also inhibits enzymes which promote tumour growth.

In the county in Georgia where the famous Vidalia onions are produced the stomach cancer rate is only one-third as high as the rest of the United States. Studies in China have likewise shown a link between onions and a reduced rate of stomach cancer. Quercetin is also believed to reduce the risks of melanoma (skin cancer).

Yellow and red onions (not white onions or garlic) are rich in quercetin. Quercetin also combats viruses, bacteria, fungi, inflammation and histamines. Onions are an important food to have in your diet, best eaten raw or only lightly cooked.

Glutathione, you will recall from the previous chapter, is a endogenous antioxidant which is particularly effective at preventing free radical chain reactions. Not only do we produce glutathione, but this important cancer-fighting compound is found in many foods. Best sources include: avocado, asparagus and watermelon. Other good sources are: broccoli, cauliflower, citrus fruit, peaches, potatoes and strawberries.

Grapes : Red grapes are an excellent source of antioxidants and anticoagulants. They also have quercetin (see onions).

Ginger : is a strong antioxidant which protects against cancer. It is also a powerful anti-inflammatory agent.

Garlic : Studies have shown that garlic may be a sort of natural chemotherapy. A study found that ajoene, a compound in garlic, was three times more toxic to cancer cells than normal cells. Also garlic may be a natural biological response modifier (a modern type of cancer therapy). In the laboratory, sulphur compounds in garlic significantly enhanced immune cell response (macrophages and T-lymphocytes). Dr. Daniel Nixon of the American Cancer Society believes that garlic may also stimulate the liver to remove toxins from the body.

In addition to fighting cancer, garlic has been demonstrated to reduce blood pressure and improve cholesterol metabolism.

Citrus Fruits : are rich in natural vitamin C important to protecting cells. They also contain carotenoids, coumarins, flavonoids, glutathione, glucarate, limonoids and terpenes which are natural anticancer agents. One analysis found that citrus fruits possess 58 different anticancer agents, more than any other food. Researchers suspect that the synergistic effect of these various agents is particularly helpful in cancer protection. Citrus fruits are especially good at preventing pancreatic cancer, which is a difficult cancer to treat once it develops.

Broccoli : Very potent anticancer food containing beta carotene, glucarate, glutathione, indoles, lutein, sulforaphane and vitamin C.

Beta Carotene is another important antioxidant which fights free radical damage. It has also been shown to directly inhibit cancer cell growth. Also, the intestinal tract can convert beta carotene into retinoic acid, which is recognised as an effective drug against bladder and blood cancers. Low serum levels of beta carotene have been associated with a number of cancers (lung, digestive tract, cervix and uterus). Numerous studies have shown that daily consumption of even moderate amounts of beta carotene can dramatically reduce cancer risks. Also a Harvard study found that regularly eating foods rich in beta carotene can reduce the risk of stroke by two-thirds. As a good general rule you will find dark orange vegetables or dark green leafy vegetables to be excellent sources.

Beans contain protease inhibitors and phytates; they are also rich in fibre and folic acid. Beans help prevent breast, colon and pancreatic cancer.

Alcohol, especially red wine, receives lots of good press about its beneficial effects on the cardiovascular system. With regard to cancer alcohol doesn't enjoy a good reputation. Just two drinks a day can raise the risks of breast cancer by 50 per cent according to a meta-analysis done by Matthew Longnecker of the Harvard School of Public Health.

Drinking to intoxication is particularly dangerous because it suppresses the immune system and allows tumours to spread. According to Dr. Gayle Page of the University of California at Los Angeles, a single episode of binge drinking can incite cancer to spread.

A 17 year study of 26,000 Japanese found that drinkers were four times as likely to develop cancer of the sigmoid colon. Beer drinking has been shown to be particularly dangerous for developing colon cancer. The same study found that beer drinkers were 13 times more apt to develop colon cancer. A meta-analysis of numerous international studies has also found a strong link between beer drinking and colon cancer.

Heart Disease

Thankfully the diet which will protect you against cancer will also protect you against heart disease. Without repeating the discussions from the previous chapter it would certainly be helpful to review the role of fibre, cholesterol, fat, free radicals, trans fatty acids, omega-3 fatty acids, antioxidants, folic acid, potassium and sodium in maintaining a healthy heart.

Our aim is to keep the heart muscle, which beats between 70,000 and 100,000 times each day, properly supplied with blood. To do this we need to keep our arteries open and elastic, and our blood fluid and free-flowing. Nutrition, regular physical activity and stress management are the keys to maintaining a healthy heart. A normal healthy adult wishing to remain that way requires a diet with multiple portions of various fruits and vegetables, legumes, wholegrains, and low fat dairy products. Such a diet, although it contains some saturated fat and cholesterol, can be more effective at fighting high blood pressure, high triglycerides, high cholesterol and blood clotting than some extremely low fat diets. How can that be?

I'll begin with anecdotal evidence, acknowledging its obvious limitations. My mother, in stark contrast to her parents mentioned in the previous chapter, suffered from heart disease. When her blood tests revealed potential problems her physician put her on a strict diet, allowing virtually no cholesterol and minimal saturated fats. That meant margarine, ersatz-eggs, non-dairy coffee creamer (also made with hydrogenated fat), and any number of products with "no cholesterol", but often full of hydrogenated vegetable fat. She also used a salt substitute.

In the middle of this rigorous diet she came to visit my wife and me in Germany. She decided to go on a three-week vacation from her diet, because we would be on the go sightseeing, and also because many of her familiar products weren't available here. So for three weeks she had wholegrain bread with cheese and butter, foods cooked with salt and oil, occasional eggs, and plenty of fruits, vegetables and grains since we are vegetarians. She also walked considerably more in those three weeks than she would have at home. She went home expecting to be scolded by her doctor when he tested her blood. As it turned out, her results were significantly better than they had been for quite some time. None the less, she obediently returned to her former strict diet and eventually had a heart attack and by pass surgery. What could have happened in those three weeks?

Certainly the long daily walks helped. But I suspect that the fibre, vitamins, essential fatty acids, minerals and trace elements also played a role, as did the fact that she ate significantly fewer trans fatty acids. Beyond what we discussed in the previous chapter about cholesterol and dietary fat, some other nutrients may play a more important role than is widely reported.

Lecithin : Soya is not only useful in nutrition, the oil of the soya bean is extracted by industry to be used by in the production of paint. Soya oil also contains lecithin, which has to be removed to reduce paint smearing. The food industry then uses this by-product as an emulsifier, which means that it breaks down fat particles into tiny molecules. You may recall seeing lecithin on the label of various products such as cookies and chocolate bars.

Lecithin, like cholesterol, is produced in the body (providing adequate nutrients are present) and has a variety of vital functions. Nearly a third of the dry weight of the brain, and roughly three-quarters of the dry weight of the liver consist of lecithin. It also circulates in our blood to breaks down large cholesterol particles into smaller molecules which are then able to penetrate arterial walls to be used by tissue cells. This removal of cholesterol from the bloodstream is an important aspect of combating arteriosclerosis. Arteriosclerosis is often accompanied by an increase in cholesterol and a reduction in lecithin. Lecithin is also a useful anticoagulant which helps prevent the formation of blood clots.

The adequate production of lecithin by the body requires a well-balanced diet. If, for example, you've switched to margarine, eliminated all eggs and nuts, and you don't eat any cold-pressed polyunsaturated oils you may not be producing adequate levels of lecithin. Even if you have a vegetarian diet, rely on monounsaturated olive oil and avoid dietary cholesterol and saturated fats, you may not, for reason we will see, be producing sufficient lecithin.

In order for the body to produce enough lecithin, three fatty acids (arachidonic, linoleic, and linolenic) are essential. (Antioxidants are helpful in this regard because they also protect essential fatty acids from being damaged by free radicals.) In order to get a rich supply of these fatty acids you need to consume some polyunsaturated vegetable oil. However, remember that refined oils and processed foods generally are deficient in EFA (essential fatty acids). As we've seen, some experts maintain that a deficiency in EFA is one of the major dietary problems facing America and nations with similar eating habits.

The production of adequate lecithin is further complicated because it also requires the presence of inositol and choline, which are B vitamins. In addition, to manufacture lecithin certain enzymes are required which only function when vitamin B6 and the mineral magnesium are present. The US Department of Agriculture (USDA) deems magnesium a "problem nutrient" because it is inadequate in the typical diet, and they estimate that over half of American women receive less than the recommended allowance of vitamin B6. Choline, and the amino acids necessary for its production, are also lacking in the typical diet.

In a study published in the *Journal of Nutrition* in 1990 researchers evaluated the role of lecithin in controlling cholesterol in rats. Previously we mentioned LDL, the so-called bad cholesterol. There are actually other types of lipoprotein in the bloodstream. For example, there is also VLDL (very low density lipoprotein) and IDL (intermediate density lipoprotein). Think of VLDL as a jumbo LDL particle. As you might expect, lecithin went to work quickly on the jumbo particles, but it also raised the level of HLD (the good cholesterol). According to the researchers, "Lecithin induced a striking reduction in the plasma levels of very low density lipoprotein (VLDL), intermediate density lipoprotein (IDL) and low density lipoprotein (LDL) cholesterol as well as an increase in the level of high density lipoprotein (HDL) cholesterol... Apoprotein A-1 was unexpectedly present in VLDL, IDL and LDL after feeding rats the hypercholesterolemic diet and disappeared only after lecithin feeding."

Except for pregnant women, any normal healthy adult can quickly determine if lecithin can improve his or her serum cholesterol. Ask your physician for a cholesterol test and then explain that you will be taking a lecithin supplement for three months. Within three months you will be able to dispense with expert opinion and objectively judge for yourself the effectiveness of lecithin. Then send me an email with your results!

I lowered my serum cholesterol by twenty per cent without reducing my HDL level, just by adding soya to my diet and taking a 1200mg supplement of lecithin. Also during this time I re-introduced eggs into my diet.

Eggs, you may recall, were vilified in the 1970's and 1980's. Now it appears that saturated fat is four or five times more likely to produce heart disease than dietary cholesterol. Yet, for a normal person the American Heart Association still recommends no more than 300 mg of dietary cholesterol daily, and only 200 mg if you have high serum cholesterol. A single egg contains around 200 mg, so if you eat one egg you can't even have low-fat milk on your morning cereal. Or can you?

Again I asked myself, how did my grandfather live to be 90 if, counting baked goods and sauces, he ate perhaps four eggs daily, or up to 800 mg of cholesterol just from eggs? Eggs are nutritionally quite remarkable, they contain lecithin, all of the essential amino acids (including methionine required for the production of choline), vitamin A, vitamin B12, iron and protein. Although I'm certainly not recommending that anyone follow his example, obviously his diet, rich in lecithin and antioxidants, allowed his body to cope quite well with dietary cholesterol and saturated fats.

And a recent laboratory study seems to back up my grandfather. Researchers fed a group of 70 young men a high fat diet with up to 14 eggs per week for five months and measured biochemical risk markers for coronary heart disease (CHD). The researchers concluded, "...no significant differences in lipoproteins or coagulation factors occurred between groups. It seems that egg intake in this range did not influence CHD risk markers in these subjects. Recommendations to lower risk should probably concentrate on a reduction in fat and not cholesterol intake."

So if you gave up eggs sometime ago because of medical advice, you might want to consider broaching this subject again with your physician. There are some people whose serum cholesterol is negatively influenced by dietary cholesterol, but generally most people can eat eggs reasonably (three or four per week) without any problems.

Soya : Dr. James Anderson of the Metabolic Research Group, VA Medical Center & University of Kentucky did a meta-analysis of 38 studies on the role of soya in reducing the risk of coronary heart disease which appeared in the *New England Journal of Medicine* in 1995. Dr. Anderson writes, "Soya protein was associated with a 9.3 per cent reduction in serum cholesterol, a 12.9 per cent reduction in serum LDL-cholesterol, and a 10.5 per cent reduction in serum triglycerides. All of these decreases were statistically significant. Serum HDL-cholesterol increased by 2.4 per cent, a non-significant increase. These findings had a strong consistency because 34 of 38 studies reported that soy protein intake decreased serum cholesterol levels."

Of particular interest is that the higher the initial cholesterol level the greater the effect of soya at reducing it. People with biggest problems will be helped the most. Alcohol, particularly red wine, has received widespread publicity with respect to reducing the risk of heart disease. Strangely, few people have heard much about the potential of soya. Dr. Anderson commented, "Since every one per cent reduction in serum cholesterol decreases estimated risk of heart attack by two or three per cent, this serum cholesterol reduction has the potential to reduce risk for CHD by 18-28 per cent."

Alcohol is a contentious issue with respect to health. Moderate drinkers, especially of red wine, have been estimated to have a 30 to 40 per cent reduction in cardiovascular mortality. Moderate drinking is considered one to two drinks daily. Alcohol may do this in two ways, by elevating the production of HLD "good cholesterol" and by helping to prevent blood clots. Moderate alcohol consumption also appears to protect against stroke.

Thus in the United States some researchers estimate that annually perhaps 80,000 people could be saved from premature death from CHD. Cheers to alcohol, or jeers to alcohol?

The prophet Muhammad forbade alcohol, maintaining that its destructive effects outweigh its positive effects:

> *They question thee about strong drink and games of chance. Say: In both is great sin, and some utility for men, but the sin of them is greater than their usefulness. II. 219*

Naturally Muhammad was correct in His assessment. Yes, moderate consumption of alcohol can potentially save up to 80,000 Americans *over the age of 45* from heart disease, but alcohol related accidents, homicides, cirrhosis, and hemorrhagic stroke currently cost the lives of over 100,000 young Americans *under 45*. Traffic accidents are responsible for more deaths of individuals between six and 33 than any other form of accident, and over half of all fatal accidents involve alcohol. Of course alcohol has other non-fatal consequences for society, for example, researchers monitored 1,500 cases of abused women calling a hotline in Philadelphia and found that over half of the husbands involved became violent after drinking. Child neglect, physical and mental child abuse, rape, assault, robbery, and critical lapses in judgement are all positively correlated with alcohol.

Generally for Bahá'ís the consumption of alcohol is prohibited, except under advisement by one's physician:

Nevertheless, intoxicating liquor, if prescribed by a physician for the patient and if its use is absolutely necessary, then it is permissible.

'ABDU'L-BAHÁ

This appears to be the message of the researchers, Drs. Pearson and Terry, reporting in the *Journal of the American Medical Association*:

Although we agree that public health recommendations cannot indiscriminately advocate alcohol consumption, we wonder if physicians, on a case-by-case basis, could be the solution to this conundrum...Since alcohol will continue to be available, the physician has the key role in ensuring that its well-documented detrimental effects are minimized...

Dr. Paul Ridker of Boston's Brigham and Women's Hospital, a leading investigator in this field, has said publicly that physicians should not advise patients to drink to reduce disease risk, rather he states that preventing smoking is the key to reducing heart disease, and states that certain common medications have the same beneficial effect as alcohol.

Recently some interesting research results have been published about the protective effects of red wine. Researchers believe that antioxidant phytochemicals (polyphenols such as catechin, quercetin, resveratol) in the skins of red grapes are responsible for protecting against LDL oxidation. You may recall that many of these polyphenols are also in green tea, onions, grapes and berries. Tannins in red wine (and green tea) also help prevent blood clotting.

In one study published in the *American Journal of Clinical Nutrition* and reported by Reuters, researchers gave male subjects between 35 and 65 either a half bottle of red wine, polyphenols as capsules, or ten per cent vodka and a lemon soft drink daily. After two weeks they measured plasma lipids peroxides, which is a by-product of the oxidation of fat. Vodka had no effect, but red wine lowered oxidation by 32.7 per cent and the capsules worked essentially as well, lowering it by nearly 29 per cent.

So in this case, for those who don't drink alcohol, phytochemical supplements can offer most of red wine's protective benefits, moreover, there are many other ways to raise HDL levels. If you eat the foods listed here it is highly unlikely that you will need alcohol to protect your heart, but if you are at risk this is a matter to discuss with your physician.

Beans : A cup of beans per day can quickly lower LDL cholesterol by 20 per cent and over the long term it can raise HDL by around 10 per cent.

Garlic : Numerous controlled studies have demonstrated that consumption of garlic can raise HDL and lower LDL. For example, researchers at Bastyr College in Seattle, Washington, found that the oil in three cloves of garlic administered daily lowered total cholesterol by seven per cent and raised HDL by 23 per cent in one month! Other studies have shown that garlic can reduce cholesterol by up to 15 per cent, and it also dramatically improves blood clotting factors.

In numerous double-blind studies garlic has been shown to dramatically reduce blood pressure. This may be due in part to adenosine, a smooth muscle relaxant, abundant in garlic and onions. This may relax the smooth muscles of the blood vessels.

Raw Onions : Professor Victor Gurewich of the Harvard Medical School began testing onions, a known folk medicine cure, in his laboratory. He found that ½ a raw onion daily produces about a 30 per cent increase in HDL in persons with heart disease or elevated cholesterol. Onions, raw and cooked, are acknowledged as powerful blood clot inhibitors.

Tea : Phytochemicals in green and black tea reduce blood coagulability, inhibit platelet clumping and enhance clot dissolving ability, and reduce cholesterol deposits on arterial walls. In Japan researchers found that catechin, a tannin in green tea, was as effective as aspirin in blocking the clumping of platelets. They also found that tea appears to assist the body in warding off the build-up of arterial plaque. Japanese researchers determined that drinking green tea daily lowers the risk of stroke by half.

Salmon : increases HDL and lowers triglycerides. (see Omega-3)

Olive oil : Switching from butter, margarine and refined polyunsaturated oils to olive oil can have a dramatic impact on the long- term health of your heart. Olive oil reduces LDL without reducing HDL, also it has antioxidant properties which cut the oxidation of LDL significantly. In most recipes olive oil can be substituted for butter without any problems, this is an easy and effective way to improve your diet.

Nuts : Dry roasted nuts without added oils are very beneficial to a healthy heart. Nuts are loaded with important nutrients such as magnesium, potassium, zink, B vitamins, vitamin E, selenium, and important fatty and amino acids. One study measured a simple low-fat diet against a low-fat diet with 20 per cent of calories from walnuts. The low-fat diet decreased cholesterol by 6 per cent, but those who also ate walnuts reduced cholesterol by 18 per cent. In a study of the generally nutrition-minded Seventh-Day Adventists, researchers identified regular consumption of nuts as the most significant food for preventing heart attacks. Those who regularly ate nuts cut their chances of heart attack by approximately half.

Avocados have lots of monounsaturated fats, but Israeli researchers demonstrated that a diet with avocados is superior to a very-low-fat diet in reducing cholesterol. Those on the avocado diet lowered total cholesterol by 8.2 per cent without lowering the level of good cholesterol. On the other hand, the very-low-fat diet lowered "good" HDL by 14 per cent, while only lowering total cholesterol by around five per cent.

Avocados also have important antioxidants which protect against free radical damage.

Apples : Pectin, the soluble fibre in apples, not only fights colon cancer, but it lowers cholesterol and raises HDL.

Carrots : Two carrots a day can significantly lower total cholesterol and raise HDL. This amount can also reduce the risk of stroke by nearly 70 per cent.

Grapefruit : has important antioxidants which protect the heart, and the pulp around the individual segments has a soluble fibre, galacturonic acid, which is very effective at lowering cholesterol. This fibre is not present in juice.

Saturated Fat : Butter, whole milk, cheese, beef, pork, and poultry skin are the major sources of saturated fats. Reducing saturated fats is one of the most effective ways to reduce serum cholesterol and lower the risk of heart disease. Eat low-fat dairy products, and if you eat meat, trim away the fat. Eating saturated fat increases the viscosity of blood, which means that the bloods doesn't flow as freely. This generally results in higher blood pressure and allows blood clots to form more easily.

Spices : Ginger, cloves, cumin and turmeric inhibit the production of thromboxane and, like aspirin, are very effective at inhibiting platelet clumping.

Sugar : As we saw in the previous chapter, the presence of insulin stimulates the production of LDL (bad-cholesterol) and retards its breakdown.

Excessive sugar intake also increases triglyceride levels which further increases the risk of heart disease. Dr. Michael Miller, a cardiologist at the University of Maryland, recommended in the *Journal of the American College of Cardiology* that the normal level of triglycerides should be lowered to maximal 100mg. Currently a reading between 100mg and 200mg is considered normal. In an 18-year study of 350 men and women Dr. Miller found that such levels were a major risk factor. Dr. Miller recommends regular exercise, a low-fat diet and foods rich in omega-3 fatty acids.

Bee Pollen is something which I first encountered in Germany. Although it isn't specifically a food for the heart, it is, however, like eggs another one of the most nutritious foods known. Designed for reproduction, bee pollen is naturally laden with a full range of key nutrients. Vegetarians in particular might want to occasionally eat some bee pollen, since it is a more abundant source of amino acids than even beef, cheese or eggs. Moreover, beyond providing all 22 amino acids, it is rich in B vitamins, fatty acids, complex carbohydrates, and it contains 27 minerals.

Omega-3 : You will recall that omega-3 fatty acids assist the body in relaxing the bloods vessels and they also inhibit blood from clotting which can cause a heart attack by blocking an artery to the heart, or result in a stroke if the flow of blood to a portion of the brain is blocked.

Omega-3 fatty acids are found in nuts and seeds (and particularly flaxseed oil and deep water fish).

Summary

Basically the healthy diet which protects you from cancer also protects you from heart disease, stroke, diabetes, senility and a host of problems. Nevertheless, your genetic predisposition, metabolism, allergies and a number of factors should also be taken into account when determining your particular diet. Be very cautious with fad diets, or any extreme diets — always discuss such diets with a knowledgeable physician or dietician. In general you can follow these suggestions from the previous chapter which are worth repeating:

1. Eat more fresh fruits & vegetables, legumes, wholegrains, and nuts.
2. Drink more water and eat more fibre.
3. Avoid unnecessary free radical exposure and discuss antioxidant supplements with your physician.
4. Avoid refined foods, fats and oils.
5. Reduce your overall fat intake, especially trans fatty acids and saturated fats.
6. Cook with monounsaturated oils, not with polyunsaturated oils.
7. Cold-pressed oils such as flaxseed, pumpkin and walnut should be used for salad dressings — never heated.
8. Eat less protein in the form of meat, eat less simple carbohydrates and more complex carbohydrates.

9

VEGETARIANISM AN IDEA WHOSE TIME HAS COME?

We're basically a vegetarian species and should be eating a wide variety of plant foods and minimising our intake of animal foods.

Dr. T. Colin Campbell
Nutritional Biochemist, Cornell University

Tradition, the way it is, is only an idea that has had widespread acceptance for a protracted period of time. But now we have to find new, better ideas. Just because something is a tradition does not, in itself, make it a good idea.

Linda McCartney
Noted vegetarian
& animal rights activist

The time will come when meat will no longer be eaten. Medical science is only in its infancy, yet it has shown that our natural food is that which grows out of the ground.

> *Truly, the killing of animals and the eating of their meat is*
> *somewhat contrary to pity and compassion, and if one can*
> *content oneself with cereals, fruit, oil and nuts...and so on, it*
> *would undoubtedly be better and more pleasing.*
> *But eating meat is not forbidden or unlawful, nay, the point is*
> *this, that it is possible for man to live without eating meat and*
> *still be strong...*
> *When mankind is more fully developed, the eating of meat*
> *will gradually cease.*
>
> *'Abdu'l-Bahá*

I'm not aware of any statistics concerning the per centage of Bahá'ís in traditional meat-eating countries who are vegetarians. My personal estimate would be around 10 to 20 per cent — somewhat higher than the general population, but definitely still a minority. The topic of vegetarianism is likely to elicit a lively discussion among Bahá'ís as it does in the general population, which a letter written on behalf of Shoghi Effendi in 1931 reflects:

> *...if man can live on a purely vegetarian diet and thus avoid*
> *killing animals, it would be much preferable. This is, however,*
> *a very controversial question and the Bahá'ís are free to*
> *express their views on it.*

Until very recently vegetarianism was considered rather wacky or odd by most people, and nearly all physicians and dieticians deemed it a danger to health. It seemed highly unlikely at the turn of the 20th century that medical science would show that fruits, vegetables and grains would eventually replace meat as the food of choice. Yet in the later stages of the 20th century there is no question that medical science began to demonstrate the superiority of a vegetarian diet. Myriad studies have shown that vegetarians as a group are healthier than the general population, although such studies frequently contain the caveat that the results might be skewed because vegetarians tend to have healthier lifestyles.

For the time being certainly no one whose livelihood depends on meat needs to worry, as there probably won't be any radical shift away from meat. However, the process of mankind becoming vegetarian will remain constant, albeit gradual, for a number of identifiable reasons.

Aesthetic Reasons

As a vegetarian I find it all but impossible to treat the slaughter of animals in a detached and circumspect manner. To write honestly about my motivations entails a degree of forthrightness which is unavoidably provocative. The word *meat*, to me, is an euphemism, as are *beef, pork, mutton* and *venison*. They allow us to put what we are eating out of our minds. Learning German and being exposed to German cuisine made becoming a vegetarian much easier for me, because, as I consciously translated the words, I was acutely aware of what was literally being served. "Fleisch", the German word for meat, is frightfully similar to the word flesh in English. And in fact "Fleisch" also means flesh with no distinction between man and animal. Moreover, in my case such things as pickled lungs, tongue, hog ankles, blood sausages, brains, kidneys, liver and flesh-cheese quickly evoked images of a gruesome inventory rather than an appetising menu.

I recall years ago watching an interview with a vegetarian on television. She was being attacked on all sides and finally she said in exasperation, "*If you choose to make your body a graveyard that's your prerogative, but please respect my right not to do so.*" That was a very powerful statement. Surely most people would feel extremely uncomfortable entering a morgue where flesh, bones, and various organs were prominently on display. Yet meat-eaters by and large have no qualms about entering a butcher shop to purchase the flesh and organs of animals.

A typical meat-eater finds the flesh of a cow or a pig highly appetising. Then based on culture various meats (such as horse, sheep, rabbit, deer, rat, cat, dog, monkey, snake, bear, racoon, and squirrel) are eaten with varying degrees of enthusiasm. After more than a decade of not eating meat, I sometimes find it difficult to convey to meat-eaters just how unsettling it can be for some vegetarians to be put in a situation where they are served meat. I say some vegetarians, because certain vegetarians who abstain from meat purely for health reasons aren't necessarily bothered by the idea of eating animal flesh.

The only way I can find to explain my attitude toward eating meat is to ask someone from a culture which doesn't eat dogs to imagine what it would be like to be served the family dog or cat. After so many years of abstaining from meat I no longer see any difference between eating a cow or a dog. Thus it isn't simply a question of being a good-sport and eating what is offered, for me eating meat is consciously eating a cadaver, carrion, corpse, carcass, dead body or whatever name one chooses. Admittedly that is harsh, but perhaps it will help some to understand a vegetarian's perspective.

In a letter written on behalf of the Universal House of Justice in 1977 the following advice was offered:

> *Here too, as in all other things, the believers should be conscious of the two principles of moderation and courtesy in the way they express their opinions and in deciding whether they should refuse food offered to them or request special foods. There are, of course, instances where a believer would be fully justified in abstaining from or eating only certain foods for some medical reason, but this is a different matter and would be understood by any reasonable person.*

Thus, the vegetarian can easily find himself in a rather problematic position. Luckily, today most airlines now offer vegetarian meals if you order them a few days prior to departure, and many restaurants now offer some meals for vegetarians. If I'm invited to a meal, I usually respond that I'd love to come, but I'm a vegetarian and I don't want to cause any trouble for the host. Most people are very accommodating and I find it is becoming easier in social situations to avoid meat without hurting someone's feelings. Of course, it would be a great mistake during a meal to explain why you don't eat meat (even if asked), because frankly you will ruin the appetite of most meat-eaters by reminding them of what they are actually eating.

Naturally, sometimes there is no escaping a difficult situation. Once my wife and I were visiting an island in the Pacific and we were invited by a lovely family into their home, and although we asked them very courteously not to cook any meat for us because we were vegetarians, something must have been lost in the translation. Perhaps they thought we were trying to be polite since meat was a special treat for them. Finally that evening as the guests of honour we were each served our own chicken with its claws still intact. They didn't have electricity so in the darkness they probably didn't notice how ashen we suddenly became. So fighting back nausea I held the claw in my hand and did my best not to insult our hosts. It was a nightmare which only another vegetarian could appreciate.

Yes in order to survive I would eat meat if there were no other alternatives. Obviously, we humans have been graced by nature with the ability to grow accustomed to any numbers of foods which, for the uninitiated, might appear repulsive. This trait is doubtless vital to our survival, but fortunately for people in many nations, it is now easy to live without eating meat. The primary obstacle nowadays is avoiding uncomfortable situations where we are forced to do something we find repulsive, or risk hurting someone's feelings by declining to eat meat.

Ethical Reasons

Anyone who has been around dogs or monkeys knows that they have personalities, experience joy, sorrow, and any number of emotions and feelings. They see, hear, taste, touch and smell and are often very much integrated into the lives of the families to whom they belong. The owner of such an animal can readily understand the aesthetic and ethical implications of eating that particular animal.

When humans are dependent on the hunt for survival, then they are generally in harmony with nature. The hunted animal continues to live in its natural surroundings and man is one of many predators. In this situation, where there is no viable alternative to meat, then there really isn't an ethical argument to be made against meat. Indeed we saw in many primitive cultures that the hunter actually thanked and asked forgiveness of the spirit of the animal whose life he took.

The swift and humane slaughter of an animal which has enjoyed fresh air and the freedom of movement on a farm does not violate any Bahá'í laws, although as we have seen it would be preferable not to do so. However, it's another matter when a calf stuffed in a box, separated from its mother, pumped full of hormones and antibiotics in loathsome conditions and slaughtered before it has ever seen the light of day. When animals become industrial products they no longer live in their natural surroundings, and they are sometimes held captive in cruel and horrific conditions. Their entire existence is marked by callous inhumanity and they exist solely to satisfy human cravings for their flesh. They are merely living industrial products, treated as though they were devoid of any feelings or sensations.

Bahá'u'lláh has designated humanity as the stewards of nature, who are charged to manifest kindness when dealing with all living creatures.

> *Look not upon the creatures of God except with the eye of kindliness and mercy, for Our loving providence hath pervaded all created things, and Our grace encompassed the earth and the heavens.*

These words from 'Abdu'l-Bahá leave little doubt that we should be concerned with the plight of animals:

> *The feelings are one and the same, whether ye inflict pain on man or on beast. There is no difference here whatever. And indeed ye do worse to harm an animal, for man hath a language, he can lodge a complaint, he can cry out and moan; if injured he can have recourse to the authorities and these will protect him from his aggressor. But the hapless beast is mute, able neither to express its hurt nor take its case to the authorities. If a man inflict a thousand ills upon a beast, it can neither ward him off with speech nor hale him into court. Therefore is it essential that ye show forth the utmost consideration to the animal, and that ye be even kinder to him than to your fellowman.*

*Train your children from their earliest days to be infinitely
tender and loving to animals. If an animal be sick, let the
children try to heal it, if it be hungry, let them feed it, if
thirsty, let them quench its thirst, if weary, let them see that it
rests.*

*Most human beings are sinners, but the beasts are innocent.
Surely those without sin should receive the most kindness and
love...*

Finally in the Most Holy Book, the *Kitáb-I-Aqdas*, Bahá'ís
are enjoined:

*Burden not an animal with more than it can bear. We, truly,
have prohibited such treatment through a most binding
interdiction in the Book. Be ye the embodiments of justice and
fairness amidst all creation.*

Thus, in my opinion, if a Bahá'í eats meat he or she should try
to purchase the meat of animals which have been treated
humanely whenever possible. Granted, such meat is more
expensive, but medically it's worth the extra expense, because of
the organic feed and the lack of antibiotics and hormones. More
importantly, it's the right thing to do.

Medical Reasons

Treating animals as products also has implications to meat-eaters.
The NBC Nightly News reported on Aug. 24, 1997 that in the
United States there were seven million cases of food poisoning
every year. (Actually the Center for Disease Control estimates 30
million cases of food-borne illness yearly.) With Dr. Neal Bernard
of the Physicians Committee for Responsible Medicine they
discussed the contributing factors. Modern industrial feed was
cited as a problem. A ton of alfalfa feed costs about $125, so many
meat producers began to look for cheaper alternatives. And this is
what they came up with, a mixture of grain plus:

chicken manure,
cattle blood, bone and hide,
pet remains,

restaurant leftovers,
deep fryer fat,
cardboard, newspaper and cement dust,
and road kill.

This cuts the cost of feed in half, but also poses health risks. The spontaneous heat generated by chicken manure is 140° F, but salmonella only dies at 145° and E. coli at 155°. E. coli can pass through the relatively mild stomach acids of cows and then flourish in the intestines. In the slaughterhouse faeces with E. coli can't be avoided, so the potential for contamination is always present. In addition, the E. coli, which normally would be killed by human stomach acid, is now acid-resistant and can also pass through the human stomach into the intestines.

Interestingly, when cows are fed hay or grass they don't have problems with E. coli. The meat industry, instead of switching feed, is proposing giving cows anti-acids so that the bacteria can't become acid resistant.

Moreover, cattle are by nature vegetarians, but they are now being fed flesh, blood and bones (even of their own species). This can and has resulted in the development and spread of dangerous diseases, and may have consequences of which we are as yet totally unaware.

In order to stimulate growth and combat the danger of infection based on overcrowding, animals are indiscriminately given antibiotics on a prophylactic basis. Consequently humans absorb them through meat-eating and a contaminated water supply, with the result that various pathogens such as pneumonia, meningitis, gonorrhoea, and salmonella are becoming more resistant to antibiotics. Also to boost profits animals are given hormones to accelerate their growth, which may also pose a danger to human health.

Another problem is that cattle ingest huge quantities of pesticide residue because they have to eat tremendous amounts of plant food to maintain their large frames. Meat has as much as 14 times the pesticide residue as plant food. In a chain reaction of one fish devouring another, fish can likewise accumulate tremendously large concentrations of cancer-causing agents which are found in polluted water, e.g., PCB's and dioxin. Thus basically the lower on the food chain one eats the better.

Humanitarian and Ecological Reasons

Livestock over-grazing is the primary cause of topsoil loss through erosion. Livestock and food animals produce massive quantities of faecal matter and urine (vastly more than humans) which often flow unfiltered into ground water, rivers, lakes and the ocean. For example, factory farms in the United States produce 1.4 billion tons of animal excrement yearly. An industrial hog-farm which is being planned in the state of Utah will produce more faecal matter than the entire population of Los Angeles. In previous centuries when isolated farm animals grazed on open fields they posed little problem to the environment. Now, however, the enormous number of commercial animals concentrated in a single spot poses a serious threat to the environment. Our soil, water, and air are jeopardised, among other things, through the ammonia in urine, the phosphorus in manure, and the production of methane gas. Each year millions of tons of methane gas, which contribute significantly to global warming, are produced by livestock and sheep. In fact, in the European Union such gases make up 41 per cent of greenhouse gas emissions.

It's difficult to imagine, but even a small island like the UK has over 60 million sheep, cows and pigs and several hundred million chickens and turkeys. It is estimated that it requires from 2,500 to 5,000 gallons of water to produce just one pound of beef. Even more alarming is the fact that for every pound of meat which is produced, more than ten times as much vegetable protein must be fed to the producing animal. The amount of grain and soya beans fed to livestock in the United States could feed over a billion people. An acre of land which produces around 200 pounds of beef can produce over 20,000 pounds of potatoes. In other nations an equally absurd system has evolved, in which poorer nations produce crops which are exported to developed nations as animal feed. Then small nations like the Netherlands even export the resulting animal faeces back to the developing nations for disposal. There are over 14 million pigs in southern Netherlands, or more than 9,000 pigs per sq km!

Each year in South America cattle ranchers destroy rain forests equal in size to England. Environmentalists estimate that since 1970 twenty million hectares of rain forest have been burned and destroyed by cattle ranchers and over 1.4 billion tons of carbon dioxide have been released into the atmosphere.

Even a cursory consideration of these arguments should make it clear that as the world population increases we must gradually reduce the consumption of meat and animal products in order to feed everyone and prevent the destruction of our environment. Dr. Campbell, mentioned previously in connection with the China Study, reports that Chinese government officials have recognised the implications of such developments:

> *Usually, the first thing a country does in the course of economic development is to introduce a lot of livestock. Our data are showing that this is not a very smart move, and the Chinese are listening. They're realizing that animal-based agriculture is not the way to go.*

In addition to conserving the earth's resources, Dr. Campbell also estimates that if the United States would adopt a plant-based diet it would result in $120 billion in reduced health care costs. These financial resources could, for example, be used to clean the environment which would then result in additional health benefits for society.

Health Reasons

The deluge of information which touts the potential health benefits of a vegetarian diet probably plays the greatest role in people abstaining from meat. Dr. Benjamin Spock, the world's most revered pediatrician, caused quite a stir in 1998 by recommending a vegetarian diet for children over two years of age in the seventh edition of his book, *Baby and Child Care*. This book, first published over 50 years ago, is the most widely read book after the *Bible*. Dr. Spock even went so far as to recommend a vegetarian diet, which excludes eggs and dairy products.

A few weeks prior to the book's publication Dr. Spock died at the age of 94. He rejected pleas to at least offer an alternative to the vegetarian diet, stating that many diseases such as obesity and atherosclerosis begin in childhood and he wanted to be on the forefront of the growing awareness of the link between animal food and disease. He maintained that children today are in worse physical condition than ever. As expected, his recommendation has been met with lots of dire warnings about its possible deleterious effects. In any case, a parent choosing to follow his advice should be very well informed about nutrition and should take steps to insure that a child receives adequate vitamin B-12, vitamin D and zinc.

It turns out that at the age of 91 Dr. Spock was extremely feeble and unable to walk unaided. He then adopted a plant-based diet and, according to his wife, he lost 50 pounds, regained the ability to walk, and recovered his overall health and energy. These dramatic results obviously motivated his thinking, and while such dramatic results are possible on the individual level, what broad advantages does a vegetarian diet really offer?

Cancer
As we have seen, red meat and saturated fat have been positively associated with colon, pancreatic, prostate and breast cancer. Professor Nick Day of the University of Cambridge and the European Prospective Study into Cancer has said that vegetarians might have 40 per cent fewer incidences of cancer than the general population. Several independent studies have confirmed this assertion, for example, a study of 23,000 Seventh Day Adventists, who have a very high per centage of vegetarians, found cancer mortality rates to be 50 to 70 per cent lower than the general population, even after adjusting for smoking and alcohol.

Heart Disease, Hypertension and Stroke
In 1987 the Oxford Vegetarian Study concluded that vegetarians had markedly lower incidences of coronary heart disease than the general population: 24 per cent lower for vegetarians and 57 per cent lower for vegetarian. Vegetarians also have less hypertension

than the general population. In an 11-year study of around 200 individuals by the German Cancer Research Center in Heidelberg researchers revealed that vegetarians were 50 per cent less likely to die of heart disease or stroke than the general population. Researchers at Loma Linda University concluded that men between 45 and 64 who ate meat even once daily tripled their risk of dying from heart disease. A Dutch study of people between 65 and 97 found that vegetarians had healthier hearts than meat-eaters ten years younger.

As indicated previously, researchers are often cautious of such results because long-term vegetarians are often non-smokers who have other healthy lifestyle habits. For this reason researchers from the WHO devised a study to measure the short-term effects of a vegetarian diet. They selected a group of 406 men who were meat-eaters and who had had a heart attack within the previous 48 hours. They then gave half of the group a vegetarian diet and the other group a normal diet including meat. After six weeks the meat-eaters had 43 per cent more deaths, 48 per cent more complications, and 66 per cent more heart attacks. The men in the vegetarian group lost an average of 7.5 lbs and their cholesterol dropped by an average of 20 points.

Another study evaluated the blood of vegetarians in the United States against the general population and found these important results:

Total cholesterol	- 23 % lower
LDL "bad" cholesterol	- 30 % lower
HDL "good" cholesterol	- 8 % higher
Triglycerides	- 27 % lower

Researchers have also quantitatively demonstrated that over a year or more a vegetarian diet can widen arteries and blood vessels in those with coronary disease.

Other Benefits
Vegetarians are three times less likely to develop kidney stones. They have an enhanced immune system, as demonstrated by a study done by the German Cancer Research Center. White cells of vegetarians, compared to meat-eater, were found to be twice as

effective in destroying tumour cells. Researchers in Norway found that a vegetarian diet relieved symptoms of rheumatoid arthritis in 90 per cent of sufferers. A vegetarian diet lowers the risk of obesity, diabetes, kidney damage, and osteoporosis.

> *It is therefore quite apparent...man's food is intended to be*
> *grain and not meat.*

'ABDU'L-BAHÁ

Clearly these words have been confirmed by science, refer to the following note for the position statement of the American Dietetic Association on vegetarianism.

Conclusion

There are ethical, moral, aesthetic, environmental and medical reasons for becoming a vegetarian. Even if you don't give up meat, you can begin to eat meat more responsibly. That entails reducing your overall consumption and looking for meat, eggs and dairy products which come from animals held humanely. If you are interested in becoming a vegetarian or learning more about the vegetarian point of view, the Vegetarian Society maintains an excellent website at: http://www.vegsoc.org.

10

FITNESS AND WEIGHT

Walking uplifts the spirit. Breathe out the poisons of
tension, stress and worry; breathe in the power of
God. Send forth little silent prayers of goodwill
toward those you meet.

O.P. Ghai

Although fitness is a very broad topic, about which
countless books have been written, it is possible to pare
the information down to a bare but useful minimum.
Swimming is a particularly healthy exercise, as is cross-country
skiing, and there are of course mechanical aids such as rowing-
machines, and any number of treadmills, walking devices, and
even Nordic skiing simulators. But the most accessible, least
complicated and least expensive exercise is good old walking. Like
the evening meal, walking can be a group pastime for the entire
family.

Walking on the Road to Health

A brisk half-hour walk five times a week is very conducive to good
health. Walking also has a few advantages over jogging for the
average person. First, brisk walking is a low-impact form of
exercise, so there is minimal risk of injury to muscles, ligaments,
joints and bones. Yet brisk walking still allows one to boost

endurance, burn calories, and speed-up his or her metabolism without causing the release of excessive free radicals.

How fast is brisk? An experiment designed to answer this question was carried out by Dr. John Duncan of the Cooper Institute for Aerobics Research and reported in the *Journal of the American Medical Association (JAMA)*. A group of 102 premenopausal women were divided into three groups which walked three miles (4.8 km) five times weekly at varying speeds.

Group 1 took twenty minutes per mile, or only three miles per hour. They achieved a heart rate which was 55 per cent of the maximum predicted rate. After six months they increased their ability to process oxygen during exercise by 4 per cent.

Group 2 took fifteen minutes per mile, or four miles per hour. They reached a heart rate of 68 per cent of the predicted maximum. After six months their oxygen processing increased by 9 per cent.

Group 3 took only 12 minutes per mile, or five miles per hour. Their heart rate was 86 per cent and their oxygen processing increased by 16 per cent. According to Dr. Duncan this group had the same health benefits as they would have had jogging nine minute miles.

Although during the course of the experiment each woman walked nearly 400 miles, there was not a single injury to muscles, joints etc. So depending on your initial level of fitness you can start at any group level and move up gradually.

Dr. Andrew Weil is also a great believer in the health benefits of walking. In addition to the physical benefits of walking, Dr. Weil points out that the cross-patterned movement of walking also quiets the central nervous system. That is, your right arm and left leg move forward at the same time as does your left arm and right leg. This activity, according to Dr. Weil, generates electrical activity in the brain which is soothing to the entire nervous system. Dr. Weil considers walking a very important factor in the body's ability to heal itself.

Weight Loss

Again this is a huge subject, which has developed into a multibillion dollar industry in North America, and experience has shown that trends which develop in America are often destined to be repeated in other countries years later. Despite countless diet books, expert advice, special diet foods, weight loss programmes, artificial sweeteners, low-fat foods, non-fat foods and sugarless drinks the proportion of overweight Americans continues to grow dramatically. In fact, Americans are heavier today than at any time since statistics have been gathered. Obesity is linked to a wide array of illnesses including, heart disease, diabetes, high blood pressure, pulmonary disease, cancer and arthritis. Next to smoking, obesity is the second leading cause of preventable death in the United States. Annually it is estimated that there are 300,000 deaths resulting from obesity.

Beyond the human costs, in 1996 in *JAMA* the National Task Force on the Prevention and Treatment of Obesity estimated that obesity costs the United States nearly $70 billion annually in excess medical expenses and lost income. When the $30 billion cost of diet programmes, products and foods are added we are looking at a staggering $100 billion cost of obesity.

Much ado has been made about the fact that the per centage of fat in the American diet has declined from over 40 per cent in the 1970s to just about 34 per cent in the nineties. Yet few people realise that on average Americans now consume about ten more pounds of fat each year. How can that be? It's simple, the average total number of calories in the American diet has risen markedly, thus 34 per cent of a bigger pie means more total fat, even if the per centage is reduced.

There is a widespread notion that eating low-fat or non-fat processed foods means that you can jump from a few cookies to an entire bag, since, after all, they are low-fat. In reality, if you look at the labels carefully you will discover that the difference in calories between low-fat products and regular products is often quite small. For example, one-half cup of fat-free pudding, 140 calories; regular, 160. Additionally, in a 1996 report by the US Surgeon

General on physical activity and health, it was estimated that 25 per cent of Americans are completely sedentary and 46 per cent are not regularly active. That means that over 70 per cent of Americans aren't physically active. So it is no surprise that now one in three Americans is overweight, compared to only one in four in 1970.

Some Lean Advice

Short and sweet, diets don't work. In fact, they are often part of the problem. Our eating patterns send our bodies important signals which allow us to adapt to a wide variety of situations. If someone is in a situation where there are regular periods of hunger and deprivation, then the body takes steps to ensure that the metabolism doesn't run at full throttle so that vital energy can be preserved. These signals are the same for nomads in the desert or affluent Americans. Thus if someone goes on a radical diet and rapidly loses a great deal of weight, the body registers the situation with alarm. It may even burn muscle in order to make up for missing carbohydrates, and muscle loss, as we will see, compounds the problem. Then after the crash diet the dieter usually regains the lost weight. The next time the dieter goes on a crash diet, the body responds, "Look out, we're in trouble again, slow things down." If this yo-yo pattern continues, eventually the metabolism slows to such an extent that crash diets no longer bring the sought after weight loss.

So if diets don't work, what does? Establishing healthy eating and exercising patterns early and sticking to them for life. The chapter on nutrition outlines what constitutes healthy eating habits, but to recap briefly: lots of fruits, vegetables, legumes, whole grains, and water; moderate amounts of low-fat dairy products, eggs and deep-water fish; small amounts of fats and sweets. To maintain a healthy weight you should be eating nearly 60 per cent of your calories as carbohydrates, 25 per cent or less as fat, and about 15 per cent as protein.

Regular exercise is critical to maintaining a healthy weight. First, exercise burns calories, and paradoxically exercise seems to stem the appetite rather than stimulate it. Further, exercise builds muscle which, even unused, burns calories more efficiently than other tissues. For this reason, men have a natural advantage over women. Also, nature seems to seek a higher fat level in women perhaps to prepare them for maternity. Unfortunately, as we age both men and women have a tendency to lose muscle mass, thus there is a gradual slowing of the metabolism. The result is that even without eating more we tend to put on weight.

Tips

1. Instil healthy eating and exercise habits in children. An obese child has a considerably greater chance of becoming an obese adult.

2. Avoid fast-foods and processed foods. Even for experts it's difficult to guage the calories and fat in fast food. A group of 203 dieticians was asked to estimate the amount of fat and calories in five restaurant meals and they were off considerably. When, for example, presented with a meal of a hamburger and onion rings they estimated 863 calories and 44 grams of fat, but the meal actually had 1,550 calories and a whopping 101 grams of fat! That is way too much, especially if you consider that a sedentary 120 pound person should only be eating 1,500 calories per day. And we have to imagine that the person who had the hamburger and onion rings, surely would eat various other snacks, desserts, soft-drinks, etc., throughout the day. Obesity is the obvious consequence of such eating patterns.

3. Cook from scratch when possible. First, that gives you the opportunity to use ingredients with nutritional value, like whole- grain flours, etc., and the advantage of eliminating unnecessary additives, salt, sugar, and hydrogenated fats. Secondly, when you see how many cups of sugar, eggs, salt and fat a recipe calls for, it allows you to judge just what you're eating.

4. Think long-term. Take a series of small attainable steps, rather than going on a dramatic fad diet. For example, over the course of a year such simple steps as switching from regular dairy products to low-fat can have dramatic results

— and this is something which can be effortlessly done. Another example would be to substitute a glass of mineral water with a slice of lemon for a daily second cup of coffee with cream and sugar. Eating a piece of fruit instead of a candy snack. These small consequent steps can save you thousands of calories over the course of a year.

Even eliminating only 100 calories daily adds up to 36,500 calories in a year. Because 3,500 calories equal about one pound of body fat, you're looking at a loss of about ten pounds with minimal effort, moreover, done this way you are apt to keep it off.

5. Never skip breakfast. Breakfast should be a major meal with plenty of complex carbohydrates and fibre. This will give you plenty of glycogen which your brain, liver and muscles use as fuel, and it will dampen your appetite. By skipping breakfast you'll eventually get jittery, bad-tempered and perhaps develop a headache, then, instead of eating something nutritious, you will be disposed to grab sweets and snacks.

6. Drink plenty of water throughout the day and eat an apple as a between-meals snack. Apples contain pectin which is a good appetite suppresser. In Germany many people mix about a tablespoon of vinegar into a glass of mineral water a few times a day, this is purported to stimulate the metabolism and dampen the appetite. I haven't seen any data confirming these and other benefits of vinegar, but it does seem to work.

   Researchers in the UK, however, have demonstrated that about 3/5 teaspoon of mustard or hot chilli sauce added to a meal caused the metabolism of test subjects to increase by about 25 per cent. Over the course of three hours they burned about 50 more calories. In mice ginger has been shown to cause about a 20 per cent increase in metabolism. Some researchers believe that many spicy foods stimulate *thermogenesis*, or the burning of calories.

7. If you are going to eat sweets do it early in the day and rarely in the evening or at night.

8. Eat supper early. Eating and snacking in the hours before bedtime is a bad idea, since such calories are likely to be stored as fat.
9. Walk and exercise regularly. Also take the stairs instead of the elevator when possible.
10. Finally, be patient and don't get discouraged. If you've already gone on lots of diets and had lots of weight fluctuations, you need to settle in on a lifestyle of healthy responsible nutrition and exercise. In such cases exercise is especially important since you are in effect sending the body new signals that it will need to burn more calories since it is now in a new situation. Above all, be consequent.

11

ALTERNATIVES

Do not allow difference of opinion, or diversity of thought to separate you from your fellowmen, or to be the cause of dispute, hatred and strife in your hearts. Rather, search diligently for the truth and make all men your friends.
What does it mean to investigate reality? It means that man must forget all hearsay and examine truth himself,
For he does not know whether statements he hears are in accordance with reality or not.
The shining spark of truth cometh forth only after the clash of differing opinions.

'Abdu'l-Bahá

Real gold does not fear the heat of even the hottest fire.

Ancient Chinese Proverb

The Debate Rages on

As I begin this chapter the respected *New England Journal of Medicine* has just published a scathing editorial attacking alternative medicine. This is a particularly lamentable development because surveys have shown that in recent years people visit practitioners of unconventional therapies more often than they do their physicians. The greatest danger of alternative medicine is that serious medical conditions will go undetected, or that essential medical treatment will be shunned in favour of alternative treatment. When physicians take an adversarial stance towards alternative medicine they may actually foster the vary tend which many of them scorn.

This can result in at least two harmful consequences. First, even some of the most ludicrous therapies can potentially produce a powerful placebo effect which a dismissive physician can quickly destroy. Secondly, a physician who does not enjoy a patient's total confidence increases the risk that this patient will avoid vital medical treatment in favour of unconventional therapy. A much better approach, which some medical schools are now implementing, is to at least educate physicians about the basics of several unconventional therapies so that they can better counsel patients. If a physician finds no organic problem, then most natural or unconventional therapies should not pose a problem. A doctor needn't endorse alternative therapies, a simple statement like, "well after you try it I would be interested in hearing how it works," would suffice. The patient would then be motivated to please the physician and might indeed overcome a stress-related or self-induced condition. Moreover, *some* natural remedies can actually aid the healing process

For example, my first encounter with herbal medicine was about 15 years ago when my general practitioner here in Germany prescribed echinacea and bee pollen for a cold. Since I've discovered echinacea, which I take at the first appearance of cold symptoms, my annual full-blown cold has become a distant memory. I have absolutely no doubts that this herb works, but such anecdotal evidence is often dismissed as meaningless.

Recently I saw a study published by the American Medical Association concerning echinacea which cast doubt about the efficacy of the herb. For 12 weeks, 300 volunteers were given a placebo, an extract of *Echinacea purpurea* root, or an extract of *Echinacea angustifolia* root to see if echinacea prevented upper respiratory tract infections.

The study revealed that the *Echinacea purpurea* group had a 20 per cent risk reduction, and although the authors indicated that two other studies had produced similar results, they felt a larger sample size would be needed to rule out the possibility of chance. They also reported, "*Participants in the treatment groups believed that they had more benefit from the medication than those in the placebo group.*" Still these results were widely reported as demonstrating that echinacea has only minimal beneficial effects.

Here in Germany, however, many physicians prescribe and recommend echinacea and other natural therapies which would be deemed unproven and therefore unsound by some more conservative American physicians. Actually, it's surprising that the study showed any effect at all. Why? My German handbook on herbal medicine contains the following warning:

Important: Echinacea may not taken for more than eight weeks. When taken for longer periods there is a danger that the immune system will produce the opposite of the desired reaction!

Thus a study which administers echinacea for 12 weeks as a preventative measure is flawed from the outset. Also note that herbalists don't consider *Echinacea angustifolia* as effective against upper respiratory tract infection, only *Echinacea purpurea* is used for this purpose. *Echinacea purpurea* is usually taken in relatively high doses at the first appearance of cold symptoms. A proper study would need to incorporate this fact.

The Limits of a Closed Mind
The debate about alternative medicine reminds me of music. I've met people who consider (European) classical music the only true and worthwhile music, summarily dismissing every other form of music. Only a composer who has enjoyed extensive training in musical theory, history and composition is considered worthy.

Thus, of all the millions of musicians and composers who have lived, these persons limit themselves to the few gifted classical composers who were fortunate enough to be supported by wealthy benefactors. This trivialises the creative talents of countless gifted musicians and composers who didn't study classical music. Yet if you examine the music collection of someone who truly loves music you are apt to find that it's very eclectic. That's because a genuine music lover is able to find something appealing and worthwhile in nearly any form of music.

In a similar fashion a true healer will be interested in any and everything which will help a patient, and a healer will be apt to find some utility in a wide variety of approaches. This is possible because a healer's first priority is to treat the patient rather than fighting a specific symptom or disease. In addition to medical science a healer will rely on caring, compassion, confidence, authority, and understanding to marshal a patient's latent healing potential. Moreover, there will be a tacit recognition that God has empowered nature to establish wellness and equilibrium. Sometimes, it is more important to understand what works, rather than to be able to explain why.

The placebo is one of the most powerful medicines we have.
It's very hard to tell sometimes whether what we're doing is more than the placebo effect.

THOMAS DELBANCO,
M.D., Director of the Division
of General Medicine and Primary Care at Beth Israel Hospital

The doctor may listen and analyze in a more detailed way and use the very latest techniques and technologies. But the real physician is a healer, perhaps with a natural talent or gift of healing.

JOHN ZAWACKI, M.D., Professor of Medicine
University of Massachusetts Medical School

Predisposition

Generalisation is frequently unfair and dangerous. Indeed there is a fine line between prejudice and generalisation. The authors of the editorial in the *NEJM* engaged in a great deal of generalising, defining two groups, themselves as effective practitioners of scientific medicine and everyone else as irrational and disinterested in scientific proof. They should, however, be lauded for admitting that, "...many treatments used in conventional medicine have not been rigorously tested, either...." They write:

> *What most sets alternative medicine apart, in our view, is that it has not been scientifically tested and its advocates largely deny the need for such testing. By testing, we mean the marshaling of rigorous evidence of safety and efficacy, as required by the Food and Drug Administration (FDA) for the approval of drugs and by the best peer-reviewed medical journals for the publication of research reports. Of course, many treatments used in conventional medicine have not been rigorously tested, either, but the scientific community generally acknowledges that this is a failing that needs to be remedied. Many advocates of alternative medicine, in contrast, believe the scientific method is simply not applicable to their remedies. They rely instead on anecdotes and theories.*

Self-Deception is in the Eye of the Beholder

Everyone needs to take a deep breath and engage in some thoughtful and honest self-reflection. First, modern medicine is in part what it is today because huge pharmaceutical firms are able to patent and license drugs, reaping tremendous profits in the process. They employ large numbers of field representatives who visit physicians with gifts and product information in hand to encourage the use of their products. They sponsor medical conventions in exotic locations to promote their products, and give research study grants whose findings are designed to support their products. Many major medical journals exist thanks to the tremendous advertising budgets of drug companies. This has undoubtedly shaped the magic-bullet approach of modern medicine. Some believers in alternative medicine see this as a dark conspiracy which seeks to undermine public health to keep profits high. In reality, it's capitalism at work, with its inherent strengths and weaknesses.

This system has produced some stunning successes in the 20th century, albeit not without some tragic mistakes. These mistakes have prompted governments in nations around the world to establish agencies to monitor and control the safety and efficacy of drugs. These scientific studies are indeed rigorous, in fact, if a drug can't be patented and sold to a large number of customers then there is little incentive to develop it because of the long, arduous and extremely costly regulation process. Thus the lack of scientific studies surrounding natural remedies results from the fact that there is little financial incentive in funding them, since once the research is done no single company can reap the financial reward. It is not, as the authors suggest, a rejection of the scientific approach. Dr. Andrew Weil commented:

> *The idea that advocates of alternative medicine don't want products sold as dietary supplements to be researched is absurd. We do, and when the funding for such research is found, the research is done. Furthermore, there is plenty of data already that supports many of the claims attributed to specific botanicals but most doctors in the US don't know about it. Our colleagues in Japan, Germany, France and Russia, for example, have left the American medical establishment in the dust when it comes to research in herbal medicine.*

James Gleick, writing in the biography, *Genius: The Life and Science of Richard Feynman* describes what Feynman, one of the most gifted scientists of modern times, thought of the medical science of the mid-20th century:

> *Twentieth-century medicine was struggling for the scientific footing that physics began to achieve in the seventeenth-century. Its practitioners wielded the authority granted to healers throughout history; they spoke a specialized language and wore the mantle of professional schools and societies, but their knowledge was a pastiche of folk wisdom and quasi-scientific fads. Few medical researchers understood the*

rudiments of controlled statistical experimentation. Authorities argued for or against particular theories roughly the way theologians argued for or against their theories, by employing a combination of personal experience, abstract reason, and aesthetic judgement.

Not only have certain accepted medical therapies been demonstrated to be ineffectual, but in some instances they were actually harmful and occasionally the exact opposite of what would have helped. Nearly fifty years later, even while condemning natural and alternative therapies, the *NEJM* still has to admit that many medical treatments are unproved, and acknowledge, *"the scientific community generally acknowledges that this is a failing that needs to be remedied."*

Yet the authors attack alternative medicine for being guilty of the same thing they admit being guilty of themselves:

It is time for the scientific community to stop giving alternative medicine a free ride. There cannot be two kinds of medicine—conventional and alternative. There is only medicine that has been adequately tested and medicine that has not, medicine that works and medicine that may or may not work. Once a treatment has been tested rigorously, it no longer matters whether it was considered alternative at the outset. If it is found to be reasonably safe and effective, it will be accepted. But assertions, speculation, and testimonials do not substitute for evidence. Alternative treatments should be subjected to scientific testing no less rigorous than that required for conventional treatments.

Granted, it would indeed be helpful if consumers knew the purity and exact dosages of active ingredients in supplements. But requiring the same rigorous testing for natural therapies as for prescription drugs results in an obvious problem. If a natural remedy can't be patented, who is going to pay for the research? Governmental funding for natural therapies is only a minuscule per centage of the funding for drug research. It would be equally unfair to disallow the use of prescription drugs unless they were shown to be as harmless and free of side-effects as natural remedies are.

Make Friends of Enemies

Are physicians shooting themselves in the foot by rejecting natural remedies? At best they potentially represent a safe remedy, or at the least, placebos which the public seems to want. The *NEJM* put it this way:

> *Fortunately, most untested herbal remedies are probably harmless. In addition, they seem to be used primarily by people who are healthy and believe the remedies will help them stay that way, or by people who have common, relatively minor problems, such as backache or fatigue... . Still, uncertainty about whether symptoms are serious could result in a harmful delay in getting treatment that has been proved effective. And some people may embrace alternative medicine exclusively, putting themselves in great danger.*

Assertions, speculation, and testimonials do not substitute for evidence, but they certainly increase the efficacy of the placebo effect. However, a negative, condescending, dismissive or combative attitude from one's physician can destroy the placebo effect. Rather than viewing alternative medicine as a foe to be conquered, a physician might do well to use it to his or her advantage. If an alternative treatment poses a potential danger a physician can gently point this out and perhaps suggest a safer alternative. Even if an alternative treatment hasn't been sufficiently demonstrated to help, it still enables a physician to involve the patient in the healing process. This, as we have discussed previously, has measurably positive effects on the healing process, but sadly some physicians don't understand this. Moreover, being open to some alternative therapies helps the physician to gain a fuller measure of patients' trust and confidence, helping to eliminate the danger that they might turn their backs on conventional medicine. An oncologist who encourages a cancer patient to practise guided imagery, or a cardiologist who encourages a patient to practise yoga, qigong or some other relaxation technique certainly isn't guilty of quackery.

I guess the medical profession has become very used to thinking
in terms of doing something to a passive recipient. But
patients have to be very active participants in their own
health.

DAVID FELTEN, M.D., PH.D.,
Professor of Neurobiology and Anatomy

Don't Shoot the Psyche with Magic Bullets

Many natural therapies don't lend themselves to the magic-bullet conception of modern pharmaceuticals. There are great numbers of possible active ingredients which may work synergistically. For example, the herb echinacea which I mentioned previously isn't completely understood. One theory holds that substances in echinacea known as beta-glucans, complex sugar molecules, evoke an immune response by white blood cells known as macrophages. The macrophages mistake the beta-glucans for the cell wall of bacteria and then activate a major immune response. But that is only a theory, perhaps there is much more to it.

In Germany most pharmacists and physicians are knowledgeable about echinacea and will counsel a patient about its use. The barrier in America between conventional and natural medicine means that many people misuse a herb like echinacea. I've even seen it in vitamin supplements in the United States. I wouldn't take something routinely which would constantly reeve up my immune system without consulting my physician, but I have the advantage that my physician won't scoff at my questions.

Certainly it must be frustrating for medical scientists to see the public turning their backs on medicine just as medicine is beginning to evolve into a true science. The writers of the *NEJM* editorial appear to understand some of the origins of the problem:

> *Now, with the increased interest in alternative medicine, we*
> *see a reversion to irrational approaches to medical practice,*
> *even while scientific medicine is making some of its most*
> *dramatic advances. Exploring the reasons for this paradox is*
> *outside the scope of this editorial, but it is probably in part a*
> *matter of disillusionment with the often hurried and*

> impersonal care delivered by conventional physicians, as well
> as the harsh treatments that may be necessary for life-
> threatening diseases.

Unity Heals

The authors are correct in asserting that there aren't two forms of
medicine: conventional and alternative. There is, however,
medical science and the art of healing, and they need to be
combined. As long as beliefs and the human psyche continue to
influence human health, it appears unlikely that a cold,
impersonal, scientific and completely rational approach can take
the art out of the practice of medicine. Physicians will have to
continue to use their own humanity, the placebo effect, and
involve the patient in the healing process. The unity of patient
and physician, and the unity of mind, body, and soul are the
essential prerequisites to optimal healing. Anything which
encourages this unity without harming the patient should be
embraced.

> *Can we afford to ignore the role of emotions, hope, the will to*
> *live, the power of human warmth and contact just because*
> *they are so difficult to investigate scientifically and our*
> *ignorance is so overwhelming?*

David Felten,M.D., Ph.D.,
Professor of Neurobiology and Anatomy

If Your Mind Is Too Open
Be Careful Of What Might
Get In There

Advocates of the various unconventional, complementary or
alternative therapies need to openly acknowledge that there are,
and have always been, charlatans and quacks who take advantage
of desperate, gullible or poorly uninformed individuals. Although
there are natural and traditional therapies which certainly can be
of benefit, there are also a great deal of useless, expensive,
irrational and even potentially harmful ideas which masquerade
as therapies. Also, be aware that not everything which is natural is
harmless or effective.

This is why it is so important for physicians to be able to give wise, sympathetic and reasonable counsel about natural and traditional therapies, rather than leaving patients to fend for themselves.

Interestingly, in the same issue of the *NEJM* there was also a book review which took a much more tempered view of alternative medicine. This book is entitled. The Alternative Medicine Handbook: The Complete Reference Guide to Alternative and Complementary Therapies, by Barrie R. Cassileth. (340 pp. New York, W.W. Norton, 1998. $25. ISBN 0-393-04566-8)

Avrum Bluming, M.D., of the University of Southern California, Los Angeles wrote:

> *Responsible clinicians must be able to help their patients sort through all the therapeutic options, including those they may find unconventional, because patients increasingly want informed and shared decision making about their health.*

This book appears to be a good starting point for physicians who are willing to investigate complementary therapies. According to Dr. Bluming:

> *'The Alternative Medicine Handbook', by Barrie R. Cassileth, is organized as a reference on the most commonly used complementary and alternative therapies. Cassileth brings to this work an appropriate base of experience; she holds teaching appointments at Harvard University and Duke University, is a founding member of the advisory council to the National Institutes of Health Office of Alternative Medicine, and has published extensively on the subject in peer-reviewed medical journals. Dealing with a broad range of material, from the use of shark cartilage to the traditions of ayurvedic medicine and the tenets of shamanism, she summarizes each therapeutic approach—its history, the beliefs on which it is based, and the therapeutic claims made for it— and analyzes any research-based evidence of its efficacy. For the physician who wants to advise a patient, Cassileth offers a*

balanced approach, providing information on certain treatments that appear to be safe and of possible benefit, as well as caveats against the indiscriminate use of others.

...Following the lead of H.L. Mencken, who observed that for every complex problem, there is a simple solution—and it is wrong, Cassileth suggests that physicians should remain open to unconventional ideas but must help their patients understand the need for a scientific approach to complementary and alternative medical practices and products.

A Healthy Attitude towards Complementary Medicine

When a disease or traumatic injury strikes we need to avail ourselves of professional medical advice, although that doesn't mean that in the absence of disease we should be indifferent or passive towards our health. The maintenance of our physical health is largely in our own hands. It requires that we eat responsibly, exercise regularly, sleep sufficiently, manage stress, and regularly quiet our minds. Sometimes, particularly with stress-related illnesses and chronic degenerative diseases, conventional allopathic medicine can be augmented by alternative therapies. Alternative therapies are often designed to empower the mind, body and spirit to regain or maintain health. Thus they need not be seen as substitutes for conventional medical treatment. About 40 per cent of Americans use some form of alternative therapy annually, with back pain, anxiety, allergies, arthritis, depression and insomnia being the most common ailments treated.

Some alternative therapies are based upon thousands of years of accumulated therapeutic practice, although there is not always a great deal of scientific evidence to back it up. This wealth of observational experience, even if one disregards the philosophical underpinnings, has something to offer. As mentioned previously, even in the area of conventional medicine there is debate as to how scientific "medical science" actually is. For example, aspirin was long known and used as an effective way to overcome pain and inflammation, although physicians didn't understand why it worked. Although there is no exacting scientific explanation for it, acupuncture has been used and perfected for thousands of years in China. For that reason it was dismissed in Western medical circles, but something which happened in 1972 caused many to reconsider this attitude.

It was during this time that US President Nixon visited China, accompanied by a large entourage of advisors and reporters. It happened that James Reston, a respected reporter for the *New York Times*, had an emergency appendectomy and received acupuncture instead of conventional painkillers for post-operative pain. Reston's recounting of this "amazing" experience in the *New York Times* made the American public aware of something which for centuries had been part of traditional Chinese medicine. In Germany, acupuncture is now used by many physicians and is covered by most health insurance as a treatment for pain. I've been treated with acupuncture twice, and although I went in a sceptic with minimal expectations, I now know that acupuncture indeed works.

There are many things such as herbs, tonics and massage which have been developed over the course of time in various cultures, and indeed many of these folk remedies served as the starting point for some conventional medical treatments and drugs. Again take the example of aspirin, which is related to compounds found in willow bark, a treatment known and used by the ancient Greeks.

Perhaps we will some day see joint medical practices with allopathic physicians working together with naturopathic physicians, nutritional experts and even herbalists, where patients can easily be treated according to medical need and preference. In China, for example, there are already hospitals where allopathic and traditional Chinese medicine are practised side by side. Although we can't cover all complementary therapies, there are a few which I would like to specifically mention.

Acupuncture

Acupuncture is no0w widely known and has been demonstrated to be a particularly effective treatment for addiction and chronic pain. It is also used for a broad variety of other ailments, such as asthma, and even loss of speech due to stroke. It is likewise an effective anaesthetic for certain types of surgical procedures, such as those on the head, neck, thyroid, tonsils and even the heart, and to a lesser degree in abdominal and gynaecological surgeries.

Acupuncture is based upon a concept that *chi* (vital life energy) circulates throughout the body along pathways called meridians. Over the course of several thousand years, around 1,000 acupoints have been identified along these meridians which, when stimulated by fine needles, can alter and redirect the flow of *chi*. Researchers using techniques such as microdissection, imaging with radioactive isotopes, and galvanic skin response have confirmed the existence of meridians. Beyond the increased electrical activity along the meridians, researchers have shown that acupuncture also stimulates the release of endorphins and enkephalins (natural pain-killers) and several other neurotransmitters. Acupuncture also appears capable of blocking pain impulses from reaching the brain, and for reasons which haven't been adequately explained, acupuncture can sometimes enhance the immune response.

In particular, persons suffering from chronic pain should discuss the potential of acupuncture with their physician.

Aromatherapy

You may recall from our discussion of the limbic system in chapter 2 that olfactory sensations, unlike other perceptions, go directly to the limbic system of the brain, specifically to the hypothalamus. This portion of the brain is responsible for emotions, long-term memory, and a number of vital functions. Anyone who has been to the Bahá'í Shrines in Israel can probably attest to the emotional effects of our sense of smell. The smell of rose oil, which is ever present there, can evoke powerful memories of the experience of pilgrimage even after years have elapsed.

Practitioners of aromatherapy have identified various essential oils which have a soothing effect upon the emotional state. In particular, orange (Mandarin), rose, jasmine and camomile oils have properties which tend to calm the nerves, and lavender oil even helps induce sleep. Researchers have even demonstrated that these essential oils can alter brain waves to produce a relaxed state, or in the case of essential oils, such as basil or rosemary, they can have a stimulating effect on the central nervous system.

In addition to being linked directly to the limbic system of the brain as olfactory sensations, aromas are also so small that molecularly they are easily able to penetrate body tissue. Proponents of aromatherapy claim that essential oils have a number of therapeutic effects, such as antibacterial, anti-inflammatory, anti-viral, antispasmodic, and vasodilators. Essential oils are also useful in aiding digestion.

There are a great many essential oils used in aromatherapy and it would be impossible to mention them, but here are a few prominent examples:

Tea Tree : This particular oil is very effective in fighting bacterial, viral and fungal infections. It can be used on small wounds, scalp problems, even on the gums. In Germany, there are numerous books devoted entirely to tea tree oil uses and applications.

Peppermint : A couple of drops of this oil can be used to relieve nausea and indigestion, or rubbed on the neck to help ward off a tension headache.

Lavender : This can be used on small wounds, minor burns, insect bites and as a soothing or sleep inducing agent.

Eucalyptus : This oil is used to treat viral illnesses, such as herpes simplex and colds. It has expectorant properties and is also good as a relaxant.

There is a great deal more which you can learn about the various essential oils. If you are interested refer to *The Aromatherapy Book: Applications and Inhalations* by Jeanne Rose. Aromatherapy is useful and generally safe, although essential oils should *never* be taken internally without competent advice. They can also produce skin irritations when applied directly.

Ayurvedic Medicine

The science of life, or ayurvedic medicine, has been practised in India for thousands of years. Like traditional Chinese medicine, ayurvedic places particular emphasis on prevention, restoring and maintaining internal equilibrium, and on integrating the patient into the healing process. An allopathic trained endocrinologist, Dr. Deepak Chopra, is largely responsible for the increased attention paid to ayurvedic medicine in the West. His book, *Perfect Healing*, is a good starting point for anyone interested in learning more about ayurvedic medicine.

Practitioners of ayurvedic medicine recognise three basic metabolic types: *vata, pitta* and *kapha*. Each person is a mixture of each metabolic type, but generally one type predominates.

Vata : Persons of this type are characterised as highly energetic (but with large fluctuations), enthusiastic, impulsive, erratic, very imaginative, moody, great with ideas, but less skilled at seeing them through to conclusion. Physically they tend to be lean with prominent features and are apt to eat and sleep at all hours. They are prone to nervous disorders such as insomnia and anxiety. They tend to have cool dry skin.

Pitta : This type of person is orderly, proficient, predictable, punctual, prone to perfectionism, short-tempered, intelligent, and articulate. These people eat and sleep by the clock and tend to be of medium build, have thin fair hair, and a ruddy complexion. Their skin is often warm and perspiring and they tend to suffer from acne, stomach ailments, ulcers and hemorrhoids.

Kapha : Slow, relaxed, graceful, tolerant, forgiving, even-tempered, and affectionate are the characteristics of this metabolic type. *Kaphas* also tend to eat slowly, have a slow metabolism and are often overweight. They are heavy and long sleepers. *Kaphas* often procrastinate and are slow to change their opinions. They often suffer from allergies, sinus problems, obesity and high cholesterol. Their skin tends to be cool, pale and damp and their hair thick, wavy and to some extent oily.

An ayurvedic physician will get to know a patient, his or her personal and family history, distinguish the appropriate metabolic type, and proceed with a physical exam which consists of listening to the heart, lungs, and intestines. The physician will also palpitate, or feel the body, examine the tongue, eyes, nails and pulse in very great detail when compared to an allopathic examination.

The ayurvedic physician will, among other things, use breathing, exposure to the sun, diet, exercise, meditation, massage and herbs to treat patients. Dr. Andrew Weil cautions that many Western practitioners are Western physicians and members of the organisation founded by the billionaire, Maharishi Mahesh Yogi, and are certified after minimal exposure to ayurvedic medicine. He suggests speaking to members of the Indian community to find a qualified practitioner.

Yoga

Yoga means to unite, or literally to yoke, the individual spirit with the great universal spirit. Through yoga the individual becomes aware that he or she is not an isolated being in a sea of chaos, rather that he or she is connected or *yoked* to the universal spirit and thus linked to all creation. Achieving this unity through yoga helps the practitioner to achieve physical health, mental balance, inner peace, happiness and contentment. The individual does this by uniting the mind, body and spirit via a systematic application of physical, mental lifestyle, hygienic activities and exercises which have been developed for over 5,000 years in India. Yoga can be practised by followers of all faiths, one need not sacrifice his or her beliefs in order to practice yoga.

During the 20th century Western medical researchers have documented the extent to which yoga has enabled individuals to gain mastery over their physical frame. Many physiological processes, such as heart rate and thyroid output, which had been deemed "involuntary" or beyond conscious control, were routinely demonstrated to be controllable by masters of yoga.

Yoga places great emphasis on mastering the art of controlled breathing. Breathing is the key to controlling *prana*, or the life force. A restless mind will result in irregular, shallow and agitated breathing. This disturbance of the flow of life force will have a negative impact on the body.

Yoga also teaches practitioners to focus and quiet their minds through meditation.

Finally, yoga incorporates physical postures (*asana*), which are divided into two categories, meditative and therapeutic. Breathing, meditation and postures are interwoven in the practice of yoga. Yoga has been shown to have a positive impact on a wide range of conditions, from asthma to stress-related illnesses. It also allows its long-term practitioners to remain agile, limber and mobile in old age.

There are any number of possibilities to take yoga classes, or countless introductory self-teaching books. You might check with your health insurance company and find out if they sponsor yoga classes. A good teacher is the best method, but if you do go it alone, start slowly and exercise patience.

Traditional Chinese Medicine

As mentioned in the opening chapter, Traditional Chinese Method (TCM) doesn't treat disease, rather it seeks to bring individuals into equilibrium, ideally before disease is present. In addition to acupuncture, mentioned above, the TCM practitioner will employ diet, massage, herbs, breathing exercises, stretching, callisthenics, relaxation, meditation, and awareness to restore equilibrium. Since the middle of the 20th century in China the science of Western medicine has begun to be integrated into the practice of TCM. The government has taken steps to standardise and improve TCM by applying modern research procedures and establishing national review committees to codify effective treatments and therapies.

Diagnosis is very hands-on. The pulse is taken with great care at the radial arteries, wrists, meridian points, and the abdomen. The smell (of the breath, body and its secretions) is employed. The tongue, skin, body language, strength and tone of the voice, and general physical condition is assessed. Then a detailed history of the patient is taken. Once the diagnosis is made the practitioner will seek to address the root cause of the problem and not necessarily the obvious symptom.

In particular acupuncture and qigong appear to be especially promising therapies which are gaining in popularity and recognition, even among Western medical professionals. If you would like to learn more, read the following:

1. Chi Kung *(Qigong), The Ancient Chinese Way to Health,* by Paul Dong.
2. *Acupuncture Medicine: Its Historical and Clinical Background,* by Y. Omura.
3. *Between Heaven and Earth: A Guide to Chinese Medicine,* by H. Beinfield and E. Korngold.

Guided Imagery

We cannot talk to our immune system or our heart muscles, but guided imagery is based on the fact that our experiences, via our thoughts, are indeed communicated to the body. Taking this a step further, our focused imagination can also be used to communicate with our bodies. Externally the image is unreal, but internally it represents a perceived reality for the body. This can enable the mind to learn to communicate non-verbally with the body.

Stress, fear, anxiety, negativity, anger, rage and depression are the flip-side of imagery. They too are communicated to the body and, as we have discussed, have physiological consequences. Guided imagery is a systematic approach which teaches the individual to utilise the power of the imagination to positively influence physical well-being. Almost any condition, but especially stress-related conditions, can benefit from guided imagery. Chronic pain, high blood pressure, benign arrhythmias, and gastrointestinal problems are examples, but even cancer patients can employ guided imagery along with their conventional treatments. Indeed, some otherwise hopeless cases have been helped by guided imagery.

Subjects learn to induce an altered state, i.e., a state in which one is focused, alert yet calm, relaxed yet energised. In this state our ability to accomplish many things is greatly enhanced. During this state the subject then interposes images on the mind which the body interprets to be genuine. Optimally the imagination is supported by sensations. For example, if you have a racing heartbeat you might do something like this:

Place a few drops of orange oil on the palm of your hand. Put on some very slow music with a beat slower than a normal human heartbeat. Sit comfortably and place the palm of your hand on your heart. Close your eyes, breathe slowly, and imagine that God's love and protection is a warm, glowing orange ball. Imagine that it is focusing a ray of warm, loving and comforting light on the palm of your hand. With each breath imagine that the peace and comfort of God's love is reaching your body through your palm. When you exhale imagine breathing out the fear, anxiety and stress to make room for God's love.

There are various types of imagery:

1. *Feeling-State*: like imagining oneself floating peacefully on water.
2. *End-State*: imagining oneself achieving the desired end results, such as cancer free, winning a race etc.
3. *Energy*: similar to the image of God's love mentioned above.
4. *Microscopic*: here one learns the basics of a health problem and then imagines the body's response in microscopic detail. Symbols can be helpful in this type of imagery.
5. *Physiological*: like the above method, except without the miniaturisation. For example, imaging the blood vessels dilating.
6. *Metaphoric*: where a tumor might be envisioned as a soft glob of a buttery substance, and white blood cells as hot pellets which melt it away.
7. *Spiritual*: like the exercise mentioned above, or imagining being held in the arms of God.

If you wish to learn more, much of the above information was gleaned from the following book: *Staying Well With Guided Imagery*, by Belleruth Naparstek.

Herbal Medicine

Living in Germany, where herbal medicine is particularly popular, makes the idea of writing about it particularly daunting. Recently I was in the largest bookstore in Munich and I was staggered by the wealth of books about herbal medicine; there must have been several hundred in stock. As I see it, neither an entire chapter, much less a few paragraphs, could begin to give adequate justice to this subject. Rather than trying to broadly treat this subject, I would like to devote a few paragraphs, to one particular herb. Hopefully, you can then recognise what a fascinating topic herbal medicine is, and perhaps you will be motivated to learn more about it. Let us consider St. John's Wort which has gained considerable attention in the United States in recent years as nature's Prozac. Indeed, several studies have shown that it is very effective in relieving mild to moderate cases of depression, without the side-effects of psycho-pharmaceuticals.

In Germany, St. John's Wort has a long and rich history. How did it get such an unusual name? According to traditions in the German- speaking Alps, it went something like this. King Herod's army had been assigned the task of capturing and executing the prophet, John the Baptist. Military scouts found the house in which He was residing, and secretly placed a bundle of flowering herbs in the window so that troops would be able to identify the house on the following day. However, to their chagrin, on the next day that same herb, hypericum, was found in the window of every house. Thus the herb saved the prophet's life on that particular day, and hypericum came to be known as Johanniskraut, or John's herb. The bright yellow flowers of the plant are also generally in full bloom around the time when a religious holiday is celebrated in honour of John the Baptist on June 24th.

Nestor and Hippocrates valued St. John's Wort as did the noted Greek physician, Pendanios Dioskurides in the first century. Under the Romans hypercon became hypericum. In the Middle Ages superstition held that St. John's Wort could repel the devil, in much the same way as garlic was believed to stave off vampires. So we see that there's always been plenty of hype in *hype*ricum. None the less, there is much more to St. John's Wort than is commonly known.

One of the few side-effects of St. John's Wort is that it can cause a sensitivity to light when taken in high doses by persons with fair hair and skin. This is believed to be caused by the photodynamic effect of hypericin, a substance found in only three other plants or mushrooms. It is possible that this increased sensitivity to light is in part responsible for the increased production of the hormone melatonin after taking St. John's Wort. In studies in Germany subjects who took St. John's Wort preparations for three weeks showed a significant increase in the levels of melatonin. Interestingly, hypericin has also been shown to inhibit viruses.

Another important substance, which is found only in St. John's Wort, is hyperforin. Russian researchers have demonstrated that this substance has antibacterial properties. This is possibly one of the reasons why St. John's Wort has been used to treat wounds and burns over the centuries. St. John's Wort is also used to make an oil preparation which is applied as an anti-inflammatory, and hyperforin is thought to be in part responsible.

Quercetin is a flavonoid found in St. John's Wort which has several properties. It too has been shown to have anti-inflammatory and infection-fighting effects. Recent pharmacological research has shown that quercetin, found in St. John's Wort and other fruits and vegetables, is a mono-amino-oxidase(MAO) inhibitor, which prevents serotonin from being blocked in the brain. A depressed level of serotonin, a neurotransmitter, is associated with depression. St. John's Wort has been shown to increase the serotonin levels in test subjects. Two other flavonoids found only in St. John's Wort, biapigenin and amentoflavon, are also believed to have a calming effect on the nerves. Some herbalist believe that these compounds are responsible for the use of St. John's Wort as a treatment for nocturia (a frequent passing of urine in the night). Indian researchers have found that amentoflavon is also anti-inflammatory and is useful for digestive tract problems.

Another active agent in St. John's Wort, procyanide, is purported to have an effect on the heart similar to hawthorn (*Crataegus oxyacantha*), which is widely prescribed for heart conditions in Germany. It is thought that procyanide increases the flow of blood to the heart.

Xanthone, found primarily in St. John's Wort, is also a MAO inhibitor, but has anti-allergenic and anti-inflammatory properties as well. Finally, tannins, found in St. John's Wort, are helpful against diarrhoea. They are also thought to be responsible in part for the anti-viral properties of St. John's Wort.

Beyond mild to moderate depression, herbalists use St. John's Wort to control anxiety (angst), sleep disorders, concentration disorders, restlessness, winter depression (caused by lack of light), bed-wetting, first degree burns, small wounds, diarrhoea, hemorrhoids, herpes, headache, gastrointestinal problems, rheumatism and gout. Most Americans know St. John's Wort only in pill form; however, many herbalists consider tea to be the delivery method of choice. Moreover, it is also available in many other forms to fit the end use, such as a tincture, powder, or mixed with oil.

St. John's Wort is one of the over 300 plant-based medications which have been approved by the Bundesgesundheitsamt (National Health Office) in Germany. Approval requires that medications have been demonstrated through research, animal studies and clinical trials to be safe and effective.

Herbal medicine can be useful for less serious conditions, chronic and degenerative diseases, and as an adjunct to conventional medicine for more serious conditions. Because herbs do contain active chemical agents you should always inform your physician of any herbs you are taking. Also, if you are already taking prescription drugs it is essential that you speak with your physician prior to trying medicinal herbs.

Books by Dr. Andrew Weil are a good place to learn more about some of the more important herbs. Dr. Weil trained as a botanist before attending Harvard medical school and gives valuable insights into medicinal herbs from his studies and from his clinical experience: *Natural Health, Natural Medicine: A Complete Manual for Wellness and Self-Care; Spontaneous Healing; and Eight Weeks to Optimal Health.*

Homoeopathy

Homoeopathy, like herbal medicine, is very popular in Germany, where it was in fact founded in the 18th century by the physician Samuel Hahnemann, although, like many aspects of medicine, it was also alluded to by Hippocrates nearly 25 centuries ago. Homoeopathy is linked to Hippocrates' Law of Similars (like cures like) and is derived from the Greek words *homoios* (similar) and *pathos* (suffering).

Dr. Hahnemann had been experimenting on himself by taking a Peruvian bark (cinchona), which was known to be an effective treatment for malaria. Paradoxically, within a short time he began to experience periodic fevers, a symptom of malaria itself. This was the spark that ignited his interest in finding substances which produce disease-like results. Conventional allopathic medicine, as we know, has always sought medicines which produce the opposite results and thus eliminate symptoms. Dr. Hahnemann, however, believed that by giving the body a substance which produced a similar effect, it would ultimately enable the body to overcome the disease.

Homoeopathy and allopathy are nearly direct opposites in other areas. With allopathic drugs the stronger the dose the greater the effect, but in homoeopathy there is the Law of Infinitesimal Dose, which states that the more diluted the dose, the greater the effect. In fact, some homoeopathic remedies are so diluted that chemical analysis can no longer detect active ingredients. Conceptually, this is where homoeopathy becomes difficult for me to accept, none the less, numerous clinical trials demonstrate the efficacy of homoeopathy. Its safety and effectiveness make it difficult to dismiss, and that is certainly the reason for its widespread use.

Finally, the last major difference to allopathic medicine is that homoeopathy is based upon the holistic conception of medicine.

The same symptoms in three individuals can produce three different homoeopathic approaches, based on the totality of the individuals involved. Keep in mind, however, that because of the difference of approach, homoeopathic treatments are generally not compatible with conventional medicine.

Fasting

The Bahá'í fast, wherein for 19 days prior to the beginning of spring adult Bahá'ís refrain from eating and drinking between sunrise and sunset, is primarily a spiritual exercise and would not fall under the heading of a classic healing fast.

Heilfasten, German for healing fast, is a widespread practice and a recognised treatment for a number of ailments. In Germany I know of over thirty clinics and sanatoriums which offer healing fasts under medical supervision. Moreover, countless general practitioners throughout Germany supervise local groups and individuals on periodic fasts. Fasting's proponents in Germany often refer to it as an *operation without blood*, because of the dramatic effect it can produce on certain physical and emotional ailments. Of course, in spiritual matters the association of fasting, prayer, reflection and meditation is nearly as old as recorded history itself. It has long been recognised that one who fasts allows the spirit to feast on the food of the soul.

Yet, if the body is so dependent on nutrition, how could a fast possibly heal or aid in maintaining health? That's certainly a valid question, and indeed many conventional dieticians and physicians, especially in the United States, reject the therapeutic effects of fasting. The theory behind a healing fast goes something like this:

* When the body doesn't receive any food it attempts to compensate and maintain the status quo. To do this the liver will begin to burn stored sugar for energy, and after a couple of days the sugar reserves in the liver and muscles will be depleted.

* Once the stored sugar reserves are used up the body will begin a programmes to conserve energy. Important organic

functions will be switched to a mode which encourages quietness, recuperation and relaxation.

* Because digestion requires the expenditure of lots of energy (nutrients, oxygen and blood), this energy can suddenly be directed to other bodily systems involved with self-regulation. Thus, cell growth, the immune function and the processes of elimination will be positively influenced.

* The body's natural wisdom will prevent it from cannibalising important tissues, unless a fast is carried on to excess. This means that after sugar reserves are depleted the body will begin burning fat reserves for energy. In this process chemicals such as pesticides, heavy metals and toxins stored in fat tissue will be released at a time in which the body's ability to eliminate toxins is enhanced.

* The body, following the law of nature, will also begin to attack old and weaken cells, or non-essential tissues which resulted from infections. The nutrients from these tissue cells will be recycled for their nutrients. Then the body is put into a prime position to begin the process of rejuvenation.

* Because of the reduced fat intake and the increased burning of body fat, the level of serum or blood fat is reduced. Thus the blood becomes thinner or more fluid allowing an increased supply of oxygen to reach the cells throughout the body. Also the transportation of white blood cells is improved, resulting in an improved immune response.

* Some people are unknowingly allergic to various foods. In such cases a fast will result in a reduction of inflammation of the digestive tract. Moreover, eliminating the allergens during the fast allows the immune system to marshal it resources for more productive tasks. (When breaking a fast one can sometimes use this opportunity to discover food allergies by systematically reintroducing foods into the diet.)

* Finally, the state of mental clarity and spirituality achieved during a fast also contribute to the total positive physical effect of the fast. Indeed, I'm sure that nearly anyone who has fasted will count the spiritual aspect as the most important aspect of the fast.

Probably the most difficult period of a fast for most people occurs during the first few days. During that time one can develop headaches and become rather irritated; however, the good news is that if you manage to make it to the third day, such problems, along with the sense of hunger, are usually overcome.

The conditions helped most by fasting include: allergies, arthritis, bladder, cardiovascular disease, digestive problems, headaches, heart disease and hypertension, kidney and skin.

Conditions which prelude fasting: tuberculosis, cancer, hyper-thyroidism, ulcers, chronic digestive tract infections. Everyone should consult a physician before undertaking a fast, and anyone with any pre-existing medical condition should never undertake a fast without medical supervision.

There are various types of fasts. The two main types are water fasts and juice fasts, each with its advantages and disadvantages. Fasting is generally combined with moderate exercise, such as walking, cycling, hiking or swimming. Springtime is generally considered the optimal time to fast because of the extra fat put on for winter and the process of renewal associated with spring. Finally, it's important to be well informed before beginning a fast. You might refer to *Fasting Signs and Symptoms - A Clinical Guide*, by Trevor Salloum.

The information in this section was gleaned from *Heilfasten*, by Gerhard Leibold, Falken Verlag.

Osteopathy

Derived from the Greek word for bone, Osteon, the first medical school for osteopathy, was founded by an American physician, Dr. Andrew Still, in 1892. Today there are osteopathic medical colleges in North America and Europe with several thousand osteopathic physicians in most English-speaking countries.

In the United States it could be considered inexact to deem an osteopathic physician a practitioner of alternative medicine. An osteopath undergoes basically the same training as a conventional physician, and they pass the same licensing examination before practising medicine. However, in addition to the conventional medical curriculum, osteopaths learn a medical approach which could be considered more holistic than conventional medicine, and they specifically learn to restore equilibrium to the musculoskeletal system. It is believed that chronic muscle tension and restricted joints play a role in a number of ailments, not only by wasting energy, but also because of superficial breathing patterns.

Imbalances are diagnosed by examining such things as the patient's symmetry, motion, mobility, gait, posture, reflexes and muscle tension. Treatments include mobilising or delicately moving restricted joints, quick jerks to restore severely restricted joints, postures which cause tense muscles to relax, manipulation of muscles and soft tissues, and nutritional guidance. Finally there is a speciality involving cranial manipulation, which admittedly seems quite strange, but can produce some very dramatic results (see *Spontaneous Healing* by Dr. Andrew Weil).

Conclusion

Admittedly, this has been a cursory review of only a small number of the alternative treatments available. Since naturopathic and orthomolecular medicine were mentioned previously they were not included in this section. There are some other therapies which I would have liked to have included, but for lack of space. They include, biofeedback training, goggle-therapy, hydrotherapy, hypnotherapy, light therapy, music and sound therapy, and neuro-linguistic programming (NLP).

Personally, I feel it is more important to find the right personal physician before one begins to seek out alternative practitioners, although many of the therapies mentioned above, such as yoga and qigong and guided imagery can be used by nearly any healthy adult without risks. The best situation to find oneself in, however, is to have a medically trained physician in whom you trust, and who is open and informed about natural, traditional, nutritional, and complementary healing methods. Ideally, such a physician will also recognise the inherent power of nature, along with importance of the mind and spirit in human health. Then you will be in a position to enjoy the benefits of alternative medicine, without sacrificing the wisdom, experience and diagnostic capabilities of a trained physician. Such a physician, once found, should be treasured.

> *The art of healing comes from nature*
> *and not from the physician.*
> *Therefore, the physician must*
> *start from nature and with an open mind.*

Paracelsus

To learn more about alternative therapies refer to *Alternative Medicine and The Definitive Guide.*

12

FUTURE MEDICINE

I n nearly every aspect of life, humanity is inexorably advancing towards global unity. Mankind, after a long and tumultuous childhood and adolescence, stands poised to reach maturity in the 21st century. Despite a wide array of severe and weighty problems, this coming of age will also have far-reaching positive consequences for people everywhere. In the 20th century many of our brightest minds were engaged in the design and development of weapons of war, and a substantial portion of our GNP was wasted in preparing for war and rebuilding after the devastation of war. Hopefully, in the century 21st, these tremendous financial and intellectual resources finally will be channelled into endeavours which will elevate the station of man, rather than those which threaten our very existence. In the 1930s, as the world careened towards a world war which would end with the first use of atomic weapons, Shoghi Effendi outlined the development of the future Bahá'í world order. In the passage below we see his vision of the impact that global unity will have on medical science. Now nearly 70 years later, his ideas no longer seem like utopian dreams, rather they could easily serve as a blueprint of where the unimaginable strides in technology and human ingenuity can take us.

The enormous energy dissipated and wasted on war, whether economic or political, will be consecrated to such ends as will

*extend the range of human inventions and technical
development, to the increase of the productivity of mankind,
to the extermination of disease, to the extension of scientific
research, to the raising of the standards of physical health, to
the sharpening and refinement of the human brain, to the
exploitation of the unused and unsuspected resources of the
planet, to the prolongation of human life, and to the
furtherance of any other agency that can stimulate the
intellectual, the moral, and spiritual life of the entire human
race....*

SHOGHI EFFENDI

Through our God-given gifts we are beginning to unlock our
own genetic code, making possible the realisation of these lofty
goals, perhaps dreamed of, but never seriously contemplated
before. The 20th century marked the end of the era of disease
treatment, and the 21st century will usher in the era of disease
prevention. Rightly, many people are fearful of the impending
genetic revolution. The implications of genetic research mandate
that societies protect themselves against a multitude of potential
dangers — biological, environmental, ethical, social and moral.
None the less, the prospective benefits to humanity can scarcely
be imagined.

Small Wonders

As mentioned previously, the human genetic code consists of
about three billions chemical letters which are organised to make
around 100,000 genes. Our genes are responsible for producing
protein molecules, such as hormones and enzymes, which
regulate our biological functioning and allow us to develop into
mature healthy beings. Variations in our genes, however, can
result in faulty proteins which produce disease. Alzheimer's,
cancer, heart disease, diabetes, arthritis, multiple sclerosis, cystic
fibrosis and sickle-cell anaemia are all believed to have genetic
components. Indeed, ultimately scientists believe that virtually all
diseases will be linked to genetics. Eventually, scientists hope to
understand the function of every human gene, and in the coming
decades and centuries they envision that humanity will be able to

correct malfunctioning genes and prevent disease. Although we currently stand in awe of the progress of modern medicine, one can hardly imagine how rudimentary our current art of medicine will appear to future generations.

Scientists have already embarked on a massive research study known as the Genome Project with the goal of deciphering human DNA. The goal is to have the work completed by the year 2005, but as of 1998 only around 100 million letters, or roughly 3 per cent, of our DNA have been decoded. Simultaneously, other scientists are busy deciphering the genetic codes or viruses, bacteria and parasites in order to devise methods of overcoming them based on their specific genetic makeup.

Problem genes are being identified by comparing the genetic make-up of a group of people suffering from a specific disease to the genes of the general population. Through this process scientists then isolate those genes which are different in the group being studied. Once these genes have been detected researchers can then zero in on the precise functioning of the genes in question. Once this is understood, using biochip technology revolutionary, new medicines can be developed which target the specific genes in question. These drugs will be quicker, safer and more effective.

In fact, genetic research will result in a flood of new diseases, yet no one need be concerned. Puzzled? In reality there won't be any additional illnesses, rather our taxonomy, or classification of existing diseases will be greatly expanded and differentiated into myriad sub-classifications. Treatments, as well, will be highly specialised to enhance or neutralise the effects of individual genes.

In the not too distant future you will be able to visit your physician and with a single drop of blood it will be possible to scan your genetic code with a disposable biochip, and within a very short time determine your genetic predisposition to an array of diseases. Initially, before medical science develops widespread gene therapies, this will be a mixed blessing. Imagine learning in youth that within a few years you are destined to be permanently incapacitated, or die prematurely. Should a physician withhold such information and allow a patient to at least enjoy a few years of carefree living, or inform them so that they can chart their own destiny, even if it means placing a very heavy burden on that person's shoulders?

Many anticipate that a new medical speciality will emerge. These physicians will be genetic counsellors, who understand the results of genetic testing and explain therapeutic options, or offer psychological support when there are no available options. Finally, they will provide lifestyle counselling for warding off relevant genetic predispositions. This type of counselling will probably begin very early in life, long before a person reaches adulthood, making it easier to instill living patterns which are scientifically sound for a particular individual. By enabling physicians to concentrate on preventing disease, Shoghi Effendi's vision of "*raising of the standards of physical health*" and a "*prolongation of human life*" appears inevitable.

Potentially there is also the possibility that genes which control the ageing process will be manipulated to further prolong the human lifespan. Scientists have already identified strings of specialised DNA at the end of chromosomes called telomeres which are shortened each time a cell divides. Once a certain minimum length is reached this causes the cell to enter into a phase of senescence, or gradual decline. Researchers have already demonstrated that cells in test-tubes can substantially increase their longevity when the telomeres are rebuilt.

Doubtless, at some point it will likewise be possible for physicians to assist in the "*sharpening and refinement of the human brain*" through gene therapy. Right now that sounds frightening, but recent breakthroughs in brain research have opened the possibility of increasing cognitive abilities even without genetic interference. Now that scientists are coming to understand the process of how the brain is wired, it is becoming clearer that stimulation of the human brain should begin very early in life. Peaceful and stimulating interaction (verbal, musical, visual, etc.)

combined with optimal nutrition allow the brain to better form the connections which will determine future cognitive abilities.

Genetic research isn't just about disease, it will also allow us to understand why some people are taller than others, more intelligent, more athletic, more musical and any number of possibilities. Also it appears that genes will eventually be identified which are at least partially responsible for such things as sexual orientation, shyness, risk-taking and violent behaviour. Whether or not we act on this information will doubtless be one of the most controversial questions in the coming decades.

Certainly it isn't difficult to imagine people in the 22nd century living to an average age of 120, for the most part free of disease, and with an average IQ of 150. Perhaps this estimate is far too conservative. Even now researchers are manipulating the genes of animals so that they can produce the proteins which defective genes can't. This may allow people suffering from some diseases to live completely normal lives by simply taking these proteins in one form or another. Also, scientists are genetically engineering animals so that they can serve as organ donors, moreover, these organs will eventually overcome the problem of rejection. This, however, may be superseded by a more elegant and humane solution. Scientist are working on the discovery of a genetic mechanism which will allow them to use the same sort of "inducing molecules" which embryos use to cause cells to become organs, tissue, bones, etc. The discovery of the so-called "hedgehog genes", which are the genes responsible for the few regenerative processes active in adults humans, appears to lend credence to the possibility of such developments. Thus it is conceivable that in the future scientists will be able to regenerate body parts.

With respect to intelligence, if parents are given the choice between letting nature take its course, or having a child with the genetic make-up associated with genius, who knows, perhaps an IQ of 200 will one day be commonplace for people in the 22nd century. Suppose scientists are able to encode information on a chip made of living material and then implant it into a human being. Could someone have a wealth of reference information implanted in his or her brain, which could be combined with the creativity and innate intelligence common to humans? Yes, it's a frightening scenario, but also undeniably fascinating. And after a few generations of such individuals, where might that take humanity? If history is any indication, we can't even begin to imagine the technological strides of future centuries, especially if it were indeed a race of geniuses.

Biological Therapies against Cancer

With respect to cancer, it was previously mentioned that for most of the 20th century the customary medical approach was to surgically remove the tumour, expose the surrounding tissue to radiation, and with chemotherapy in effect poison both healthy and cancerous cells in an effort to give the body a chance to start anew. This approach is now being augmented with an array of new and innovative methods of fighting cancer. Perhaps the most promising and appealing therapies are those which either emulate, stimulate or enhance our own natural healing mechanisms. These therapies are referred to as biological therapy, which can include immunotherapy, or biological response modifier therapy.

You may recall BRMs (biological response modifiers) from our discussion of food strategies for overcoming cancer. BRM can ward off cancer in several ways:

1. By curbing, controlling, or cutting off body responses that allow or contribute to cancerous growth.
2. Making cancer cells more vulnerable to the body's immune response.
3. Enhancing the body's immune response to better cope with cancerous cells.
4. Interfering with or reversing the process whereby normal cells become cancerous.
5. Interfering directly with the growth process of cancerous cells.

Some of these BRMs include agents which we have mentioned previously, such as: interferons, tumour necrosis factor and interleukins. In addition, such methods as cancer vaccines, monoclonal antibodies, and colony-stimulating factors are being researched.

Interferons

There are three basic categories of interferons: alpha, beta and gamma. Each is a form of cytokines which occur naturally in the body. You may recall from the section on food strategies that researchers have found that yogurt significantly enhances the production of gamma interferon. Scientists have identified at least three different ways in which interferon helps the immune system to overcome cancer:

1. It stimulates the immune response against cancerous cells, in particular T cells and B cells.
2. It encourages some cancerous cells to revert back to normalcy.
3. It suppresses the growth and development of some cancerous cells.

Interferon was the first BRM to be approved by the US Food and Drug Administration as a cancer treatment. It is used in the treatment of certain types of leukemia, Kaposi's sarcoma, and may someday be used for some forms of kidney, lymph-system, colorectal, multiple myeloma and melanoma cancers. Currently, alpha interferon is receiving the bulk of the attention.

Interleukins (IL)

Interleukins, like interferons, are cytolines and are produced naturally by the body. Interleukins play an important role in the immune system, in particular by stimulating the growth and activities of immune cells. For example, once a lymphocyte has been stimulated by IL-2 it is known as a lymphokine-activated killer cell (LAK). Such cells are known to be effective at destroying tumour cells. Researchers have found that when lymphocytes are removed from a patients blood and stimulated with IL-2 in the laboratory, they become LAKs and can be returned to the body to enhance a patient's immune response against tumours.

Interleukins have shown promise against advanced kidney cancer and advanced melanoma, and are being tested against colorectal, ovarian and small cell lung cancer.

Tumour Necrosis Factor (TNF)

Like interferons and interleukins, TFN is also a cytokine which occurs naturally in the body. You may recall TFN from our discussions on the immune system, where it was seen that a high fever stimulates the release of TNF. TFN triggers the immune system to fight cancerous cells, but it also directly destroys them by damaging the blood vessels in tumours, although this process isn't as yet completely understood.

TFN administered in high doses is toxic, so therapies are being investigated which target a specific tumour site with TNF.

Colony-Stimulating Factors (CSFs)

These too are naturally occurring agents in the body. They bolster cell division in bone marrow, where our various white blood cells, red blood cells, and platelets are produced. This can help the body to better deal with infection and other problems which result from chemotherapy. There also appears to be a general enhancement of the immune system resulting from CSFs.

Monoclonal Antibodies (MOABs)

This is an example of human ingenuity. Perhaps you recall the discussion of antigens and antibodies in chapter 2. When certain immune cells encounter foreign substances (antigens) they produce a protein called an antibody which correlates to the invading substance. We have millions of different antibodies which are both inherited and produced by exposure.

With MOABs, researchers inject human cancer cells into mice so that their immune systems will produce antibodies against the cancer cells. Then, using a cell called a hybridoma generated in the laboratory, researchers commingle it with the mice cells which produce the antibody. The hybridoma then manufactures the cancer antibody (MOAB) indefinitely.

The MOABs can then be used on patients to improve the immune response against certain types of cancer. MOABs can also be bonded with anti-cancer drugs, radioactive substances, BRMs, or specific toxins; then, when the antibody (MOAB) attaches to the tumour it can directly deliver the toxin, etc., to the targeted tumour.

MOABs are being tested against colorectal cancer, lung cancer, leukemia and neuroblastoma.

Tumour Vaccines

Researchers are also working on anti-cancer vaccines. As with other diseases scientist are attempting to use a vaccine so that the immune system will cause some T cells and B cells to transform themselves into memory cells so that they will develop a specific immune response. In this case they are attempting to elicit this response against cancer cells, rather than a foreign antigen. Thus cancer cells would be readily attacked by the immune system before tumours could develop. Such vaccines are being studied in relation to a number of cancers.

Other Advances in Cancer Treatment
Angiogenesis Inhibitors

Cancerous tumours remain small if they aren't supplied with nutrients. At some point a small tumour releases a chemical messenger which causes blood vessels nearby to grow capillaries to support the tumour's growth. As the tumour and blood vessels grow, this new opening to the circulatory system also enables cancer cells from the tumour to spread more easily throughout the body. This process of building blood vessels is known as angiogenesis.

Scientists have discovered hundreds of substances which are angiogenesis inhibitors. A drug from the 1950s, originally prescribed to relieve morning-sickness in pregnant women, is a powerful angiogenesis inhibitor, which, by cutting off the foetus from blood supplies, resulted in serious birth defects. Now this drug, thalidomide, is again being researched as an anti-angiogenesis tumour suppresser.

We saw that certain foods, soya in particular, exhibit angiogenesis properties which some biological therapies mimic.

Researchers are now investigating several avenues of blocking angiogenesis:

1. By blocking the required enzymes for blood vessel growth.
2. By blocking a tumour cell's receptors for growth hormone.
3. By attacking the blood-vessel cells directly.

Anti-Metastatic Facotrs

Metastasis is the spreading of cancer. Scientists have identified enzymes which cancer cells use to enter the bloodstream and spread. Tests have already begun on drugs which may inhibit metastasis.

Oncogene Inhibitors

In addition to using growth hormones naturally occurring in the bloodstream, tumour cells also produce them by turning on so-called *oncogenes*. In order to deprive tumour cells of this growth factor scientists are developing drugs which inhibit the oncogenes.

Radiation

In the past the difficulty with radiation was that it damaged and destroyed healthy cells along with cancerous ones. Now using 3-dimensional imagery physicians can implant radioactive *seeds* directly into a tumour with great precision. This minimises the damage to healthy tissues.

Preventative Drugs

Scientists are developing drugs which mimic the preventative properties of food. Tamoxifen and raloxifene, like soya, prevent certain cancer cells from getting estrogen, which they require for growth. Retinoic acid (which we learned in the chapter on food strategy can be produced by the body from beta carotin) is a drug which prevents the recurrence of some types of cancer.

Again, food is a powerful means of preventing cancer in healthy people, and it should be used as an adjunct to medical treatment; however, it is not a substitute for professional medical treatment once cancer has been diagnosed.

And Beyond

Space won't allow us to delve into the advances which are occurring in all of the medical specialities. Lasers, computer imaging, genetics, fibre optics, miniaturisation and revolutionary materials are but some of the factors which are dramatically changing modern medicine. Yet, as we mentioned previously, this technification of medicine has also exposed a deficit on the part of those who are responsible for selecting and training physicians. A true healer cannot simply rely on technology, there must be a spiritual connection between the patient and the physician. This, as we have seen, enables the individual to move from being a recipient of treatment, to becoming a participant in maintaining and restoring health. This innate internal strength is and should remain integral to medicine, regardless of technological innovation.

What will be the impact of the Bahá'í community on the future of medicine? It is my personal hope that Bahá'í scientists, medical researchers and physicians will be instrumental in combining physical healing with spiritual healing, in elevating the station of nutrition in medical science, and in using human ingenuity to free mankind from the pain and suffering of disease. Of course, this is more than my personal longing, the Bahá'í writings clearly support such developments:

> *These investigations you have so painstakingly pursued in the field of medical science, and on a subject which is still puzzling the minds of all the leading scientists in the world, cannot but be of a captivating interest and of a great value to all medical research workers.*
>
> *It is significant that you as a believer should have undertaken a work of this nature, as we all know that the powers released by the Manifestation of Bahá'u'lláh in this day are destined, in the course of time, to reveal themselves through the instrumentality of His followers, and in every conceivable field of human endeavour.*

That you should increasingly prove, through your confirmed researches in the domain of medicine, to be one of those instruments, is the fervent hope of our beloved Guardian.

from a letter written on behalf of Shoghi Effendi

Apart from these developments, there is another aspect of the Bahá'í community which could potentially have a meaningful impact on the medical community. The Bahá'í Houses of Worship scattered around the world are noted for their aesthetic beauty, harmony with their surroundings, openness, peacefulness and tranquillity. A House of Worship, however, is in reality only a part of the institution known as the *Dawning-Point of the Remembrance of God.* This institution encompasses the House of Worship and the various social needs of the surrounding community such as hospitals, orphanages, schools and universities.

Although it is a House of Worship, it is also connected with a hospital, a drug dispensary, a traveller's hospice, a school for orphans, and a university for advanced studies. Every Mashriqu'l-Adhkár is connected with these five things.... Make these matters known to the beloved of the Lord, so that they will understand how very great is the importance of this 'Dawning-Point of the Remembrance of God.' The Temple is not only a place for worship; rather, in every respect is it complete and whole.

'ABDU'L-BAHÁ

Traditionally, hospitals have been organized for doctors, for auxiliaries, for insurance companies — everybody but the patient.

RON ANDERSON, M.D.

For too long hospitals have been designed and organised in a utilitarian fashion, ignoring the psychological implications of immediate surroundings for the patient, while focusing on the establishment of a physical plant which is efficiently cleaned and operated. The typical hospital is large, threatening, depressing and impersonal, with dreary artificial lighting, stale air laden with disinfectant, and isolated from nature and the community. There are exceptions, but surely most people can readily identify with this description. This has a direct effect upon the patient's healing potential.

> *For example, studies suggest that a patient who can look out the window during recovery from some specific types of surgery stays there a shorter time than the patient who can't look out a window. The environmental circumstances of the hospital make a difference in how well a patient recovers. There's a lot of literature on that, although basically it's been ignored, because for many decades we've practiced medicine more for the benefit of the staff and the hospital than the benefit of the patients. And that is something that has to be changed.*

David Felten, M.D., Ph.D.,
Professor of Neurobiology and Anatomy

Hopefully, future Bahá'í architects will work closely with psychologists, sociologists, artists, landscapers and health care professionals to design hospitals which will mirror the unique spiritual and aesthetic characteristics of the Houses of Worship. Perhaps the concept of a large imposing hospital will give way to a scattered collection of clinics which are proximate, yet distinct, integrated into their natural surroundings, while affording patients and health care workers natural light, fresh air, and verdant gardens. Interiors should not only be functional, but pleasing in form and colour and as 'Abdu'l-Bahá wrote, in *every respect complete and whole.*

Such developments will no doubt have a positive impact upon the spirit of the patient and the health care worker, which will in turn contribute to physical and emotional health. Rather than isolating the sick in cold impersonal bunkers, we will allow them to continue to be part of that institution which is the *Dawning-*

Point of the Remembrance of God. Finally, beyond the purely physical aspects of health let us not forget that Shoghi Effendi indicated our final goal was to, "... *stimulate the intellectual, the moral, and spiritual life of the entire human race.*"

$$\boxed{13}$$

PATIENTS AND PHYSICIANS

Finding the Right Physician

Many people make a serious mistake by waiting to find a physician until they need one. Next to finding one's spouse, finding the right physician is one of the most important decisions we face. Chances are that it might take some time and effort, therefore you should never wait until an emergency or an acute situation to begin your search.

Talking to friends, colleagues, neighbours and people with whom you worship is a good starting point. If you know any health care professionals such as nurses, physical therapists or pharmacists they can often give you some useful insights and recommendations. If you are interested in finding a physician who has a more holistic approach, you might find like-minded people at a health food store, organic grocery, or a yoga class. The important thing is to begin seeking before an acute situation occurs.

Unfortunately, modern health insurance often places considerable constraints on patients and physicians alike. Patients sometimes can't choose their own physician, and physicians are often restricted as to how they can treat their patients. This type of hurried, assembly line medicine drives a wedge between patients and physicians. Expensive equipment, costly malpractice insurance, complicated billing procedures, enormous responsibility, emotionally charged situations and a ceaseless flow of new and essential information make the practice of medicine a very demanding profession.

Dr. Herbert Benson, mentioned previously, advises people to trust their instincts and first impressions when evaluating a physician. He points to research from the social sciences which shows that people are quite adept at interpreting body-language, tone of voice, facial expressions and many such things which enable us to intuitively make correct decisions. He further advises that if you already have a physician, you should reflect upon the care you have received. Has your physician ever offered a non-drug-related solution to a medical problem? Do you feel you have your physician's full attention? Is your physician interested in you and your family situation? Has your physician ever asked for your thoughts about the source of a problem?

If you have an interest in such things as nutrition, natural remedies, mind/body medicine, and stress-management techniques you should ask your potential physician how he or she feels about them. This will give you a good opportunity to see if you are on the same wavelength and help you evaluate a physician's knowledge of those health-related issues which interest you. However, you should keep in mind that because of the litigious culture in some countries, physicians are often acutely aware of potential lawsuits. This forces them to be cautious and conservative (which frequently translates to an emphasis on drugs, along with aggressive and invasive procedures). Moreover, most health insurance companies will neither reimburse physicians for unorthodox therapies nor for the time they spend counselling patients about such therapies. Finding the right physician is difficult, but finding the right physician/healer is especially difficult.

If you are facing serious illness, Dr. Bernie Siegel, also mentioned previously, offers some good advice for finding a physician. If you have found the right general practitioner, he or she can generally help you by recommending a good specialist. But a good peer relationship doesn't necessarily mean that a good doctor/patient relationship will ensue. Dr. Siegel stresses the importance of building a relationship with your physician and establishing a framework in which teamwork and mutual trust prevail. He also encourages patients to be the ones to initiate a sense of closeness and intimacy. However, he also advises that if you don't get back an honest and human response, you should get up, leave the room and continue searching for the right physician.

For more information refer to: *Love, Medicine & Miracles*, by Bernie Siegel, M.D.; *Peace, Love & Healing*, by Bernie Siegel, M.D.; and *How To Live Between Office Visits*, by Bernie Siegel, M.D.

(I highly recommend Dr. Siegel's books for anyone confronting serious illness);

Timeless Healing, The Power and Biology of Belief, by Herbert Benson, M.D. (Demonstrates the power of mind/body medicine, spirituality and the importance of the doctor/patient relationship); and *Spontaneous Healing*, by Andrew Weil, M.D.

Dr. Weil is the physician millions of people wish they had. This book is a wealth of information about a wide variety of subjects such as the spontaneous remission of disease, nutrition, herbs, relaxation, exercise and traditional medicine. Dr. Weil also outlines the basis of a paradigm shift in medicine which he calls integrative.

Being a Good Patient

To build any successful relationship you need to master the skill of empathy. As mentioned above, physicians work under a great deal of mental and emotional stress. Time is generally of the essence in a physician's office, because illness and injury can't be scheduled. A good patient will recognise the limitation of a physician's time, not that you need to feel rushed, but you need to be empathetic.

In order to save time you might spend some time preparing for a routine visit to the doctor. For example, you might want to make a few notes of specific things you want to ask. Hopefully, you'll see your physician only for regular examinations or socially.

Remember, medical care is centred around disease, while a good patient needs to understand the principles which foster health. Since such a great number of health problems are stress-related, psychosomatic or a result of poor nutrition and inadequate exercise, there is a great deal you can do to reduce the need of seeing a physician.

If you work at establishing a state of equilibrium with your mind, spirit and body, you will become more aware of what's normal for you. You'll get a sense of when you can work at your own problems and when you need your physician's advice. Of course, if you sense that something is *really* wrong you should never hesitate to visit your doctor. However, if you consult your home medical reference manual and do all in your power to assist the *physician within*, chances are that in a few days the body will solve most problems itself.

When you have a physician in whom you trust, then it is vitally important to follow his or her instructions carefully. Never interrupt a treatment plan or therapy without advising your physician. People often take antibiotics until symptoms subsist and then stop. This can have serious consequences, because bacteria which aren't completely overcome can develop a resistance and return with a vengeance. Also, it is important to take medicine at the intervals prescribed, if necessary use an alarm clock to remind yourself of the time. Finally, never mix non-prescription medications or herbal remedies with prescription drugs (even for non-related illnesses) without consulting your physician.

When serious illness does strike, then you need to move from being a good patient to becoming what Dr. Siegel describes as an *exceptional patient*. Dr. Siegel and his wife formed a group called ECaP (Exceptional Cancer Patients) which has served as the basis for countless support groups for cancer patients. He maintains that the most important direction we can go isn't north, east, south, or west, but inside ourselves. Illness is a second chance to go farther into ourselves and begin to understand the preciousness of life, to understand more of the meaning of life, and to take advantage of life's opportunities.

Dr. Siegel writes that exceptional patients learn to say yes to themselves and no to others when necessary. They are willing to learn from others, but they make decisions themselves. They confront their fears and use the energy of anger for positive ends. They practise altruism, not out of duty, but out of love. They look for people who are worse off than themselves and help them. They learn to live in the present, not dwelling in the past or worrying about the future. They get in touch with their true selves, and learn that healing powers come from unconditional love and being able to forgive. They have a sense of humour and can laugh at themselves. They let go of what they can't change and put themselves in God's hands. They find something they love to do and dive into it completely, letting it function as a form of meditation. They participate in and are informed about their treatment, which means rejecting the idea of being submissive (patient). They risk being called difficult or uncooperative. They know that nothing is impossible and they believe in miracles.

Reforming Medicine from the Bottom up

It's understandable that many physicians gradually begin to view their patients as potential litigants. In a sense, there is surely a degree of self-fulfilling prophecy in such an attitude. The problem is compounded when a once idealistic physician begins to erect emotional barriers to protect himself or herself from the pain and responsibility of dealing with those who are suffering. Eventually an efficient, detached, impersonal and mechanistic routine is developed and meshed with an aggressive and invasive form of medicine which leaves patients feeling powerless, alienated, demeaned, violated, helpless and insignificant. A person feeling thus is much more apt to sue for malpractice than a patient who enjoys an intimate relationship with a physician. Few patients who trust, respect and value a physician will take him or her to court.

Thus it would seem that the best approach for protecting oneself from lawsuits is to establish a genuine relationship with patients, treat them with compassion, concern and empathy, and to involve them in the healing process.

In his book, *Spontaneous Healing*, Andrew Weil makes a plea for a reform of medical education, but also expresses his cynicism of the chances of any truly meaningful change. Some of his suggestions include:

1. Study of the philosophy of science, based more on quantum physics than on the Newtonian mechanistic approach and the Cartesian dualism. A recognition that physical events can sometimes result from non-physical actions, and that observation can potentially influence the outcome of events.
2. The study of the history of medicine, which should also include major systems like traditional Chinese medicine, homoeopathy and osteopathy.
3. Emphasis on the inherent healing power of nature and the body. An emphasis on mind/body interactions, including placebos, medical hexing (planting negative thoughts in patients), and psychoneuroimmunology.
4. Instruction in spirituality, psychology, and communication.
5. Practical experience in nutrition, exercise, relaxation, meditation, and visualisation.
6. Basic knowledge of alternative medicine. Students should learn how to design and conduct medical research and how to evaluate the research of others.
7. Less emphasis on memorising facts and more emphasis on the general structure of medical science and how to access medical information more effectively, especially with respect to the computer.

I'm not aware of any statistics about the proportion of physicians in the Bahá'í community, but unquestionably it is considerably higher than the general population, undoubtedly because of references to the medical profession found in the Bahá'í teachings which were mentioned previously. In all probability this trend will continue. Thus, until there is a reform of medical education, future Bahá'í medical students with foresight can plan their undergraduate elective courses so as to acquire knowledge about subjects which will help them later in their careers. For example, they might consider subjects such as nutrition, sociology, counselling, communication, comparative religions, medical history, and psychology. On a personal level, yoga, meditation and visualisation can also help them to focus and cope with the pressures of higher education, and later with the demands of practising medicine.

STAYING POSITIVE

Your thought, spiritual and positive, will spread; it
will become the desire of others, growing stronger
and stronger, until it reaches the minds of all men.

'Abdu'l-Bahá

We live in a world full of nay-sayers and pessimists and it's easy to allow negative influences to colour our thoughts. Negative feelings such as fear, uncertainty, pessimism, hopelessness, and despair can alter body chemistry, suppress the immune system, and jeopardise health. On the other hand, optimism, certitude, faith, hope, and altruism enhance the immune response and contribute to health. The exceptional patient described by Dr. Siegel in the previous chapter is, in reality, a person who embodies the wisdom and spirituality found in the world's sacred scriptures. Even when illness strikes, we can consciously decide if it is a physical crisis or a spiritual challenge.

Given that the soul is immortal, our primary concern should be the development of a healthy spirit. Fortunately, nature's plan, confirmed by scientific research, is that spiritual health and virtuous conduct are conducive to physical health. Yet, life in general, and health in particular, are temporal and destined to fade. When physical illness strikes this is but a bump on the road to a higher state of being. Shoghi Effendi described it very succinctly:

> *Though willing to share to the utmost the temporal benefits and the fleeting joys which this earthly life can confer, though eager to participate in whatever activity that conduces to the richness, the happiness and peace of that life, they can, at no time, forget that it constitutes no more than a transient, a very brief stage of their existence, that they who live it are but pilgrims and wayfarers whose goal is the Celestial City, and whose home the Country of never-failing joy and brightness.*

We can't control many of the physical and material aspects of life, but our inner-life, our spiritual reality, and our expression of unconditional love towards all living creatures is firmly within our control. When you view existence from this perspective you can begin to realise that there is no reason to be filled with fear, uncertainty, hopelessness, etc. Most people would be willing to spend a night in miserable physical conditions, if they were then rewarded with a palace and material comforts for the rest of their lives. You might therefore think of the trials of this life simply as brief tests which allow you to store treasures in the spiritual realm. Recall Bahá'u'lláh's words:

> *Sorrow not if, in these days and on this earthly plane, things contrary to your wishes have been ordained and manifested by God, for days of blissful joy, of heavenly delight, are assuredly in store for you. Worlds, holy and spiritually glorious, will be unveiled to your eyes. You are destined by Him, in this world and hereafter, to partake of their benefits, to share in their joys, and to obtain a portion of their sustaining grace. To each and every one of them you will, no doubt, attain.*

On the collective level we know that news is fixated on crisis and conflict, and portrayed with no small degree of cynicism and pessimism. It's easy to get sucked into this worldview, but we also have the guiding vision of the Bahá'í revelation. We know that the disasters and conflicts which afflict mankind are the birth pangs of an era of global unity. In the 20th century Bahá'ís witnessed that WWI spawned the League of Nations and WWII resulted in the founding of the United Nations. How rewarding it must be for Bahá'ís who lived through the two world wars to now witness the European Union, in which traditional enemies are unified to a degree never imaginable even half a century ago.

In the middle of the Cold War the Bahá'í vision of global unity was scoffed at by many as absolute utopia. We were told that dictators and totalitarian regimes never relinquish power, it would take centuries, if ever, for the communist countries to evolve into democratic nations. Then we were told that Jews and Arabs could never make peace, nor could the divisions in South Africa be overcome without a bloody revolution. So even in the face of continual bad news, collectively as Bahá'ís it should be quite clear that there is no reason to despair. These conflicts and catastrophes are the unavoidable growing pains of mankind's turbulent adolescence and approaching maturity. Our task is building unity at every level of human existence, from the individual, to the family, the community, the nation and finally the entire planet. This is the supreme and inevitable goal towards which we aspire.

Scientists can be Pessimists too

In 1980 Professor James Fries of Stanford University developed an hypothesis called the *compression of morbidity*. Dr. Fries theorised that instead of the continuous physical decline and increasing disability which begins in mid-life, if people would adopt a healthy lifestyle they could live relatively healthy lives into their 80s at which time they would begin dying at an accelerated rate. Sounds like a logical idea which would be advantageous for the individual and society, right?

Pessimists and sceptics in the scientific community immediately attacked Professor Fries theory, warning that large numbers of people adopting such healthy living habits would be harmful for themselves and for society. How? The sceptics agreed that people would live longer, but they maintained that they wouldn't live better. They would simply live more years suffering from disability and chronic illness. Not only would the individuals suffer, but society would have to carry the financial costs of caring for them. Of course this type of reaction by knowledgeable scientists reinforced the attitude of people who have unhealthy lifestyles. "What's the point, I'd rather die than waste away in a nursing home."

Fortunately, Dr. Fries designed a major study to test his hypothesis. For 32 years he and fellow researchers have been following a group of 1,741 men and women who graduated from the University of Pennsylvania in 1939 and 1940 (the observation of this group began before Dr. Fries developed his theory). In April of 1998 he published some initial findings in the *New England Journal of Medicine* which strongly support his hypothesis.

Subjects were placed in three risk groups (high, moderate and low), based upon three modifiable factors which are recognised as affecting health: smoking, being overweight and physical inactivity.

Although the average age was only 75 at the last assessment, it is clear that those in the low-risk group not only live longer, they are also healthier at every age. They experience only half as much chronic disability, and on average the age at which they experience even minor disability is 73, compared to 66 for those in the high-risk group. Future assessments should even be more telling.

Positive Expectations

New techniques in computer imaging are helping to change the way in which we understand human perception. Previously, we considered our inner reality to be the effect of information flowing into the brain as sensory perceptions. Now, however, scientists are learning that our thoughts, beliefs, desires and expectations can affect our biological mechanism and impact upon our cells, tissues and organs. Researchers are discovering that our perceptions are not only influenced by outside stimuli, but that our expectations of what will occur , based on previous experience, are extremely significant. It appears that nature has provided humans with an ability to anticipate the outcome of events based on experience.

Researchers conducted an experiment in which subjects were given a drug which causes a surge of adrenaline. Based upon expectations communicated to them, they experienced euphoria, anger or no reaction at all. Of course this is the basis of the placebo effect which we have discussed previously. You should never discount the power of your expectations on your physical well-being, nor should your physician.

You will recall that patients who thought they were receiving chemotherapy, but who were receiving a placebo, developed the symptoms associated with chemotherapy, a significant number even lost their hair. Interestingly the reverse is also true, 42 per cent of subjects who thought they were receiving a drug to prevent baldness, but received a placebo, stopped losing hair or even increased the amount of scalp hair.

At first glance it seems rather silly to question the efficacy of surgical operations which haven't been subjected to the rigours of double-blind tests. Yet, as we saw earlier, pseudo heart operations in the 1950's were shown to be as effective as the actual operation. More recently, surgeons in Texas began a study to test arthroscopic knee surgery. Patients with sore and worn knees were given general anesthesia and one of three operations: scraping out the knee joint, washing out the knee joint, or nothing. When nothing was done, the patients still received general anesthesia and small incisions around the knee, so that they couldn't determine what had been done. Two years after the placebo operation these patients reported the same amount of relief of pain and swelling as the patients who had actual operations.

In Venezuela a study was conducted on asthmatic children in which they sniffed vanilla as they used bronchodilators twice a day. Eventually the smell of vanilla alone produced a third of the increase in lung capacity produced by the bronchodilator.

According to Dr. Marcel Kinsbourne, a neuroscientist at the New School for Social Research in New York:

> *The brain generates two kinds of activation patterns, which arise from networks of neurons firing together. One type is set in motion by information flowing into the brain from the*

outside world — smells, tastes, visual images, sounds. At the same time, the cortex draws on memories and feelings to generate patterns of brain activity related to what is expected to happen. The top-down patterns generated by the cortex intersect smoothly with the bottom-up patterns to inform us about what is happening. If there is a mismatch, the brain tries to sort it out, without necessarily designating one set of patterns as more authoritative than another.

We need to harness this tremendous potential, rather than treating the placebo effect as something to be derided. When you eat, relax, exercise, laugh, help others, and pray, learn to expect that bottom-up brain patterns are sending powerful and positive signals to your body which will gradually improve your health.

Conclusion

If not smoking, staying trim and exercising can have such a dramatic impact on the length and quality of life, just imagine the impact which vegetarianism, healthy nutrition, worship, remembered-wellness, stress-management, visualisation, proper breathing, yoga or qigong, spirituality and altruism could have.

The key is to make healthy choices part of your daily routine. At first you will have to make conscious choices, but eventually you will internalise healthy behaviour and it will become second nature to you. What initially seemed like a sacrifice will one day allow you to look back and wonder how you could have ever lived so recklessly. You will learn that happiness is superior to pleasure, and wisdom is greater than intelligence.

Wellness requires an active balanced mind, a vibrant loving spirit, and a body strengthened by nourishment, exercise and rest.

SOURCE MATERIALS
(ALSO INDIVIDUAL FOOTNOTES FOR COMPLETE LISTING)

American Institute for Cancer Research. Spring 1996. Newsletter 51.

American Journal of Clinical Nutrition

Asimov, Isaac. 1965. *The Human Brain*. New York: Mentor Books.

Bahá'í Writings, compiled by Alan Bryson. 1998. *Enlightened Views*. New Delhi: Sterling Publishers Private Ltd.

Benson, Herbert, MD, with Marg Stark. 1996. *Timeless Healing, The Power and Biology of Belief*. New York: Scribner.

Bhagavad Gita. E.H. Palmer translation on CD ROM.

Bible, King James Version.

Burton Goldberg Group. 1993. *Alternative Medicine, The Definitive Guide*. Puyallup, Washington: Puture Medicine Publishing, Inc.

Carper, Jean. 1994. *Food - Your Miracle Medicine*. New York: Harper Perennial.

Paul Churchland. *The Engine of Reason, The Seat of the Soul*.

Confucius. *The Doctrine of the Mean. The Great Learning*. CD ROM.

Conkling, Winfred. 1996. *Natural Medicine for Arthritis*. New York: Dell.

Cooper, Kenneth, MD. 1994. *Dr. Kenneth H. Cooper's Antioxidant Revolution*. Nashville: Thomas Nelson Publishers.

Devaraj, T.L. 1998. *Speaking of: Ayurvedic Remedies for Common Diseases*. New Delhi: Sterling Publishers Private Ltd.

Editors of Prevention. 1993. *Food and Nutrition*. New York: Berkeley Books.

European Journal of Clinical Nutrition.

Ghai, O.P. 1992. *Health: Quotable Quotes*. New Delhi: Sterling Publishers Private Ltd.

Gleick, James. 1993. *Genius: The Life and Science of Richard Feynman*. New York: First Vintage Books.

Gore, Al. 1993. *Earth in the Balance: Ecology and the Human Spirit*. New York: Plume Books.

Herodotus. 400BC. *The History of Herodotus*. Translated by George Rawlinson. CD ROM.

Hirschsteiner, Tanja. 1998. *Von Apfelessig bis Weissdorn*. Munich: Graefe und Unzer.

Hornby, Helen Bassett. 1994. *Lights of Guidance*. Bahá'í Publishing Trust of India.

Institute of Noetic Sciences with Willian Poole. 1993. *The Heart of Healing*. Atlanta: Turner Publishing, Inc.

International Journal of Immunotherapy

Journal of the American Medical Association.

Journal of Lipid Research

Kreuter, J.H. 1989. *Die sanfte Art des Heilens: Homoeopathie*. Niedernhausern: Falken.

LeVay, David. 1988. *Human Anatomy and Physiology*. Suffolk: Hodder and Stoughton.

Levin, J.S. 1994. "Religion and Health: Is There an Association, Is It Valid, Is It Causal?" Social Science and Medicine.

Mansmann, Vinzenz. MD. 1997. *Total Erschoepft: Mit Naturheilmitteln zu neuer Energie*. Munich: Graefe und Unzer.

Matthews, D.A., D.B. Larson, and C.P. Barry. 1993. *The Faith Factor: An Annotated Bibliography of Clinical Research on Spiritual Subjects*. Vol.1 John Templeton Foundation.

Miketta, Gaby. 1992. *Netzwerk Mensch, Psychoneuroimmunologie: Den Verbindungen von Körper und Seele auf der Spur*. Stuttgart: Georg Thieme Verlag.

Moyers, Bill. 1993. *Healing and The Mind.* New York: Main Street Books.

Naparstek, Belleruth. 1994. *Staying Well with Guided Imagery.* New York: Warner Books.

Netolitzky, Hansjoerg. *Innere Medizin in Frage und Antwort.* Stuttgart: Georg Theime Verlag.

Nyanatiloka, compiler. *The Word of Buddha.* CD ROM.

Oxman, T.E., D.H. Freeman, Jr. and E.D. Manheimer. 1992. "Lack of Social Preparation or Religious Strength and Comfort As Risk Factors for Death After Cardiac Surgery in the Elderly". *Psychosomatic Medicine 57.*

Pharmaceutical Information Associates, Ltd. March 1994. "Molecule of the Year: p53". *Medical Sciences Bulletin.*

Pschyrembel, Willibald, MD. 1975. *Klinisches Woerterbuch mit Syndromen.* Berlin: Walter de Gryter.

Qu'rán. Translated by Mohammed Marmaduke Pickthall.

Schiller, P.L., and J.S. Levin. 1988. "Is There a Religious Factor in Health Care Utilization?: A Review". *Social Science and Medicine 27.*

Scientific American, Sept. 1992.

Shambhu Nath, Pandit. 1991. *Speaking of: Yoga, A Practical Guide to Better Living.* New Delhi: Sterling Publishers Private Ltd.

Siegel, Bernie, MD. 1993. *How To Live Between Office Visits.* New York: Harper Colins.

The Bantam Medical Dictionary. 1982. New York: Bantam Books.

The New England Journal of Medicine.

Weil, Andrew, MD. 1995. *Spontaneous Healing.* New York: Alfred A. Knopf.

WHO, *Fact Sheet N 127.* August 1996. Tobacco Addiction.

WHO, *World Health Report.* 1995.

Zeltner, Renate. 1998. *Die Kraft der Heilpflanzen: Johanniskraut.* Munich: Deutscher Taschenbuch Verlag.

Zohoori, Elias. 1985. *Throne of the Inner Temple.* Jamaica: University of the West Indies.

Some Useful Websites

(many sites have links to various other sites of interest)

http://home.t-online.de/home/a.bryson/ (My homepage)

An opportunity for you to make comments, also information and links concerning the **Bahá'í Faith**.

http://www.aicr.org/aicr.htm (American Institute for Cancer Research - Online)

Lots of useful information about foods which help to reduce the risk of cancer, also lots of useful information and links for people with cancer.

http://www.heartinfo.org/nutrition/nutrhrtdisease1297.htm (Nutrition and Heart Disease)

http://www.englemed.demon.co.uk (Latest Medical News)

This site will also send you an email newsletter of important new medical research findings.

http://www.healthnet.ivi.com/onhealth/common/htm/ hpnutr.htm (Nutrition & Fitness)

http://www.mb.sympatico.ca/Contents/Health/DIRECTORY/ B1.html (Alternative Medicine Directory)

http://navigator.tufts.edu/ (Tufts University Nutrition Navigator)

Very good site for reliable information and links about nutrition.

http://www-sci.lib.uci.edu/HSG/Nutrition.html (Virtual Nutrition Center - Martindale's Health Science Guide)

Lots of useful information and links.

http://www.drweil.com/ (Dr. Andrew Weil's Website)

Lots of information on vitamins, herbs, and natural medicine.

http://www.excite.com/health/

Lots of links and medical headlines.

http://dir.yahoo.com/Health/

Lots of links and medical headlines.

http://www-english.lycos.com/health/

Lots of links and medical headlines.

http://www.cnn.com/HEALTH/

Lots of links and medical headlines.

Extensive site with a great deal of useful information.
http://www.nytimes.com/
You'll need to register, but the *New York Times* is one of the finest
  newspapers available. The Science/Health section is very
  good.

Of allied interest

You need these books. For better health and longer life. For more up-to-date information on medical treatments.

A product of the combined knowledge and experience of medical experts this series offers a clear look at sickness and therapy — therapy which uses both alternative care and conventional medicine.

You owe it to yourself to own this Health Update.

This series has been taken from Health Update, a monthly bulletin of the Society for Health Education and Learning Packages.

All You Wanted to Know About :

* These titles are not from Health Update bulletin

Books by Grand Master Choa Kok Sui
Modern Founder of
Pranic Healing & Arhatic Yoga

1. **The Ancient Science and Art of Pranic Crystal Healing**
   ISBN 81 207 2220 5 Rs. 250

2. **Miracles Through Pranic Healing**
   ISBN 81 207 2218 3 Rs. 300

3. **Advanced Pranic Healing**
   ISBN 81 207 2219 1 Rs. 250

4. **Pranic Psychotherapy**
   ISBN 81 207 2221 3 Rs. 100

Books on Health & Cure Series

Write for a Complete Catalogue

STERLING PUBLISHERS PRIVATE LIMITED
L-10, Green Park Extension, New Delhi-110016
Tel : 6191023, 6191784/85; Fax : 91-11-6190028
E-mail: ghai@nde.vsnl.net.in